HELPING YOUR AGING PARENTS

A Practical Guide for Adult Children

James Halpern, Ph.D.

McGRAW-HILL BOOK COMPANY

New York   St. Louis   San Francisco
Toronto   Hamburg   Mexico

1 2 3 4 5 6 7 8 9 D O C D O C 8 7

ISBN 0-07-025586-5

LIBRARY OF CONGRESS CATALOGING-IN-PUBLICATION DATA

Halpern, James.
  Helping your aging parents.
  Bibliography: p.
  Includes index.
  1. Parents, Aged—Care—United States. 2. Parents,
Aged—United States—Family relationships. 3. Adult
children—United States. I. Title.
HQ1063.6.H35 1987   646.7′8   87-5272
ISBN 0-07-025586-5

Book design by Kathryn Parise

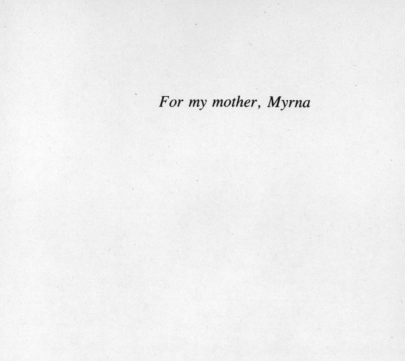

For my mother, Myrna

Acknowledgments —————————————

I would first like to thank all the elderly parents and adult children who took the time to fill out questionnaires and be interviewed. Thanks also to research assistants—Janet Guidice, Melissa Signor, and Melissa Smith—who helped develop, distribute, and analyze the questionnaires, as well as conduct interviews and gather source materials.

The information and advice provided by Susan Mende, Diana Price, Vivian Ubell, and Judy Walker was very much appreciated. A special thank you to the people who read the manuscript and made valuable comments and suggestions: editor Mrs. Lou Ashworth, Dr. Lou Cassotta, Mr. Paul Grabbe, Ms. Francey Oscherwitz, and Dr. Bernard Weitzman. Research assistant Mary Ann Schroeder did a superb job of gathering and organizing materials on nursing homes, dying, and funerals. She also made insightful comments and useful suggestions from beginning to end. I also want to thank my son, Nathan, who provided inspiration and my wife, Ilsa, who supported and helped me with the entire project from its inception.

NOTE TO READERS

In this book "she" is used generally to refer to an elderly parent, primarily because there are more elderly women than men.

Contents

Chapter 1

Introduction

The attachment between children and parents is from any psychological perspective the most fundamental and important connection in our life. As Daniel Callahan says,

> Parents stay in our memory and exert their influence even in the face of distance or active hostility. Whether we like it or not we are in some sense always one with our parents, both because of the unique circumstances by which we came to know them and because of the long period of nurturance when we were utterly dependent on them....The emotional and biological bond between parent and child gives the relationship a permanent and central place in our lives, quite apart from whether it turns out well or poorly.[1]

Many adult children experience a time of relative calm in their relations with their parents. This is the time when, if all goes well, adult children are able to take care of themselves and perhaps care for children of their own, while the parents adjust to and enjoy their independence—no longer worrying too much about their children.

As all relationships are precarious, it is virtually inevitable that even the best of parent/child relationships shifts—sometimes suddenly, sometimes gradually—as aging parents begin to experience problems that are associated with old age. Aging parents often lose energy, income, mobility, health, friends and family to sickness and death. Most importantly they lose a degree of independence. As aging parents experience these problems and others, adult children are often confused and troubled. Most parents want to impose as little as they possibly can on their children. They often cover up their problems in the same way that their children hid their problems decades earlier. Other elderly parents make their unhappiness known all too clearly, contributing to feelings of guilt, resentment, and helplessness in the adult child. However long it is delayed, eventually it becomes clear that elderly parents need some kind of help that they didn't need in the past. When an elderly parent lives alone, the most likely caregiver is an adult child. This shift often intensifies the relationship and creates a good deal of emotional turmoil.

Most adult children help because they feel that to do so is the fulfillment of a felt responsibility. However, many feel sad, confused, guilty, or angry, as well (see Chapter 3, "The Facts: Numbers and Feelings"). Although this can be a very difficult stage of life, the process of helping an aging parent can also give an adult child an opportunity to change, clarify, and improve this most important of all relationships.

Your Attitude

In order to help your parents it is important to have the information necessary to give appropriate advice, make the right decisions, and handle your responsibilities adequately. Many practical issues are discussed throughout this book, but there is just as much emphasis given to other, less tangible aspects of helping. Your attitude, style, and personality are the most fundamental aspects of the helping process. You may know, for example, that your parent needs to exercise in order to remedy a physical problem. You may have all the appropriate and relevant information, but you also need helping skills in order to be effective. If you are too aggressive or not assertive enough, you will not be of help. Some general guidelines are presented in Chapter 4, "Guidelines for Helping."

Self-Help

This book is intended subsidiarily to help an aging parent, but its focus is more on helping you—the adult child—in this task. Perhaps the most difficult aspect of helping is not the sacrifice of time or money, but rather, the emotional suffering. This book provides advice and insight concerning the emotional issues surrounding the problem of helping aging parents. If your parent is having problems connected with aging, it is understandable that you would feel concerned and upset. It is not, however, necessary to feel depressed, exhausted, or panicked. You can help a parent and at the same time feel sane and healthy yourself. This will be of as much benefit to you as to your parent. Some specific suggestions for coping with the stress that is often a result of helping elderly parents is offered in Chapter 5, "The Stress of Caregiving."

There are important decisions that we as a society must make concerning the fact that there are many more elderly people, living much longer than ever before. Later in the book there will be discussions of demographics, surveys, research findings, and the like. But as important as it is to study and reflect on the social, political, and economic aspects of the problem, to guide us in the future, you need information to help you now. In addition to dealing with the emotional issues, in the following chapters I intend to cover the many practical issues that you must face when you help your aging parents.

This book is therefore meant to be more helpful than theoretical. Its purpose is to help you to help without becoming overwhelmed. This is important for a number of reasons. First, you can be of more help to your parents if you know what you are doing, if you know the relevant facts, if you know the alternatives and are reasonably cheerful. If you are always resentful and anxious, you will probably not be of much help. Second, there is the possibility that you may be needed to help an elderly parent for many years, and it is no fun to feel miserable most of the time. Third, and I believe most important, if you can find a way to change the way you act with or feel about your parent so that you feel less emotionally reactive, less upset, you stand a very good chance not only of helping your parent but of altering all your relationships so that they can be more satisfying. It is sometimes hard to accept the fact that your relationship to your parents is so fundamental that to improve it can lead to positive changes in your other relationships. If you can be present and accounted for in relation to your parents—present without anger, guilt, or exhaustion—you will likely be able to be more honest and to feel better about your other relationships. As the noted family therapist Elizabeth Carter once remarked, "Moving an inch with your parents is like progressing a mile with the rest of the world."

Change Is Possible

If you have had a difficult relationship with your parent or parents over a long period of time, you may believe that it is not possible for this to change. It is not easy to change the way you behave with your parents, but change is possible. Often, although a relationship is unsatisfying, people resist change because they prefer to deal with the familiar. If you change your actions, you are entering into an unknown region. As badly as you think you want to change a troubled relationship, you also don't want to leave the comfort of the known. Change can come about when you reveal to your parents what you are feeling, what upsets you, what your fears are, and what you want and need from them. This means taking the risk of being assertive, but not aggressive, and often represents a departure from previous modes of interaction. Changing the way you relate to your parents may, in the short run, create discomfort; however, there are significant benefits.

Finding Out

This book draws on many sources of information. One source is my own clinical work as a family therapist. As will be discussed in Chapter 2, "A Family Systems Perspective," it is virtually impossible to understand the problems of one family member without understanding the ways in which these problems affect and are affected by other family members. Many of the suggestions offered in the book are based on family therapy interventions. In Chapter 4, "Guidelines for Helping," a number of principles are presented and discussed that are based on the theory and practice of not only family therapy but psychotherapy as well.

A second source of information is the research done by other professionals. There has been a growing interest in the problems of the aged and their families, and this book attempts to report on the basic findings of many other social scientists, scientists, and therapists in gerontology and related fields.

Additional information came from the results of an original questionnaire that was distributed to elderly parents. In this questionnaire parents were asked to indicate the areas in their lives that were troublesome as well as to indicate which problems they would like help with from their children. In this way we were able to look at the most serious problems facing aging parents—as they see it—and to see, from their point of view, which problems they would like help with from their children. Parents were also asked to give or send an identical copy of the questionnaire to one of their adult children. The children were asked to examine the same list of problem areas that their parents had examined and to indicate which problem areas they believed their parents regarded as the most serious, as well as to indicate whether they—the adult children—could be of help in these areas.

The questionnaires were distributed both to parents who had children living close by and to parents in retirement communities, whose children were likely to live much farther away. The responses to the questionnaires revealed the parents' main areas of concern as well as whether the children accurately perceived their parents' problems. The potential and real areas of understanding and misunderstanding between elderly parents and their children are presented throughout the book. Previous research and the results of this questionnaire indicate that the major concerns of the elderly are *health, emotional,* and *practical* issues. In Chapter 6, "Emotional/Psychological Concerns," some of the causes of the emotional problems that afflict the elderly—ageism, retirement, loneliness—will be examined, and suggestions on how to be helpful will be offered. Of greatest concern to elderly people is physical health. Chapter 7, "Your Parent as Patient," focuses on current findings in health psychology: how you can help your parent as she copes with stress, disease, doctors, hospitals, medications, and the like. In order to empathize with an elderly parent it is necessary to have some understanding of the physical side of aging. Chapter 8, "Physiological Problems," is devoted to a current discussion of the normal physiological changes that occur with age: how to accommodate them and stay healthy, as well as how to recognize the most common diseases. Elderly parents want to remain self-sufficient, but they and you may need some practical assistance. In Chapter 9, "Practical Concerns," problems such as finding social services, senior centers, home care workers, and information about housing and legal services are discussed. Although only a small percentage of elderly parents are in nursing homes, a discussion of types of nursing homes, how to select a home, and how to help a parent in a home can be found in Chapter 11, "Nursing Homes." In Chapter 12, "Dying, Death, and Funerals," information is provided to help you cope with the confusion and sadness that comes when your parent is dying. There is also a discussion of the stages of dying; how to be of help as your parent dies; funerals, and mourning.

A fourth source of information for this book has been conversations with people—both elderly parents and adult children. Although their results are presented throughout the book, a number of these intensive interviews form the basis of Chapter 10, "When a Parent Moves In." In this chapter the typical problems and points to consider before and after a parent moves in are discussed.

The Elderly and Frail Elderly

There are few things that are true everywhere and for all times. Aging is one of the few universal truths. There is a genetically determined maximum number of years that people can live— between 90 and 100. In all cultures and in all times the last decades of life are marked by physical and mental deterioration. It is also nearly universally true that societies divide the group referred to as "old" or "aged" into two categories—those who can manage their own daily affairs and needs, with some assistance from others; and the second are those who may be totally dependent on others, who require virtually total supervision and custodial care. In this book a distinction is made between the elderly and the frail elderly. If your parent is frail or infirm, your choices are somewhat more limited and you face a more painful situation.

The vast majority of elderly parents in our society are quite competent, and most of the suggestions in this book are for adult children whose parents are capable of taking care of themselves to some degree. In such cases it is important to allow elderly parents to function for themselves as much as possible. The best help is often the least help.

Changing Families

In the 1980s we have witnessed a dramatic transformation in the ratio of adult children to elderly parents in the western developed nations. This change is greatly affecting many of our lives directly. At the turn of the century 3 million Americans (1 out of 25 persons) were over 65. By 1980 that number had increased to 25 million, or one out of eight people in the country. There are more elderly parents living longer lives, and having fewer children to care for them. Many adult female children, the traditional caretakers, are in the work force. The nature of the family is also changing rapidly. For every two marriages there is one divorce. More than half the children born in the 1980s are likely to spend a portion of their childhood *not* with a two-parent family. In other words, the "traditional" two-parent family is not only not traditional, it is becoming the exception. There are more and more "blended" families, single-parent families, couples who are not married, and so on. An aging person today may find that her grandchildren no longer live with her child; she is much more likely to find herself in the role of a stepgrandparent; she may have developed an excellent relationship with a son- or daughter-in-law and find her child remarried to someone else. When an elderly parent needs help and looks to her adult children, she may find that there is less stability, clarity, and predictability. She may not be sure about who to ask.

Daniel Yankelovich, in his book *New Rules,* wrote:

> One of the most far reaching changes in norms relates to what parents believe they owe children and what their children owe them. Nowhere are the changes in the unwritten contract more significant or agonizing. The overall pattern is clear: Today's parents expect to make fewer sacrifices for their children than in the past, but they also demand less from their offspring in the form of future obligations than their parents demanded of them.... Sixty-seven percent [of adults surveyed] believe that children do not

have an obligation to their parents regardless of what their parents have done for them.[2]

In the next few decades we will see whether the changes in family structure—the increased divorce rate, dual-career marriages, and the like—do in fact lead to a decrease in the levels of affection and responsibility that adult children feel for their parents. However, for now, it seems that American children still think, feel, and act in accordance with the biblical injunction to honor their fathers and mothers.

Although Yankelovich's data suggests that adult children don't think that children, in general, are obligated to help their parents, in fact, adult children behave very responsibly. In one recent study, investigators conducted one- to two-hour interviews with a principal married member of 206 American families. Respondents were presented with the following scenario: "Mrs. M's husband died recently and since then she has been feeling rather useless. Now at age 68 she has decided she would like to live with her family in order to help care for the children and help out in other ways." Respondents were then asked, "Would you be inclined to have this older person live with you if she was your mother?" In the United States 84.3 percent said that they would.[3]

There has been a sharp decline in the number of elderly parents who actually live with their children, and there has also been a sharp drop in the number of parents receiving financial support from their children, yet this does not seem to reflect any weakening of ties. Most elderly parents live a short distance from and have very regular contact with at least one of their children. Adult children are also still very reluctant to place parents in nursing homes. Elderly parents who are frail, sick, or housebound are twice as likely to be at home as to be in an institution.[4]

Alternatives and Decisions

It is astonishing to see how often people "drift" into an unsatisfying situation with an elderly parent, just as they have drifted into other major life decisions. Some people get married, have a child, take a job, volunteer to take a parent to the doctor every week, and even invite a parent to move in, without investigating or considering the alternatives.

If one or both of your parents needs help, you and they have a great many choices and alternatives to examine and discuss. You need to have discussions with them to formulate what their options are; discussions with your own family to see how everyone feels about the alternatives; and discussions with your siblings, perhaps your parents' siblings, and other involved family members and friends. You may need to call a meeting and gather all the relevant people—including your parents—together to discuss the alternatives and decide on a plan. Oftentimes, the person you least expect help from—that distant aunt on the other side of the country, or your uninvolved brother—is able and willing, if she or he is asked respectfully to help your elderly parent.

Aside from other family members and friends whom you can talk with, there are professionals, agencies, volunteers, and many avenues of support for you and your family. Many people are unaware that their community has volunteers who will provide services such as bringing meals to the elderly or taking them to the doctor. The more choices you have, the less burdened you are. The central purpose of this book is to provide you with more choices as you help an elderly parent. Increasing your choices means knowing the relevant information and practical possibilities that are available to you. It also means being able to face clearly emotions like guilt, anger, embarrassment, and confusion, so that you can make rational choices and decisions.

An Important Limitation

Many of the suggestions and recommendations made in the following pages are based on research findings that may, in turn, have been based on small or select samples. Yet, even if the researchers used large, representative samples, the findings may have little relevance or applicability to your situation. For example, although research indicates that health is a major problem for the elderly, it may not be a problem at all for your parent. Although the research indicates that most elderly people would like to have more information about their illnesses, your parent, if ill, may be happier with less information. In other words, it is important to examine the recommendations and suggestions made in the book not as prescriptions but as ideas for your consideration.

It is hoped that an understanding of the examples and cases presented throughout the book as well as the suggestions made in reference to the cases will be useful for the reader. However, the book is not custom-made. Everyone's situation is unique. The suggestions made for one individual may not be perfectly suitable for another, or applicable to your situation, though some variation of it may prove to be useful. The book attempts to deal with the most common kinds of problems faced by elderly parents and their adult children. I hope the suggestions made will have some degree of applicability to your situation.

Chapter 2

A Family Systems Perspective

It is impossible to assist a parent if you can't think clearly because you are beset with crippling emotions. One way to lessen the negative impact of these emotions, to increase your choices and be freer, is to try to take a broader perspective than most of us normally do. Sometimes we have difficulties helping an elderly parent because we take a worm's-eye view of the problem. It is often helpful to take a wider, or bird's-eye, view of the problem. Such a view is offered by family systems theory and is illustrated by the following story.

The American explorer Robert Peary reported that he spent one day traveling directly north to the pole. At day's end he unhitched his dogsled and took readings to determine how far he had traveled. To his great surprise he found that he was farther south than when he had begun. How could this be? There was no question that he was traveling north, and he knew that he hadn't gone over the top of the pole. Peary discovered that while struggling to go north he had been on an iceberg that was carrying him south by more rapid ocean currents.[1]

You absolutely cannot understand your own situation unless you understand what is happening around you. Peary could not tell where he was until he understood his surroundings—the environment. The same is true when we try to understand the problems of children or adult children or the elderly. We are not isolates. We have friends, communities, cultures, and, most importantly, we have families.

The Family Life Cycle

Public policies affecting the elderly sometimes assume that they have no children, no families. And many adult children are surprised and overwhelmed when their parents have problems associated with aging. Why are they so surprised? Although you know on some level that your parents will get old, become weak, and die, there is the sense that it happens to other people's parents, not to yours. Adult children often feel that their parents will always be able to take care of themselves, be depended upon, not be dependent on them. Many adults who are in middle age, who have been reasonably successful in jobs or careers, who have intimate relationships with people their own age, and who have friends and well-adjusted children, are completely unprepared for the problems that arise when their parents have difficulties associated with aging and need their help. Adult children tend to be better prepared for other stages of the family life cycle. They are more actively involved in making decisions about getting married or having a child. They don't usually prepare so well for the time when a parent will need their assistance.

The problems involved with aging are no more the sole problems of the elderly than are the problems of growing up solely the problems of children. When an infant is struggling with colic, it is certainly his problem, but as every exhausted parent knows, it is their problem as well. Infancy is a stage of development not only for the infant; it also involves adults learning how to be parents and grandparents.

A family systems perspective suggests that although individuals go through transition periods in life, it makes more sense to consider individual stages in the context of changes in the family system or organization. Changes in your family structure are the best predictors of stress and change in your life. When someone leaves home, gets married, has children, has children leave home, divorces, or remarries, the entire family makes a transition. You may not think that your child's departure for college will have a tremendous impact on you or your marriage, but like Commodore Peary you would do well to consider the impact of the forces around you. All relationships change when someone comes into or goes out of the family organization. This is why there are so many books on such things as how to have a successful marriage, how to bring up children, or how to survive a divorce. When your parents get old and need your help, you go through just as significant a transition period as you do when you get married or have a child. It is a new stage in the family life cycle, and it requires new adaptations. Although your parents may feel that the problems associated with aging have an effect only on them, this is not the case. You may believe that your parents' problems do not really affect you, but if you feel confused or unhappy and are unsure why, you may be floating south on your family iceberg.[2]

There are few books that focus on the relationship between adult children and their elderly parents. Although the vast majority of adult children want to be helpful, they often have little understanding of the physical and emotional changes that come with age. Many do not understand their parents' needs and are unable to offer the best advice and be of the most help.

Amy—A Case Study

Amy, 32 years old, has short dark hair, a trim figure, sparkling eyes, and speaks with energy and enthusiasm. She just graduated from social work school and has been living with her boyfriend, Marcus, for three years. Amy says she feels happy about most aspects of her life, except that she is having problems with her mother.

The difficulty began when Amy's father died two years ago. Amy's mother, Ruth, age 68, lives about a 45-minute drive away from Amy. Since her father's death, Amy visits Ruth much more often and feels Ruth to be more demanding—especially in an emotional sense. Ruth is quite healthy but says that she feels lonely and wants Amy to do more for her—to listen to her, to drive her places, and to visit and call more frequently. Amy's mother has actually begun to say things like, "It's very important that we spend time together because you just don't know how much longer I'll be around." Amy feels guilty, angry, and very stressed in relation to her mother, but her greatest concern is for the future. She is worried that her mother's aging will become more and more of a problem for her.

Not only is her father gone, but her sister, Robin, won't have anything to do with their mother. Robin, 42 years old, is married to an internist, Gregory, and has three children. Amy believes that Robin was really the favorite child while they were growing up. Robin was a very sensitive and insecure child. Amy remembers that Robin often cuddled with their mother and that it was Robin who made their mother most proud by getting good grades and academic awards. Now Robin won't even talk to Ruth. This is because when Robin got married, her parents disapproved of the marriage. No one is quite sure why Robin's husband was so disliked, but he and Robin both felt rejected and insulted. Neither of them will now get involved with Ruth, whom they see as cold and unemotional.

Amy also has a younger brother, Eric, who is 28 years old. Eric cannot be of too much help because he just started work as an engineer in a different part of the country. No wonder, then, that Ruth, finding her son far away, her eldest daughter estranged, and her husband dead, has come to depend on Amy. Amy, beneath her anger and guilt, feels frightened by the likelihood that she will come to have more and more responsibility for her mother. She is not sure how much time she wants to or ought to allocate to Ruth. She finds it difficult to listen to her mother's never-ending stream of complaints and annoyances. She wants to be helpful but doesn't know how to do this without sacrificing herself. She is angry with her brother, who seems to have gotten himself out of the emotional quagmire with not much expected of him, and angry with her mother whom she blames for estranging her sister. As for her sister, Amy feels puzzled. She would like to ask her sister to be more involved, but Robin won't let Amy even mention Ruth's name, and Amy does empathize with Robin. Nevertheless, Amy feels she has been abandoned by her sister as well as by her brother, and forced into the role of caregiver. When Amy tells her trouble to her siblings, Robin's advice is, "Don't get so involved. Take care of yourself"; while Eric says, "Gee, I'd love to help out. I feel really bad for you. It's too bad I live so far away." Amy feels trapped, almost as though she has lost her ability to choose, and sees no possibility of finding a satisfying solution. Lately she has begun to think that she would probably be better off if she simply resigned herself to the situation.

Some Facts in Amy's Case

Adult children are less likely to feel the need to be helpful when both parents are alive. Amy's father's death was the event that triggered the shift in the family life cycle. Another common transition point is marked by a shift in the physical health of a parent. Amy's parents had been able to support and help each other. There were difficulties, to be sure, and had her father lived longer, Amy might have eventually been called upon; but the sudden death created a vacuum, and among the siblings it is Amy who is feeling the pressure to fill it.

The case also illustrates the most common aging parent/adult child bond—that between mother and daughter. An aging parent in need of help is more likely to be a woman, primarily because women live longer than men. And, although certain sex-role stereotypes have changed, it is still very much expected that the daughter will assume most responsibility for taking care of a parent. Amy's mother, Ruth, needs and wants more from her children. It is not a coincidence that Amy's brother is on the other side of the country. Ruth makes fewer demands on and has fewer expectations of Eric. Although he is a good son who is concerned about his mother, he gets and feels much less pressure than Amy. Eric feels that Amy is a little "hysterical" about the situation, and Amy finds herself wondering at times if he is not right. Amy is not fully aware that her added responsibility and pressure have to some degree been determined by her sex. The statistics show that the majority of aging parents live close to one of their adult children and that this child is most likely to be female. Eric is similarly unaware that his greater mobility and more relaxed attitude are a result of sexist expectations. Of course, gender is only one of the variables that determine who feels responsible for an aging parent. In some families there are just daughters, in others just sons, and others are mixed, with a son taking on the role of principal helper. In one family studied, an aging parent spent three months a year with each of her four children. This is not a common, and usually not a successful, arrangement. In most families one child takes on the major responsibilities for the parent, and there is no question that the child is most often female.

When a parent begins to need help from a child, not only

parent/child relations but sibling relations also change. The unresolved issues between siblings come to the fore just as parent/child issues do. The question of who put Amy "in charge" of Ruth is a difficult one to answer. What besides sex of the child determines who feels or becomes responsible? Interviews and case studies show that the "favorite" child is not necessarily the most likely to help. Many less-favored children are greatly involved with their aging parents. It may be that the favored child feels more secure or less guilty, having already pleased a parent, whereas a less-favored child may still feel the need to get close to a parent and/or win her approval.

Freud said that the goal of psychotherapy was to replace neurotic misery with normal human suffering. This is really not an overly pessimistic remark. It means that there are many good reasons for people to be unhappy. If your parent is physically ill or has recently lost a close friend, it is appropriate for her to be upset. It is not the goal of psychotherapy to take the pain out of life. However, Freud believed that it was possible to change certain feelings, thoughts, and behaviors so that there could be less unnecessary pain. In the case above we can see that Ruth and her children needed to be sad and to mourn the death of Ruth's husband. However, because of the estrangement between Ruth and Robin, and Eric's lack of involvement, the family is having extreme difficulty making the transition to the next stage in the family life cycle. Some of the family's difficulties appear not to be necessary and could be changed. Everyone would be better off if Robin and her mother had a better relationship. Why don't they?

Problems Are Ineffective Solutions

When there is confusion and unhappiness in a family because a family member is acting irresponsibly or inappropriately, it may be helpful to take a step back from your emotions and the immediate situation. There is often a method in people's madness. Irresponsible behavior sometimes has very beneficial effects. The cause of a "problem" can often be found by looking at its positive results. For example, if your sister is irresponsible, you are likely to be seen by the rest of the family as the favored child. You may inadvertently contribute to the problem by your own actions. You may complain about your sibling's lack of involvement; yet, when your parent needs assistance you quickly come to her aid. This may lead your sister to feel unnecessary and more distant. She may withdraw further as you—feeling more resentful, more essential, and more favored—do more. Perhaps your uninvolved sibling helps you to maintain the favored status that you desire.

In a similar "systems analysis," if your sister is always too upset to help you with your parent, you are forced to keep yourself emotionally stable. Many people who are easily upset pull themselves together if they feel needed. You may feel yourself to be the "stronger" sibling and complain about the "weaker" one. However, the stronger sibling usually benefits by playing the more stable role. You may be contributing to your sibling's instability by treating her as less competent than she really is so that you can feel more competent and strong. She may consciously or unconsciously play a less stable role in order to help you.

Finally, if your mother complains incessantly, it may give you an opportunity to call one of your siblings frequently to share your burden. Your mother's complaints could also remind you that you and your mother both miss your father. Such _consequences_ of problem behavior are clearly not trivial. Think about what the symptoms or problems of one family member allow other family members to do. If you consider that the problem may be an unconscious attempt at a solution, you may be able to come up with a better, less painful solution. _Symptoms or problems serve a function, which is why they are so hard to get rid of_. Consider that when a family member appears to have a problem or a symptom, it can have beneficial effects. Think about what the beneficial effects are, and explain to the problem person that you realize that you and the rest of the family have contributed to the problem and that some other solution needs to be worked out. It is sometimes hard for us to appreciate this point of view. However, when someone is being difficult or has a problem, he or she is the person who suffers most. Such suffering can only be endured if it helps the family. People are willing to make drastic self-sacrifices (although they are not conscious of doing so) to help the family organization. If you discuss the problems in the family in such a way that you stop blaming particular members, and realize that everyone plays a part in the difficulty, change is more likely to come about.[3]

If Amy considered the beneficial aspects of the rift between her mother and sister, she might be able to help them find a better solution for the situation. Amy recalled that Robin was always the favorite when they were growing up. Now Robin and Ruth aren't speaking. Once again, such things don't just happen. As Robin was growing up she was extremely close to her parents. No one understands why Robin's parents rejected her husband and caused such a problem in the family, but there is always a reason. The family members each have their own explanations, often filled with blame, but the truth almost always involves the "invisible loyalties" that motivate family members. Often the meanest or most incomprehensible behaviors are expressions of loyalty to other family members. Although Robin was so close to her parents, she married a partner who was unacceptable to them (often, such a partner is one who has different religious or political beliefs). In this case the parents felt they had to reject the marriage, but it allowed Robin to break from them and devote her energy to her husband. In order to make her marriage work, Robin needed to pull away from her family. Her parents unconsciously knew that she needed help with the separation and pushed Robin away with the one blow that would force her to be aware that her main priority should be her husband—they rejected him. This rejection and the estrangement which followed probably hurt the parents more than it did Robin, but it was good for the marriage. The proof is that the couple have three children and are doing well. These are the kinds of sacrifices that parents make for children (children, of course, do the same) without anyone being aware of them, including the parents. Had these issues been worked out more consciously, Robin and her parents could have accomplished the separation while still preserving the relationship.

Amy doesn't realize how much she gains by the distance between her mother and sister. Amy feels saddled with more responsibility and pressure, but it is a position that she would not relinquish easily. If she was more aware of these family dynamics, she could choose to be somewhat less involved with her mother and allow her sister to become more involved. She could do this by pointing out to Robin how painful it must have been for their parents to have pushed her away by rejecting her husband in order to help her marriage. If you realize that the "senseless" things family members do to one another are often motivated by a desire to help, you can sometimes figure out what positive goal the "senseless" act was meant to accomplish. This will sometimes allow family members to accomplish their goals more effectively in the future.

The Importance of Maintaining the Family Hierarchy

Amy's primary feeling in relation to her mother is anger. When she is not angry, she says she feels tired, which is probably because she is working so hard at controlling her anger. There are a great many feelings stirred up when you begin to help an aging parent. What causes the feeling of anger which is so commonly found in these situations?

When you help an aging parent, the situation does not commonly become a complete role reversal. A role reversal occurs when the child parents the parent. Unless a parent is so impaired that such a reversal is necessary, it is usually strenuously resisted by both parent and child. The resistance to role reversal is quite proper, especially when there is no real need for it. This is the primary reason for Amy's anger—she adamantly refuses to be her mother's mother. "Maintaining the family hierarchy" is another way of saying that parents should behave like parents and children should act like children. If Amy and her mother were clearer about their roles, if Amy did not feel the need to assume the role of mother, she would be more helpful and have a better relationship with her mother. Because Amy is not calm and clear about her role as child, she has become an "anti-mother." Amy's fantasy is that her mother is so needy that if she helps out willingly she will soon find herself confronted with a "bottomless pit" of requests, expectations, demands, emotionality, and complaints. In order to protect herself and her mother from this outcome, she angrily withdraws.

Amy needs to be clearer in her own mind about how much help she is willing to provide, so that she can invest less psychological energy in being an "anti-mother." She also needs to consider the possibility that Ruth can still function as a mother. In other words, at the same time that she is helping her mother, Amy should not dismiss the notion of asking her mother for help. Adult children commonly have a difficult time helping a parent and, at the same time, allowing the parent to function like a parent. Amy could ask her mother's advice on all sorts of matters. She likes Ruth's taste in art and furniture. If she was able to ask her mother for any kind of support, Amy would feel less angry about supporting her and there would be less danger of their reversing roles.

A Family Meeting

When an elderly parent has a problem, it is important to remember that the problem and its solution include many other people. That you are reading this book is an indication that you feel some responsibility for your parent. You should be careful that you do not take too much responsibility. It is likely that your parent has an informal support network of friends, neighbors, and other relatives who help her and whom she helps in return. There is also an army of professionals trained in various aspects of helping elderly people. This formal support network is discussed in Chapter 9, "Practical Concerns."

In many situations, if an elderly parent has a problem, it is not necessary to call a family meeting. However, if there is a crisis or if it appears that some major change is in the offing, it is important to discuss the possibilities with the members of your own family, your siblings, your parent's siblings, and any other people who are involved. You might consider conferring with another relative in order to decide who should be invited to the meeting. It is important to invite even a sibling who has been previously uninvolved and uninterested. If you don't, later you might hear, "If I had been consulted, I would have suggested something completely different, and much better," and there is the possibility that what you do will be undermined. Keep in mind also that less-involved relatives can sometimes offer a clearer perspective. It is important to include your parent in the conference, as well, unless she is so disabled and disoriented that such a meeting would greatly upset her. If you don't include your parent, she should definitely be told that a conference will take place, who is coming, and what is to be discussed. Her needs and feelings are the primary consideration, and it is important to minimize secrets. When secret plans are made, people begin to feel suspicious, paranoid, excluded, uninvolved, and disrespected. None of these feelings are conducive to effective development and implementation of a plan. At the meeting everyone should have an opportunity to talk about what the problems are. For example, can your parent continue to live by herself, and, if not, what are the various alternatives; how can decisions be made and actions be taken?

The Problem of Overinvolvement

At this point it may not be necessary for Amy's family to meet; but if her mother comes to need more assistance, a conference might help them to resolve some of their problems. A family meeting might help Amy to realize that she is overinvolved with her mother, and that she can alter this situation.

People in families care a great deal about one another. More common than uninvolvement between elderly parents and their adult children is *overinvolvement*. Amy feels so upset by what is happening to her mother because she is too involved with her. You don't feel guilty or angry about someone whom you are not passionately attached to. Amy might feel better if she was a bit more distanced from her mother. She could accomplish this by making a conscious decision about how much help she is willing to offer. She could tell her mother in advance when she plans to visit, and she could also regularize the phone contact between them. This would enable Amy to feel more in control, and also make their contact more predictable—"Mom, please try to call me on Wednesday or Saturday." Such formal arrangements often make relationships less intense and less passionate. Eric can be reminded that he can call or write more regularly. He can also be told that he could invite his mother out west for a vacation or provide financial support if needed. If there was more distance between Amy and her mother, Robin and Eric would probably find themselves more involved. Such is the nature of families: change in one relationship always changes other relationships.

Chapter 3 _____
The Facts: Numbers and Feelings

The facts that psychologists work with are behavior and experience. Facts are not matters of opinion. They cannot be talked out of existence or wished away. The scope of the subject of this book—the relationship between aging parents and adult children—can best be understood by first examining the basic facts.

Some of the facts in this chapter are presented in terms of the numbers of demographic study. The demographics indicate that we are in a period of transition and suggest that this is a difficult time for aging parents and their adult children. The conclusion that adult child/elderly parent relations are in a period of flux is supported by another set of facts—our feelings. Feelings, although changeable, private, and precarious, are experienced directly; if you feel sad or confused, this feeling is just as much a fact as that in 1980 over 25 million Americans were over 65. The facts—both numbers and feelings—are always changing. The numbers have changed since 1980. Feelings also change. The fact that feelings about our elderly parents can change is certainly one of the underlying premises of this book.

More Elderly Parents

One of the most striking changes taking place in our country has sometimes been referred to as "the aging of America." In 1900, 3.1 million Americans were 65 years of age or older, but by 1980 the number had increased eightfold, to over 25 million. At the turn of the century about 4 percent of the population was over

65; now the estimates are about 12 percent or one in every eight Americans. It is expected that the ratio of elderly to nonelderly will be 1 to 5 in 1990 and 1 to 3 in 2025.

Not only are there more older Americans, older people are living much longer. In 1900 the average man had a life span of 46 years. Today the average 65-year-old man can expect to live until 79 and the average 65-year-old woman until 84. The fastest growing age group in the United States is the 75-plus category. In 1900, fewer than 1 million Americans were 75 or older and 100,000 were over 85. By 1980 there were almost 10 million over 75 and 2.3 million over 85 (22 times as great as at the turn of the century). From 1960 to 1982 alone, the 85-plus population jumped 165 percent.

The diseases of old age are being conquered and controlled, so that more and more people are living longer. However, the majority of the elderly are not infirm. In the 65-and-older group, 8 out of 10 describe themselves as in good or excellent health compared with others of their age group, despite frequent chronic conditions. In the 85-and-over age group, one-third are in good health, one-third are limited in some degree, and one-third need regular assistance in living. Since the turn of the century, there has been more chronic illness and less acute illness. These issues will be discussed more fully in Chapter 8, "Physiological Problems." It seems that as a person gets older, the chance of acute illness goes down and that of chronic illness goes up. In practical terms this means that larger numbers of elderly people need limited assistance, rather than hospitalization.

Sex Difference in Longevity

As older people need help, they typically look first to their spouses. However, because of the dramatically different mortality rates for men and women, many more women than men are without mates and living alone. As can be seen in Table 3-1, only 11 percent of women over 85 are married. It should be pointed out that the difference in life span between men and women continues to increase. At the turn of the century there were actually more elderly men than women. In 1960 there were 5 elderly women to 4 elderly men, and by 1982 the ratio was 6 to 4. It is interesting to speculate on

TABLE 3-1

**U.S. Elderly Population for 1980
by Age, Sex, and Marital Status**

Age/Sex	Number	% of Total Elderly Population	% Married
Age 65–74			
Males	6,755,199	26	79
Females	8,822,387	35	50
Total	15,577,586	61	63
Age 75–84			
Males	2,865,974	11	69
Females	4,860,852	19	27
Total	7,726,826	30	43
Age 85+			
Males	681,428	3	44
Females	1,558,293	6	11
Total	2,239,721	9	21

Source: New York State Office for the Aging. Data from U.S. Bureau of Census, 1980 Census Supplementary Rep., Social Security Administration, Actuarial Study No. 84, 1980.

these changes. It had been postulated that as women continued to enter the work force in increasing numbers, this ratio would shift. However, current research does not bear this out. The prediction that women would have coronaries at the same rate as men when they joined the work force has not yet come true.[1] At the present time many elderly women cannot turn to spouses as a source of help. The number of elderly women living alone has doubled in the last 15 years, so that now *most* elderly women live alone. In the over-75 age group 7 out of 10 women are widowed and live alone.

Current statistics indicate that there are more older people and that they are living longer, many of them without the comfort and assistance of a spouse, many with chronic physical problems, and a good many at the low end of the economic scale. In 1984, 17 percent of American women over 65 had incomes below the poverty line.[2]

As we will see, some of the obstacles older people face are based on myth and stereotype. However, others are all too real. There is an increased need for safety measures in the home. There is less money, and hostility or lack of awareness in the marketplace; there are problems of transportation and mobility, and sometimes isolation and loneliness. For the frail elderly or the ill, daily life becomes a battle: just finding suitable clothes to buy or the physical act of getting dressed can be a problem. Especially for those living alone, preparing a meal can be such an arduous task—beginning with food shopping and ending with dishes to wash—that it may be experienced as just not worth the effort. The elderly need allies in their struggles, and most feel that their strongest and most dependable allies are their children.

Fewer Children

If the only major change in families was that people were living longer and there were more older people than ever before, the situation would be serious but perhaps manageable. However, other significant changes taking place in families at the same time complicate the problem.

An aunt of mine told me about a saying she heard when she was growing up: "It takes one mother to raise 10 children but 10 children to help one aging mother." One fact in America today is that there are very few elderly mothers with 10 children. Today's elderly parents simply raised fewer children than previous generations and therefore have fewer descendants to call on for help. Adult children in this generation have fewer brothers and sisters to lend a hand in caring for their elderly parents.

Table 3-2 shows that in 1931 almost 6 out of 10 mothers had four or more children; by 1981 half of that percentage, or fewer than 3 out of 10, have that many. Table 3-3 shows that the majority of parents aged 65 or over have only one or two children. This makes the job of helping aging parents more difficult

TABLE 3-2
Mothers with Four or More Children (%)

Year	1931	1941	1951	1961	1971	1981
Percent	58.8	52.2	44.4	33.0	26.4	29.6

Source: U.S. Department of Health, Education, and Welfare. Fertility tables for birth cohort by color, United States 1917–73, pub. No. HRA 76-1152, Table 7A.

than ever before. There are simply fewer siblings to share the responsibilities.

Adult Female Children in the Work Force

Through many generations the work of helping aging parents has fallen largely to the female children. In one recent study, it was found that the homebound elderly were helped, in rank order, by children, spouse, relatives, and friends or neighbors. Of the children who were the major caregivers, 75 percent were women, while other relatives, friends, and neighbors providing assistance were nearly all women.[3]

One of the most commonly held beliefs, and one substantiated by the facts, is that the psychological and physical care of the aged has come predominantly from the female members of the family. Middle-aged daughters are thus said to have fallen into a "demographic double bind."[4] While middle-aged daughters have traditionally been the principal source of needed ser-

TABLE 3-3
Persons Age 65 and Over with Surviving Children

Percentage of Total Elderly Population	25	26	17	13	6	5	8
Number of surviving children	1	2	3	4	5	6	7+

Source: E. Shanas. *The national survey of the aged* (Final Rep.). Chicago: University of Illinois, 1977.

vices, more of them than ever before will have aging parents who are living much longer lives. These same daughters are much less likely to have siblings with whom to share caregiving responsibilities, and they are much more likely than before to be experiencing the additional pressures and responsibilities of work.

In Cantor's 1980 study of adult female children helping their aging parents, 60 percent were employed at the same time. These women reported that they were under severe strain. They had to balance the demands of their careers, the needs of their own nuclear families, and the needs of their aging parents. Table 3-4 shows the rapid increase in the participation of middle-aged women in the work force. However, the percentages are still changing. In 1984, 69 percent of all women between the ages of 35 and 44 were in the work force.

Illusions of Times Past

Many Americans think wistfully about how much better off older people were a few decades ago, when, among other reasons, adult children were supposedly more dedicated and responsive to their aging parents. Somehow just looking at a Norman Rockwell painting we know that grandparents used to help with the chores and assist in bringing up the grandchildren. Meanwhile, the grandchildren got into just the right amount of mischief and the parents listened to the advice of their parents and tended to their own children with just the right amount of fairness and discipline. The paintings show the supposed harmony of three-generational love, caring, and support.

Although changing demographics have altered many aspects of the adult child/aging parent relationship, it is simply not true

TABLE 3-4
Women in the Work Force

	1950	1981
45–54 years old	38%	60%
55–64 years old	27%	42%

Source: U.S. Department of Labor, 1981.

that older people were better off decades ago. Older people were more likely to be neglected and impoverished, and they certainly suffered more than the elderly of today. Social Security has helped many to maintain independence, and the support of the old by the young now occurs on a national scale through old age programs, as well.[5]

It is also not true that the support of the elderly by their adult children occurred without tension and conflict. Much evidence indicates that adult children assisted their parents out of economic necessity rather than love and devotion. In his book *Family Life and Illicit Love in Earlier Generations,* Peter Laslett shows that children would take in and care for an elderly parent who was capable of contributing to the household, but would be reluctant or refuse to care for one who was a drain or liability. Other accounts reveal that the elderly who lived in the poorhouse would be taken in by their adult children in the summer when they could help with the chores and care for the grandchildren and then be returned to the poorhouse when winter came and they were no longer needed. It is true that in many parts of rural America aging parents were well cared for by their children, but often this was because parents held title to the land, which the children did not receive until the parent died. Often the father willed land to the children with the stipulation that they care for his wife.[6]

Although the average income of families headed by someone over 65 is only half that of families headed by persons under 65, this represents a dramatic improvement over how things used to be.[7] The poverty rate for people over 65, although still high compared with that of other age groups, has shown clear improvement even in the last two decades. In 1959, 35 percent of Americans over 65 (about 1 out of 3) were considered to live in households below the poverty threshold. By 1979 the percentage had dropped to 15 percent: about 1 out of every 6 elderly Americans was considered poor or near poor. This does represent a trend for the better. The "good old days" for older Americans never really existed.[8]

Contact Between the Generations

In recent times we have witnessed a striking increase in geographic mobility among all age groups. People born in America today are-likely to move or change households about once every 7 years. Older Americans do not move around as much as their adult children, but many (some estimates suggest 1 million) have gone to retirement communities in Florida, the Ozark plateau, the Texas high country, and the sun belt. Florida has the largest concentration of the elderly. More than 20 percent of the population of the Fort Lauderdale–Hollywood and Tampa–Saint Petersburg area are elderly. Some people believe that most elderly people have moved to retirement communities and have little contact with their children or that those who haven't moved nonetheless have little contact. There is very little evidence to support any of these beliefs.

One shift that did take place was that many elderly people left the central cities to move into the suburbs. In 1979 most people over 65 lived in metropolitan areas. Now most older Americans (55 percent) live in the suburbs. Have adult children abandoned their parents? Are you more the exception than the rule because you have a great deal of concern for your parents? According to statistics, the answer to these questions is *no*. A nationwide survey reveals that 4 out of 5 older Americans have children and that almost three-quarters of these elderly parents live within half an hour of the nearest child.

Table 3-5 shows that most older Americans live less than 10 minutes away from an adult child. The table does not tell us how many of the children live close by. Which child lives close by and how that has come about is important, since the sibling physically closest is likely to be most responsible for helping.

TABLE 3-5
Proximity of Parents over 65 to Nearest Child

Travel Time	Percent
Living in same household	18
Within 10 minutes or less	34
Within 11 to 30 minutes	21
More than 30 minutes away	28

Source: The White House Conference on Aging, *Chartbook on aging in America,* Washington, D.C.: U.S. Government Printing Office, 1981, pp. 104–105.

The table also shows that almost 30 percent of aging parents do not have adult children who are living close by. Helping in such cases can involve somewhat different practical and emotional issues, to be discussed in Chapter 4, "Guidelines for Helping," Chapter 6, "Emotional/Psychological Concerns," and Chapter 9, "Practical Concerns."

From Table 3-6 it can be seen that older Americans are not only physically close to their children, but also in close contact with them. The "contact" referred to in the table consisted of an actual meeting between a parent and a child, rather than a phone call or a letter. More than three-quarters of the elderly sampled reported having had such a contact with one child in the last week, and the majority of aging parents sampled actually saw one child on the day that the survey was being done or on the previous day. Only 10 percent said that they had not seen one of their children in the previous month. This frequency of contact seems to indicate that adult children are very much involved with their parents.

The numbers that have been discussed lend factual weight to the direct experience of many adult children. Middle-aged children, both men and women, tend to be working full-time, and at the same time must cope with parents who are getting old. These adult children, especially women, feel called upon to help their elderly parents, who often live close by, and to see them often. Compared with their counterparts of 50 years ago, they have fewer siblings to assist them in this sometimes very difficult task.

TABLE 3-6

Contact between Parents over 65 and Adult Children

Most Recent Contact	*Percent*
Today or yesterday	53
Within 2 to 7 days	24
Within 8 to 30 days	12
More than 30 days ago	10

Source: The White House Conference on Aging, *Chartbook on aging in America,* Washington, D.C.: U.S. Government Printing Office, 1981, pp. 104–105.

Feelings

Social scientists tend to focus a great deal on numbers, and it seems clear that the numbers are important. Knowing the demographic patterns and trends is essential to making sound social and public policy decisions. It would not be wise to recommend social policy merely on the basis of your experiences and those of your acquaintances. Statistics also can reflect our own personal experience, and thus they often enable us to feel a connection to other people in similar situations. If you are, for example, a middle-aged woman helping to care for your elderly parent and feeling pulled by the demands of your own family and career, it may be helpful to know that you are not alone. It is also important to realize that your concerns, feelings, and problems are related to other people's and that group interests exist and group actions can be taken. For example, middle-aged working women have tried to get help with child care, but they also need assistance with their aging parents. The needs of middle-aged children as a group, regarding their parents, have not yet been adequately addressed.

The numbers, however useful, leave out one very essential aspect of the problems that adult children encounter when they attempt to help their parents—feelings. Although there have been a great many studies done on such questions as how often adult children see their parents, or how many live where, do what, and how much, there has been very little research on what it all feels like. Our personal feelings—often difficult to explain, difficult to test and examine in a laboratory, not even easy to talk about—may be what count most in any analysis of the problem.

The Difficulty of Expressing Love

The troublesome or unpleasant feelings that adult children sometimes have for their aging parents have received more attention than the positive feelings of respect, affection, devotion, or love, and yet these are the feelings that underlie most relationships between adult children and their aging parents. The primary reason why adult children get so angry and upset with, or crazed by an aging parent is anguish at the inevitability of death. Anguish is the expression of this same love. If you see a parent being forgetful, having trouble hearing, or having difficulty finding the right key, or you see her bedridden, uncomfortable, and in pain, you may be able to assist her but you cannot stop the aging process, you cannot change the fact that she will die.

Although this section of the book focuses on troublesome feelings, it should be pointed out that the most painful and problematic feelings often arise because there is a passionate attachment. We simply do not feel guilty or angry with people we do not care about.

In many relationships the direct expressions of caring and intimacy are not allowed. This does not mean that such feelings do not exist. It is not unusual for parents and children to only express positive feelings directly on birthday or Christmas cards. The direct expression of caring and affection for a parent can be helpful for us, but it can be very difficult, especially if there is little history of this type of expression. Some of us just don't have much practice. It is hard to know exactly why positive feelings are so difficult to express. Perhaps the Freudian notion that we are afraid to feel too close to our parents has some merit. Many people need to devalue their parents in order to leave them. This allows the child to become independent. Such a devaluation can continue to maintain itself even after a healthy separation has taken place and there is no further need for it.

Love, loyalty, and caring are often expressed indirectly. We will see that often the seemingly most negative feelings of parents and children are indirect expressions of love. The love that underlies the relationship is sometimes expressed in jokes, other gestures, or even as other feelings, such as hatred of a sibling who is not doing his share. Love can even be expressed as anger toward a parent, as when one feels too close and pulls back from being smothered.

Changing Feelings

It is not easy to change feelings by working directly on them. You may feel guilty or angry or exhausted in relation to an aging parent even if you know that the feelings are not appropriate or helpful to them or to you. Unfortunately, advice like, "Don't feel guilty or angry" usually has very little effect. However, feelings can be changed. If you are able to change family structure or organization, communication patterns, or attitudes, feelings can and do change. Feelings can also change when you do things differently. It is most important to remember that *small changes* can be very meaningful and very powerful.

In one family consisting of three generations—a mother, a father, two children ages 10 and 8, and the mother's mother—the 8-year-old boy was consistently getting into trouble at school. Notes came home saying that he was getting into fights frequently. In the very first interview with the family it was clear that there was much hostility between the parents. The parents could not agree on what should be done about the situation. As is so typical in these situations, when the father wanted to take a tough stand the mother would stop him because she thought he was getting too loud or tough in his attempts to discipline the child. When the parents began to fight, the child took comfort with the grandmother, who was then resented by both the mother and the father. The child would cry in the arms of his grandmother, and the whole business would usually end with both parents blaming the child's problem on the presence of the grandmother. Somehow they concluded that if she would leave, everything would take care of itself. This was a very unpleasant situation for everyone in the family. Years of analysis were not necessary to remedy the problem. Several changes in the family's pattern of interaction were effective in making a difference. The parents were advised to work together to develop a joint plan to stop their son's aggressive behavior. They had to decide on specific punishments for first, second, or third offenses. They were also advised to go out with the child and do something special—the boy loved to go to the movies, so this was the agreed-upon reward—if no notes came home. The first necessary step toward change in this family was to convince the parents to work together and cooperate. Another step was also taken to ensure the child's positive behavior. As was stated earlier, behavior problems like fighting can sometimes be faulty solutions to family dilemmas. The grandmother was, in fact, lonely and very much enjoyed being able to comfort her grandchild, but she only did this when he was in trouble and very upset. Grandmother and grandson were therefore encouraged to hug and comfort each other every day when he came home from school, regardless of how he had behaved.

Small changes can be important ones. If you are having problems with an elderly parent, there is not a great chance that you or your parent or spouse or sibling will undergo some drastic redesign of character which will make everyone happy. However, often some slight alteration in attitude or behavior can make things tolerable and perhaps even satisfactory.

Confusion

A great many people we talked with or who responded to our survey described themselves as feeling confused or frazzled or upset or undone. This is quite understandable. Whenever you enter any new role there is a certain amount of discomfort and confusion. When you take on a new job, there is a period of adjustment. You are expected to wear certain clothes, follow specified routines, and know your place in the hierarchy. A new teacher, for example, must learn to feel comfortable with the authority she has in relation to her students and learn how to adapt to the instructions from the school principal or administrator. If the teacher becomes an administrator, she will go through another adjustment period. When you take on a new role, you have a certain amount of freedom but there are actions that must be taken and words that must be spoken. When a stage actor takes on a role, he has a certain degree of flexibility, but every actor who plays Hamlet must say, "To be or not to be," although no two would say it in precisely the same way.

Perhaps a helpful way of thinking about family organization and confusion is in terms of role theory. To be a son or daughter is to have a role. In this culture, as in others, roles are in part defined in terms of other roles, namely those of mothers and fathers. Everyone knows that although there is great flexibility, the parental role is to nurture—to support, discipline, and promote the autonomy of their children until the children are able to take care of themselves. When the children become adults, there is a major shift in the roles of both parents and children. There is often a long period of time in which new, adult-to-adult relations are established. When a parent needs the help of an adult

child, there is another significant shift in roles. It sometimes
takes a while to see clearly that your parents are dependent,
vulnerable, and in need of help, and that they may be asking for
your support and assistance. When you are asked to help nurture
and care for your parents, there is not only the disorientation of
changed roles but in some instances a role reversal. When a
parent is disabled or helpless and roles are reversed suddenly
and completely, the experience can be shocking and disorienting. An elementary school teacher who, after years of teaching,
goes back to the university to get a Ph.D. and finds a former
student as her professor experiences only a small fraction of the
confusion due to role reversal that an adult child experiences
when she cares for a frail elderly parent.

All adjustments to role changes require time. The confusion
and disorientation that you experience when a parent asks for
help is likely to lessen as you get your bearings in the new role.
It can be helpful to recognize that such reactions are natural and
transitory and should not be resisted.

Lack of Feeling

There are some adult children who react to their elderly parent's
problems by withdrawing—sometimes physically, sometimes emotionally, and sometimes both. They want to pretend that it's just
not happening: their parents aren't really getting old, they aren't
really approaching death, they don't really need anything from
them. In the face of such dangerous possibilities, such adult children distance themselves from the whole situation. Perhaps they
visit less or call less and hope that someone else will step in. In
response to an elderly parent's call for help, they may find themselves getting busier than ever. This may be the child's subcon-
scious attempt to persuade the parent to look elsewhere for help
and to keep the child from feeling the emotions connected to this
change in his or her life. While it is helpful to the parent for the child
not to become overly worried or involved, ignoring the situation is
not a helpful strategy for a child to adopt. If you believe your
parents' problems are not yours but strictly theirs, you would have
to agree that a stick has one end. Explorer Robert Peary, in the
story described in Chapter 2, may have wished that he wasn't

floating south on an uncooperative iceberg, but it wouldn't have helped him to ignore the obvious. No matter how much he would have liked the iceberg to have been carrying him north or to be immobile, it wasn't. Adult children who "cut themselves off" from their parent because they find some personality trait in him or her unacceptable often develop the same personality trait and repeat the mistakes of the parent out of their unconscious loyalty. If you pretend that you are completely cut off from your parents, you do so at your own peril.

Depression

When parents show the many problem signs of aging—forgetfulness, failing health, financial struggle—many adult children feel sad. They feel that something has been lost, and it has. If your parents have a more painful and difficult life, and you see this, you should not push away your sadness too quickly. Similarly, if your parent has been diagnosed as having some physical illness and you feel distressed and sorrowful, it is important to allow these feelings their natural course. There is much in our culture that argues against having or expressing feelings of sadness or loss. This "macho" mentality, sometimes shared by both men and women, dictates that nothing is more valuable than a stiff upper lip, that these are changes which must be accepted, that you shouldn't impose your sadness on your friends and family. A slightly more relaxed version of this ethos is that it is OK to be sad about your parent's being sick or frail, but that you should get over your sorrow as quickly as possible, and you should grieve alone. It is important to question these values. Why should you feel that your friends or family are so fragile that they could not bear to hear your sorrow? They are probably much stronger than you give them credit for being, and many would probably welcome the opportunity to act like real friends or family, knowing how you are really feeling and sharing your sadness.

Adult children often need to be instructed to feel sad. This may sound somewhat bizarre—to instruct someone to feel sad—but in our culture men especially need to be taught to feel sadness about their elderly parents. If you do not allow yourself to feel a "natural" degree of sadness, it can sometimes invade and overwhelm you, leaving you more depressed.

Family therapists have noted recently that serious problems can develop in families in which there hasn't been sufficient mourning over a deceased family member. Without such mourning the loss isn't experienced fully and resolved. It is as if a ghost remains and haunts the family. This is why so many cultures and religious traditions impose or specify a period of mourning. People are instructed to sit and grieve for a period of time, say prayers, and think about the deceased and how much he is missed. It may be more important than ever to follow these rituals today, because for many people the old traditions are not maintained. Such mourning may be equally important for *living* parents.

Rhoda entered therapy because she was feeling exhausted and depressed after a recent ordeal. Her mother, who lived in a retirement community in the sun belt, had been getting progressively sicker and more incoherent, and had suffered an incapacitating stroke. After much deliberation and emotional turmoil, Rhoda arranged for her mother to go into a nursing home. When she came back home she went right back to work, hoping to leave all the unpleasant memories and feelings behind, but she couldn't. She would get overwhelmed during the day with feelings of depression. She fought them and continued working and pushing herself until she was exhausted. In therapy Rhoda came to realize that although her mother was physically alive, she had really died in an important way for Rhoda. When a person is physically alive we are not expected to feel loss, to mourn or grieve. We are expected to go on as before until there is a physical death—perhaps years later. This is unfortunate, because the stroke had resulted in a serious loss for Rhoda. It was suggested that she try to mourn the loss of her mother as she knew her. To help her gain a sense of control, it was agreed that every day for 14 days, she would look at pictures of her mother, touch mementos, and think about what her mother had been like before the illness and how much she missed her. She was to do this in the morning before going to work and was encouraged to try not to think about her mother for the rest of the day.

In this case the client was given permission to feel her loss. However, the feelings were placed within certain limits so that she had control over them. She was instructed to confine her grieving to a specified period of time, in the manner of a ritual. This had a curative effect.

Guilt

In conversations about their elderly parents, adult children often discuss guilt—the feeling that they are not doing enough, that they *ought* to be helping more, that they *should* be of more assistance. For some this is a vague, inarticulate feeling, whereas for others it is quite pronounced, dominating the entire relationship.

Guilt is the feeling that results from self-punishment, although this is rarely done on a conscious level. Instead you have a set of standards, both conscious and unconscious, regarding how you should behave and feel in relation to a parent; and if you don't comply with these standards, you provide your own negative evaluations and recriminations. You may not be conscious of the standards that you operate under and of the fact that you punish yourself, but you are aware of the feeling that arises when you inflict this punishment—the feeling is guilt.

One might think there would be a direct correlation between your level of effort and your feelings of self-satisfaction, that the more you did for a parent the less guilt you would feel. This is not so. Although a great many children do a great deal for their parents and feel little or no guilt, others doing the same amount are in a constant state of self-recrimination. Some children who do little for their parents feel guilt, while others do not. This lack of relationship between objective output and guilt is due to the fact that guilt is felt when you transgress an inner, not an objective or external, standard.

There are many adult children who spend a lot of time with their aging parents; they call every day, they shop or run errands, and still they feel guilty. If you know on a rational level that you are assisting your parents but you still feel guilty, it is important to examine your inner standards to see if they are realistic, if they make sense. Make your expectations of yourself as explicit as possible. Exactly what are you prepared to do for your parents? Are you willing to provide transportation, and if so, how much? Do you want to make periodic visits? When and how often? Do you want to invite them to live with you and prepare all their meals? What do you think are your responsibilities? It may seem artificial to make a list, but doing so helps to make you conscious of your standards. It is sometimes helpful to get outside confirmation or feedback from someone whom you know and trust—perhaps someone who knows the situation between you and your parent. Examine your list with your spouse or a trusted friend. Making conscious decisions, rather than drifting along, can be helpful in alleviating both guilt and anxiety.

Guilt can also be affected by your parent's expectations and behavior. Some elderly parents are genuinely satisfied with little support from their children, while others seem to be experts at inducing guilt no matter how much you do. A parent can induce guilt if she makes indirect requests such as, "I would like you to visit more, but I know how busy you are. I don't bother to ask because I don't want to be troublesome. I so much want you to be happy." It is difficult to respond to such a mixed message. Your parent may be angry or disappointed that you do not visit more. She is implicitly asking you to visit more and explicitly not asking for anything. Should you visit more or less, get angry at her manipulations, or be thankful because she understands how busy you are and wants you to be happy? Adult children often resolve such a dilemma by feeling guilty or by getting angry and then feeling guilty. A better solution is to be direct. "If you want me to visit more often, I'd rather that you ask. If I can make it I will, if not I'll let you know." You could also say, "I think you would like me to visit more often, but once a week is best for me."

There are other adult children who feel guilty because they are not helping very much and know it. Their difficulty is that they find contact with their parent too difficult. The only way to change this kind of situation is to make the contact more bearable.

Susan's mother, Mrs. Olivia Smith, is 75 years old. Olivia has been estranged from her husband for quite some time, and Susan has always felt sympathy for her mother. Olivia has had chronic respiratory problems for many years, but in spite of her health has always remained active in church groups and raised money for charities. Susan respects and loves her mother, but she avoids her. When they do see each other, Susan talks only about her job and this only superficially. What Olivia really wants is closeness and intimacy. She wants her only daughter to confide in her, to tell her about her hopes, her goals, and disappointments. Susan doesn't do this. She knows that her mother is very saddened by this, and feels extremely guilty, but she will not do anything to change the situation. Susan is not cold or uncaring. Her distant behavior is part of her attempt to take care of herself, to survive. Olivia is an extremely emotional person and can cry or be furious with little provocation. She is also lonely, is having trouble breathing, and is in pain. Susan is afraid of being caught up in the emotionality of her mother, and for very good reasons. Olivia is not wrong in wanting and needing more contact from her daughter, and Susan is not wrong to hold back. They are both, however, very unhappy, and Susan feels extremely guilty.

If you think that you feel guilty because you are not doing enough for a parent, you can try to find a way to do more while being very careful to protect yourself. This requires making a change, which is not easy but can be done. Susan needs to learn to preface any intimate disclosure to her mother with a warning: "Mom, I want to tell you about a problem I'm having at work, but it is no big deal and I want you not to get upset or carry on, OK?" Then if her mother begins to get distressed, Susan can say, "This is what I was afraid of. Every time I start to tell you anything that's not trivial you get upset, so how can I tell you anything important about myself? If you want me to tell you what's going on with me, you have to learn to not take everything so seriously." Such direct requests from an adult child to a parent are usually very effective. To make such a request is not insulting. It is much kinder to let someone know when they do something that interferes with your relationship, than to say nothing and be quietly resentful or guilty about not making contact.

One man complained that he felt guilty because he never visited his 76-year-old father. His father consistently made ethnic slurs which upset him. He had to learn not to ignore what his father was doing and not to argue with him but to say something like, "Dad, it really upsets me when you say that stuff about minority groups. It's up to you what you say to other people, but it drives me nuts. Can't you please try to control it?" If his father continues to make the slurs, he can say, "I told you that it hurts me when you say that stuff, and you don't stop. Are you trying to tell me to come around less? If you are, I would rather that you just say 'get lost,' because that is what I feel when you say those things." Such a direct approach differs radically from what many adult children are used to, but difficult though it may be, it is often very effective in bringing about a change in the relationship. The suggestion here is not to manipulate an elderly parent by guilt, nor to criticize his entire personality, but to make clear what you want, what you need, and what is difficult for you. Your contacts, then, need not be experienced as self-sacrificing and can therefore become more frequent and more satisfying. This would go a long way toward reducing guilt.

Anger

There is a big difference between behaving angrily and feeling angry with your parents. It is usually a good idea to avoid behaving angrily, but you may have many good reasons to feel angry. You are busy and overworked. You may not feel you have the extra time, money, and energy that is required to help your aging parent. "What right do they have to expect help or assistance from me? Damn them anyway!" It is quite normal to have such feelings on occasion. In fact, the feelings can be helpful. Anger can be protective in several ways. Some people accommodate other people much too easily. They have a hard time saying no to anyone because they try so hard to please people. It may be only when you feel angry that you can be firm about setting limits on yourself—making certain that you will not do more than what is good for you to do—so that you will not sacrifice too much. Feeling angry can also help you to regulate the distance between yourself and your elderly parents. It signals to you that you need more space, more separateness. It is a way to say to yourself, "Back off, we are too close, too involved." When you feel angry you are also feeling and perhaps expressing your independence or autonomy. If you think, "The hell with you," at a time when your independence, your possibilities and choices are actually being threatened, you may get the valuable feeling of being free. Anger allows some people to feel less trapped and more free, which at times is highly beneficial.

Some psychologists believe there is a close connection between guilt and anger. They believe that guilt arises when anger that should be directed outward is unconscious and directed inward. Therefore, the way to feel less guilty is to let the inner-directed anger out. If you feel guilty, you should get mad at someone who deserves it and you will feel better and less guilty. According to this questionable approach, something is gained if you yell at your parent and complain that she is difficult and a burden. Something is certainly gained when you can be direct with a parent. However, frequently expressing anger in order to alleviate guilt is almost sure to backfire. Rather than feeling less guilty after venting the aggression, most people feel more guilty for being nasty and rude to their parents.

There are adult children who feel angry whenever they even think of their parents. Although anger can be a very useful signal, to always feel angry is not so useful. Aside from the obvious fact that such feelings are not usually helpful to the parents, they are also unpleasant for the children. Yet, although feeling angry all the time is not fun, many adult children have difficulty letting go of the feeling. They feel locked into anger, and consider it inevitable. These feelings, however, can be changed, if you take suitable action to reduce your frustration and resentment. Clenching your jaws or muttering under your breath are not effective ways to protect your autonomy and regulate the distance between you and your aging parents. Again, try to be more direct. Often when you examine the causes of your anger you find that you have difficulty formulating what you need. Sometimes you know what you need and have difficulty saying it. What is required is to find a gentle way of asking for what you need without accusations or blame. At other times the difficulty is that you are not really aware of what you need. If you need something but don't know what it is, you cannot ask for it directly and you will undoubtedly end up frustrated. Psychological research has demonstrated that frustration often leads to aggression. If you are angry with a parent, you need to think about what it is that you want from him or her. This is not an easy thing to do. However, if anger is an especially difficult feeling for you, one way to examine what you need is to write a letter. You don't ever have to send it, but in the letter you should explain to your parent how you see your relationship and how you would like it to be. This is one way of helping yourself to think about what you want from your parent. Such an effort is a small investment to make, because if you don't know what you want, you can never be satisfied.

There are other reasons why people get and stay angry with elderly parents. A great deal of attention and research has been devoted to the phenomenon of scapegoating in families. Most often the scapegoat is a child, who by getting into trouble unifies the whole family. Everyone can say, "If it weren't for little Johnny we wouldn't have any problems and could be a perfect family." Everyone can deny the existence of his own problems and disappointments and fix the blame on someone else. Of course children are not the only targets of such scapegoating, and in some families parents and children talk about or think about how happy they would be if an elderly parent would disappear. Sometimes an aging parent consciously (or, more likely, unconsciously) recognizes the need for a scapegoat to help keep the family together and in harmony. The parent then helps the family by acting a bit ornery or difficult, keeping herself in the role of scapegoat. This enables everyone else to transfer responsibility for the difficulties onto the elderly parent.

When an aging parent becomes a scapegoat in a family, she is making the kind of sacrifice that only a loving or devoted parent or child would make for a family. In some families adult children and aging parents take this process to its most dangerous and awful extreme, which is the abuse of the aging parent.

Fortunately, at the present time, violence toward elderly parents is not a common problem. What is most common is the stress and strain that adults in mid-life experience when they assist an elderly parent. Adult children need to find ways to help without becoming overburdened and overwhelmed.

Chapter 4_____
Guidelines for Helping

Carl Jung, one of the seminal thinkers of our time, developed an extremely elaborate approach to understanding the human mind. He called his theory *analytical psychology*. Yet, even Jung recognized that there are no formulas for helping people. In his autobiography, *Memories, Dreams, Reflections,* he presents an entire chapter of clinical case studies which demonstrate that the art of helping someone often bears little relation to Jungian or any other theory. Complete silence may be as effective in one case as giving advice, making interpretations, or giving directives is in others.[1]

Later in this book (Chapter 6, "Emotional/Psychological Concerns"), there are some recommendations about how to assist an elderly parent with "life review." It is suggested that asking your parent about the past and listening to her talk about it can be an emotional help for you both. However, some elderly parents can get caught up in complaining about the same past injustice for hours on end. It may not be so helpful for you to listen endlessly, but to say, "You know, I've heard about this episode many times and it doesn't seem to get you anywhere. It also upsets me to hear about it so much. Let's talk about something else."

It is not a good idea to make rules about how to help someone. Helping is such a personal matter that one individual's solution for a problem can have absolutely no relevance to another's seemingly similar problem. Trying to apply what is helpful for one person to another can even make the other's problem worse. This chapter includes an outline of some of the most general ideas to keep in mind when helping an elderly parent. However, remember they must be adapted to your particular situation, not applied wholesale.

Offering to Help

When your parent is very sick or obviously in trouble or asks you for assistance directly, you don't have to wonder about how or when to offer help. But what if she appears to need help, or you are in some doubt and she doesn't ask? This may be one of the trickiest and most difficult issues to deal with. Many elderly people have a great reluctance to ask for help from their children. Most struggle to remain independent for as long as they possibly can. This is a very healthy and natural attitude. The more an elderly parent can do for herself, the more hopeful, vigorous, and healthy she is likely to stay. Aging parents may also be reluctant to ask their children for help because they have experienced caring for their own parents, often in their own homes. In the past it was more common for an elderly parent to move in with an adult child, whether or not it was a good or workable situation. Because many elderly parents today have painful memories of such a situation, they have vowed not to repeat this experience with their own children. Many go even further and try never to ask for help and never to discuss illness or even more minor concerns. What should you do if you think your parent needs help but won't ask for it? If you feel willing, you should take some action on your own and offer help. Then see if your offer is accepted.

Chris's mother, Mrs. Betty Burns, was in the hospital for minor surgery. Betty knew that Chris was very busy and didn't want to "impose" on her daughter. Betty was feeling anxious and upset about the surgery. She didn't think she wanted Chris to come to the hospital and see how scared she really was. Chris explained to her mother over the phone that she really wanted to come and see her. Finally Chris just went to the hospital; her mother was very glad to see her. When Betty cried a little, Chris explained that she was glad to be with her mother and that she, Betty, need not feel bad about crying.

Be sure that if you do offer help, you are willing to give it. What should you do if your offer is rejected? What if your parents tell you clearly that they really don't want you to help? In most situations the best course of action is to back off but leave the door open. There is the distinct possibility that you are being too eager and perhaps aggressive. Maybe they don't need help, or maybe they feel that someone else will be more helpful than you. You can simply say that you are concerned, that you are willing and able to help, and that they should let you know if they need you. Acting in a restrained manner is often helpful—you don't want to insist that there is a problem if there isn't, and at the same time you are indicating unambiguously that you are available.

Learning How to Listen

Sometimes it seems that it is harder to help the people we are closest to, the people in our own family, the people whom we love, than it is to help anyone else. This is because it is difficult to maintain a sense of perspective when someone we are very emotionally connected to is in distress. I have always believed that most child-care books, certainly Dr. Spock's *Baby and Child Care,* contain mostly common sense. Yet when your six-month-old infant has been screaming for an hour, or you have been up half the night trying to get your baby to sleep, common sense may be something that you have completely lost and desperately need. When you have trouble getting in touch with your common sense, it becomes very difficult to listen to anyone, even yourself. When your parents are in distress it can sometimes be so confusing and disruptive that you cannot really listen to them. To know that they are in psychological or physical pain can be excruciating, so you block it out by getting angry with them or feeling manipulated or cheering them up right away or offering premature solutions. You do this because if you really listened, there is a very good chance that you would feel sad. One way to change this is to recognize that it is OK for you to feel unhappy about the fact that your parents are having problems. You may be better able to listen to their concerns if you don't try too hard to defend against this sadness.

There are other reasons why it is difficult to listen to people in our own families. We sometimes mistake their thoughts and feelings for expectations and demands. If your mother says, "I am feeling so lonely and isolated," you may not want to hear it: not only because it will make you sad, but also because you may think that she is asking you to visit her. You may even think she is accusing you of selfishness for not having visited her more regularly over the past 20 years. Most aging parents certainly have expectations, demands, and criticisms, but you should address them only when they are stated directly. If your mother says that she is lonely, she may be simply telling you how she feels, rather than making an indirect request. If, however, you feel that she is making an indirect request, you don't have to respond in kind. You could say, "Mom, when you say you are lonely I always think you want me to come over more often. If that's what you want, I'd rather that you say it more directly. If that's not what you want, tell me, so that I don't have to feel like I'm not doing enough."

Unresolved issues from the past may also hamper your ability to listen to your parents and to hear what they are really saying. Such issues are different for everyone but there are always plenty of them. One common theme is that it is very hard for adult children to believe that their elderly parents need help. The children are too rooted in their need to be taken care of by their parents. Other adult children handle their own need to be taken care of very differently: they totally reject these feelings and become authoritarian parents to their parents. They turn the parents into children, half-listen to their problems, and offer premature solutions without understanding what their parents truly want or need.

Being Empathic

Unfortunately, we are not accustomed to being listened to with empathy or to listening to others in this way. This is unfortunate because psychological research indicates that the experience of empathy fosters growth, self-understanding, and greater self-acceptance. For all the reasons discussed above, it may be especially difficult to listen empathetically if your parent is telling you about a problem or concern. To be empathic means to get into another's shoes for a while to see how things look from their point of view. In addition to listening empathetically, it is also necessary to communicate your understanding.[2]

Suppose your father comes over, sits down, looks at the ground, and tells you that an old friend is sick and that his favorite grocery store just closed to make room for a new shopping center. Consider the following responses:

"Listen, Dad, these things happen."

"New shopping centers aren't so bad."

"Yeah, the same sorts of things happen to me."

"Your friend will get better, and that old store charged higher prices."

It is hard to listen to someone empathetically, because it can mean being touched acutely. To avoid being so affected, you relate your father's words to your own experience or to "experience" in general, or make a judgment or evaluation. When you immediately approve or disapprove of what your parent says, this is not empathy. None of the above responses are unsympathetic or insensitive, but they are not empathic. A more empathic statement would be something like,

"It sounds like a sad time for you right now—a lot of changes and some endings."

When you give a parent your attention, listen, and communicate your understanding of his experience, you have provided empathy. You let him know that you have heard him. This sort of response wouldn't need to be discussed if we were empathized with more often, but we are not.

Another obstacle to listening empathetically is that people sometimes feel that if they hear about a problem, they have to do something about it or solve it. Some problems can't be fixed but have to be endured, and empathy is all that can be offered.

The ability to be empathic is not genetic; it can be practiced and learned. When your parent shares an experience or concern, try to summarize in your own mind what is being said, and say what you hear. If your parent gives you a confused message such as, "I'm thinking of visiting my old friend in the hospital, but I don't know if he wants me to come and see him looking so ill," he is really not mixed-up. He is expressing a conflict. Rather than saying. "Well, do you or don't you want to visit him?" you could give an empathic response, which might be something like,

"It sounds like you aren't sure what would be best for him and how to reconcile his needs with what you want to do." This may not sound like you are solving you parent's dilemma, but by paying attention to what he is saying, accepting what he is saying, you may allow him to clarify what he is feeling, what he wants and needs. Try to practice giving back the core of the message that you have heard. Obviously, if this is the only way you talk to your parents, they will think you are acting weird or studying psychology or social work. It is important, however, to keep in mind that if you are going to help someone, you have to know what their world looks like to them, and they have to know that you empathize with their experience if they are going to allow you to help.

Knowing When Not to Help

Many adult children are unhappy with the way their parents live. They object to the way they dress, the way they eat, where they live, their sexual behavior, and so forth. If your aging, widowed mother has recently become interested in a man of whom you disapprove, and tells you that they are thinking of living together, you may feel upset. You may have some legitimate concerns, and voicing your concerns—once—is important for honest communication. However, advising your parent about matters of personal taste when your opinion has not been asked for, and when your parent is experiencing little distress, is not helping; it's meddling. For some adult children the temptation to meddle arises because their parents meddled in their lives earlier on. If you think that, when you were a child, your parents were overly critical of you, it does not mean that as an adult you must be overly critical of them. If you don't like their furniture, their music, their hobbies, you are not likely to be helpful by saying so. It is more helpful to be polite. Some people—whether aging parents or adult children—take pride in giving honest and what they refer to as "useful" criticism. If someone has not asked for such criticism and is not open to it, you are not helping them; you are being rude. Where matters of personal preference are concerned, unless it is quite clear to you that there is a problem, the best course of action is not to interfere.

On the issue of an elderly parent getting remarried, however, a few additional points should be made. As discussed earlier, when someone moves into or out of a family it is a time of change and stress for all concerned. If your parent moves in with someone of the opposite sex—which has economic and legal advantages—or gets married, and you are distressed, annoyed, worried, or depressed, the chances are that it is more your problem than your parent's. Many adult children are disturbed largely because they feel the remarriage to be an act of disloyalty to the deceased parent. If they accept the new marriage by supporting their parent and warmly receiving the new spouse, they may consciously (or, more likely, unconsciously) feel that they are supporting the surviving parent's disloyalty, accepting an intruder, and betraying the deceased parent. Others are concerned that they may lose out on an inheritance which they believe they deserve for the many sacrifices they have made since childhood. Most adult children control these feelings and manage a lukewarm acceptance. It should be remembered, though, that the success of a marriage is sometimes related to its acceptance by the family. If you have the opportunity to support a parent who is beginning a new relationship, you should try to be helpful.

Knowing What the Problem Is

A mother calls an adult child and says, "I have been feeling tired and depressed. I think it's serious." Consider the following responses:

> "I'm feeling the same way this morning. Maybe it's the humidity."

> "I'm sure once you've had your morning coffee and taken your walk you'll feel much better."

> "Stop complaining all the time."

> "Listen, Mother, I think you should take two aspirins and lie down. When you get up, check your pulse and blood pressure and call me back."

> "Do you think I should call Dr. Smith?"

> "I had a feeling this would happen if you spent time with Aunt

Sally. It always seems to take a lot out of you when you two get together. You ought to not let her overwhelm you. She is quite persnickety and could depress almost anyone."

Any of the above responses could be helpful. It sometimes helps to say you have the same problem, to be optimistic, to dismiss the problem, to try to solve the problem, to give the problem to an expert, or to suggest the cause of the problem. However, these responses are all somewhat inadequate because you still don't really know what the problem is. The way to be more helpful is to ask questions. Don't be afraid to make it obvious that you don't have all the answers and solutions. We sometimes want so badly to give the impression that we are knowledgeable that we are afraid to ask questions. What does your mother mean when she says "tired and depressed"? How can you suggest remedies unless you know what she is talking about? You may find out that by "tired" she means sleepy— maybe she got too much or too little sleep, or maybe she means something more serious. When she says "depressed," does she mean simply a more fancy word for "tired," or could she be thinking of harming herself? When someone says they are "seriously depressed," do they mean they are unhappy, fatigued, or sad about something that recently happened; mournful about some past hurt; generally pessimistic; or suicidal? In order to be helpful, you need to get more information. Here are some possible questions.

"What do you mean by 'depressed'?" Be sure you get more of an idea or feeling about what is happening.

"Did you just start feeling this way? When do you or don't you feel this way?" This question may prompt her to tell you what caused the problem or how serious it is. She might answer, "Yesterday, when I found out that Uncle Joe was sick," or "I have been feeling this way every morning for months." These two answers give you very different pictures of what is going on.

"Why do you think you are feeling this way?" Your mother could say, "I took a sleeping pill last night," or "I'm worried about your sister who never married." Again, with such information, you are in a much better position to be helpful.

"What have you done to solve the problem; what have you

tried?" She might answer, "I have taken two aspirins," or "I have vowed not to talk to Aunt Sally." Now you are clearer about the problem, and you won't offer solutions that have already been tried.

"Is there anything you want or need me to do?"

Allowing Your Parents to Function

Helplessness and depression are critical problems for older people. As a result of retirement (sometimes forced), lack of money and declining physical health, they are often confronted with problems about which they feel helpless. Helplessness saps motivation, disrupts the ability to learn, and produces emotional disturbances.

In an unnecessarily brutal but important experiment conducted by Martin Seligman in 1967, a dog was placed in a shuttle box—a two-room chamber with a barrier that could easily be hurdled by the dog. When the experimenters produced a moderately painful shock in one of the compartments, the dog would scramble about until it jumped over the barrier to escape the shock. When it was again placed in the compartment and shocked, the dog took much less time to hurdle the barrier, and over time it learned to avoid the shock altogether by leaping the barrier at the very first signal for a shock. This dog and others like it appeared confident and in control. They appeared to have learned that they could take care of themselves.

Other dogs, before being placed in the shuttle box, had been given a series of inescapable shocks, in closed-off compartments where all their frantic attempts at escape went for naught. After receiving the inescapable shocks, the dogs, now given the chance to escape, simply gave up. At the onset of the next shock they didn't look for escape but whined and lay down. Their previous experience with the inescapable shocks had taught them that trying would get them nowhere. When placed in a situation where action and effort would enable them to succeed, they were passive and inactive. These dogs had *learned to be helpless*. They had learned that their actions did not make any difference, and so they had become helpless and depressed. Similar experiments with cats, rats, fish, apes, and people all show that when an animal learns to be helpless it becomes less likely to take any kind of action and looks and feels depressed.[3]

Everyone needs to feel that he has *control* over his life. No matter how old or tired your parents are, they need to feel that their actions or ideas or words matter—that they make a difference. This does not mean that elderly people need to feel that they can change the world. It means they need to be in control of small but important things. When they pick up the phone, it is important that there be a dial tone and that, if there isn't, they can go next door and call the phone company or find some other solution. When they try to open the front door, it is important that they find the right key and open it. If they go to a supermarket, they need to have enough money and be able to find the right change. No matter how trivial the action may seem to be, every time you act and something happens, you learn that you have some control over the world. If you act and nothing happens, you eventually stop acting. If you press a button to get an elevator 100 times and it doesn't arrive, you will stop pressing. After a few days of such activity, you probably won't even bother to see if it is working. You will have given up on it. If you go job hunting and are not successful or receive little positive feedback, it is likely that your efforts will gradually diminish. As you get older, many tasks that were once easy become hard. If nothing happens every time your parent tries to do something, she will feel discouraged and begin to stop doing things. If her activities don't bring about results, she will gradually slow down and feel down.

This is why it is very important that you understand and respect your parent's need to have as much control over her life as she possibly can. Unless she has clearly passed the point of effective functioning, you should not decide what is best for her, where she should live, what she should eat, or how she should take care of herself. Often the best way to give help is to make sure that you do not overfunction for your parent; if you are too helpful, your parent may become helpless. Throughout the book are a variety of suggestions designed to enable you to help your parent take care of herself for as long as she can. You should remember that if your elderly parent is struggling with someone or something, you are better off not to take it over but to support her and help her help herself.

One man reported that his mother was in the hospital and was fighting with the hospital staff about the food. At first he advised her not to make waves, to calm down. Then he realized that in this case, "making waves" and being active was really the best thing for her. Hospitals sometimes do so much to and for a patient that the patient easily sinks into a feeling of helplessness, inactivity, and depression. The woman's spark and fighting were her way of combating helplessness. They were excellent signs of vitality and deserving of her son's support.

If your elderly parents have the physical capability but have "given up," the situation is far more difficult. It is much easier to help keep someone from getting depressed than it is to bring them out of a depression. Some widowed elderly who were the less dominant half of their marriage are especially likely to want someone to care for them and tell them what to do. If possible, this should be resisted. Find out what your parent wants. If he says, "I just don't know what I want, what do you think I should do?" try to be persistent: "Yes, I'm sure you know what you want, just think about it a little bit more." Once your inactive or depressed parent does something or takes an action, no matter how small, you should support and encourage it.

Asking for Help When You Need It

Helping your elderly parent is often emotionally draining. Even in the best of situations, where there is plenty of money and your parents are in reasonably good health, there will be times when you will feel stressed or depressed and need support or assistance. It is very important that you be aware that your capacity to help has limits, and when these limits are reached you need to ask someone for help. Many people have a difficult time asking for help in a straightforward manner.

One woman reported that she visited her mother every night in order to prepare her evening meals. At first she felt that this was not a big sacrifice but was in fact something she wanted to do. After a few weeks she began to feel tired out. She would leave work, go to her mother's, and race home to make dinner for her family. She began to complain to her friends, and soon she was complaining to her husband and her children. Once she came home and yelled, "Why can't you all get dinner started while I'm at my mother's?" This comes close to being a plea for help, but it isn't. It is yelling and complaining, which is not the same thing. When someone yells and complains, we try to ignore or avoid her, or we think that she is just letting off steam and that it will pass. The woman also began feeling resentful toward her sister who lived close by, for not doing her share. Even though her mother always said, "You don't have to make dinner for me every night," she believed that her mother was not telling the truth and she began to feel annoyance and resentment toward her, as well.

The above is not an uncommon scenario. If the woman had been able to ask for help directly, it would have gone a long way toward improving her situation. At the very least she should be able to ask her husband, her children, her sister, her mother, and the community for some assistance. For example, she needs to ask her husband and children for help, and it is best that she start with her husband so that they can approach the children with a united front. "My mother is going to be needing me to help her in the evenings for an hour or so. I am going to need your help and the kids' to get dinner on the table. Let's talk to the children tonight and arrange for them to set the table, wash the vegetables, and so on. If we talk to them together and get them to understand the serious nature of the situation, I'm sure they'll help out."

It is also important to be direct in asking your parents for their help as you help them. One man, aged 51, became more involved in taking care of his mother after she suffered a slight stroke. He went to her house several times a week and helped her with a few errands and chores. As soon as he would arrive, his mother would say, "I'm sorry to be such a burden," and the man would say, "It's really OK, Mom, I don't mind doing these few things for you." After not more than 2 minutes his mother would say, "I know how difficult it is for you to give up so much time for me," and go on in this way until he felt slightly crazed. He had to learn to ask his mother for help so that he could help her without going mad. The situation was much improved when he was able to say, "Look, Mom, I really don't mind coming over to do a few chores, but I can't stand it when you tell me how awful you feel for me. Please don't tell me how upset you feel when I help you. This would really be a tremendous help to me, and I do want and need your help."

Siblings, agencies, programs for the elderly run by religious and civic groups, and professionals of various sorts can all be of assistance. If you suffer silently—or even noisily—you are not helping yourself, which means you are probably not going to be of much use to anyone else. It is inevitable that your resentment will spill out, affecting all those around you.

Knowing Your Limits

We will see in the next few chapters that as our parents get older, they have to adjust to many different kinds of changes. One of the most significant of these is that they simply have less energy and strength than they had when they were younger. They cannot easily take long trips to visit their families, because such trips are tiring. However, elderly parents do take trips, and when they do, it is not unusual for them to overextend themselves and not feel well, or get sick. Adult children also have limits, and it is important that you recognize and make every effort to stay within them. This can be a very difficult assignment for middle-aged people. The elderly have typically been forced to recognize that they must slow down, while adolescents and young adults have the most energy and fewest responsibilities of any age group. If you are middle-aged and are helping an aging parent, it may be necessary for you to cut back on some other activity or activities. If you are exasperated with an aging parent, it may be because you are doing too much. It is important to examine your activities with an open mind and look for ways to make things easier on yourself. There are always shortcuts, and you must assume that if you are diligent, you will be able to find them. You probably should also examine your activities and friends to see which ones are not so satisfying and can be given up. Perhaps there is a television program that you watch regularly with little enjoyment—give it up. This can be an opportunity for you to make certain that your free time is being spent in ways that are truly satisfying.

Of course, you must also recognize your limits in relation to your aging parent. Don't say that you don't mind helping or that you want to help unless you mean it. Here the key is to *stop and consider* before offering. If, for example, your parent lives in a retirement community and is not feeling too well, it is not necessary for you to immediately say, "Do you want me to fly down and spend a few days?" If your parent needs help and calls on you, think it over; talk to your spouse or friends. If you call back an hour or a day later and say, "I've thought about it and I would like to fly down to see you," it is unlikely that your parent will be insulted that you didn't offer sooner. In fact, if you offer after you have reflected and considered, your help may be even more appreciated than if you give it automatically. Also, by waiting you may discover that it would be too difficult or not really be necessary for you to make such a trip. It is almost always a good idea not to act too impulsively, and this is especially true in relation to our parents. If you wait a bit, you are less likely to go beyond your limits out of guilt or some other emotion. Counting to 10, as the old saw says, is a very good way to take care of yourself.

Problems with Martyrdom

Some adult children feel that they can never do enough for their parents. They sacrifice time, energy, and money and continue to feel dissatisfied with themselves. They feel guilty and have the sense that they aren't doing enough. If you are one of these overly devoted children, you are undoubtedly unaware of the extent of your sacrifice. Someone who is overly dedicated to a parent would not be able to say or think, "Hey, maybe I'm doing too much." You will probably not cease your martyrdom as a result of reading this short passage. However, what follows is an analysis of such behavior.

Adult children become overly sacrificing because their parents had tremendous needs while the children were growing up. When parents are insecure, anxious, and without confidence, they are not really able to nurture and take care of their children. Such parents may appear to be taking care of their children, and probably do love them, but they are really unable to give their children the attention, understanding, and comfort they need. Instead of the child depending on the adult, the adult, who is needy and insecure, has a tremendous dependency on the child. The parent depends on the child for comfort in many ways. The parent who has low self-esteem and low self-acceptance, who is shy or reticent, *depends* on the child to always look cheerful; to achieve in school, at work, or in social situations, and to act according to the needs of the parent.

Almost all parents want what is best for their children, but some parents are secure enough to allow their children a degree of autonomy—the freedom to be themselves. Many children live their lives trying to please the internalized voice of their parents. They do well in school and find the "right" career; they are always polite and rarely get angry; they have children and work for the "correct" political cause, party, or religion; and still they feel vaguely unhappy or even depressed. According to psychoanalyst Alice Miller, these grown children can become depressed because they have been working very hard to satisfy their parents' needs, not their own. In fact, such children are not really aware of their own needs. They do not know what they want, what would bring them satisfaction, because, lacking true autonomy, they have lost a sense of self. A loss of such magnitude is bound to result in depression. A great deal of unlearning is necessary to undo the loss—mourning it would certainly be appropriate; attempting to learn that each has her own needs and discovering what they are and how to satisfy them would complete the task.[4]

Do you think your parents sacrificed so much for you that you cannot possibly repay them? Are you unable to set limits or say no to any request from them? Are you unable to see faults or flaws in them? If so, you are probably right that your parents loved you as a child and love you now. But they may have been unable to allow you to develop autonomy and be yourself. If you are already doing a lot to help your parents but feel that you could never do enough to repay them, it is likely that you have already sacrificed a great deal for them and may have given up your most valuable asset—yourself. You may not realize it, but you have been taking care of your parents all your life. You have already done plenty.

Giving Good Advice

There are many people in the helping professions who do not give advice. They believe that people are best off finding their own solutions to their problems. This is actually a very sound policy, and especially when applied to elderly people, who, for reasons already discussed, can often become passive and dependent. Whenever possible, you should stick to the position that your parent knows best what is good for her. You should try not to make decisions about what she should do, and try not to give too much advice. However, there are times when your more active participation is needed and giving advice is appropriate. This may be as minimal as recommending that your parent use a less expensive long-distance phone service or, at the other extreme, as radical as making a decision to select and place your parent in a nursing home. Some adult children are in a very good position to offer advice to their parents about the modern world. They can counsel them on financial matters—perhaps help them with their taxes, explain new tax laws, or advise them about a new car purchase. One man, over 80 years old, explained to me that although he felt independent, he greatly appreciated any advice he could get from his children about the new technologies. He was totally confused about the breakup of AT&T, for example, and counted on his children to keep him informed on what action to take. You, the adult child, may be a better-informed consumer than your parents. Ask them if they want your help. However, remember that your advice will be useful only if you know your parent's needs. This requires asking the kinds of questions discussed, and listening to the responses. When you give advice it is also important to be as clear and as unambiguous as possible. If, for example, your parent wants the name of a doctor with a certain specialty, you are not being too helpful if you say, "There's a guy named Stones or Jones on the north side of town." The doctor's name, address, phone number, and how to reach him is, of course, much more useful.

Be sure that your parent understands your advice. Just saying something does not guarantee that it will be understood. Be sure that all the components of your advice or directions are understood. One very serious problem with giving advice is that you have to be well-informed—definitely not an easy assignment, and one of the major purposes of this book.

Helping Can Help You

It is a mistake to think that helping must be draining, and that the more we help, the more our psychological and physical resources will be depleted. If you feel agitated, annoyed, impatient, or restless when you help, you will feel exhausted afterward. However, these feelings shouldn't be blamed on helping. Although there are no perfectly happy families, involvement for all its difficulties is preferable to a lack of intimacy or relationship. When you help an aging parent it brings you into contact with her in ways that may truly be enriching. The bonds that are changed and strengthened by your helping benefit everyone involved.

Increased involvement with your aging parents offers you an opportunity to reevaluate and better understand your roots, your past, your traditions. The parent/child relationship changes throughout your life, and as an adult you are in the best position you can ever be in to understand your current situation by exploring the past in a more truthful and open fashion. When you were a child, an adolescent, and even a young adult, your parents may have been reluctant to speak openly about family history. In the relationship between adult child and aging parent, there is the opportunity to repair this omission. It is also possible to lose a good deal of unnecessary self-consciousness and self-absorption when you focus on someone else and their difficulties.

The Major Concerns of Elderly Parents

In order to help your parents, it is important to know their concerns. Do adult children tend to have an accurate understanding of their parents' needs, hopes, and fears? Do they know what is most important to their parents, or do they underestimate or exaggerate their parents' concerns? Some adult children project their own concerns onto their parents, imagining that their parents worry about, think about, or need the same things that the children do. This misperception renders any sort of help useless.[5]

To address this issue, we distributed several hundred questionnaires to men and women over the age of 65, in both rural and urban communities. Respondents were told, "The purpose of this questionnaire is to gather information about your needs so that adult children may better be able to understand and perhaps assist their aging parents. The intent of this questionnaire is to determine precisely what areas elderly parents need help in."

Elderly parents were also requested to give a similar questionnaire to an adult child. The child was asked to examine the same set of concerns and to indicate how important each concern was for his or her parent.

The results of this investigation showed that, in fact, adult children have a fairly accurate understanding of their parents' concerns, although differences exist between the perceptions of adult children who live close to their parents and those of children whose parents live at a distance.

Concerns of Parents Living Close to Their Children

The following is the rank order of concerns expressed by the elderly parents in our sample. (Where the same rank order is shown, the sample ranked the items equally.)

1 Emotional (feeling lonely, in control, needed, etc.)

2 Health

3 Transportation

5 Bureaucratic mediation (dealing with government agencies, etc.)

5 Social

5 Domestic chores

7 Finances

Adult children perceived their parents' needs according to the following rank order.

1 Emotional

1 Health

3 Domestic chores

4 Transportation

5 Bureaucratic mediation

5 Finances

7 Social

The estimated ranking of concerns by the adult children who live near their elderly parents were very close to the actual ranking of concerns by their parents.

Concerns of Parents in Retirement Communities

Although the majority of elderly parents live quite close to one adult child, there are many adult children who live at a great distance from their parents. How can you possibly be helpful to an elderly parent if you live hundreds or even thousands of miles away? Previous research, supported by the information that we gathered for this book, indicates that the factor of physical distance from your aging parent is not as important as one would think in determining your ability to help.

In order to assess the problems of the elderly who live far from their children, we distributed questionnaires to people in retirement communities in Florida, Arkansas, and Texas. We asked them to indicate which areas gave them the most cause for concern. The following are their concerns in rank order.

1 Health

2 Emotional

3 Bureaucratic mediation

4 Domestic chores

5 Transportation

5 Social

7 Finances

Similar questionnaires were sent by the parents to their children in distant states. We asked the children to rank their parents' concerns in order of importance. They indicated the following.

1 Health

2 Emotional

3 Domestic chores

4 Bureaucratic mediation

4 Transportation

6 Finances

7 Social

We can see from the above two lists that the adult children in this sample are quite accurate in their perception of the *order* of their parents' needs—health and emotional issues are at the top and financial and social concerns at the bottom. However, the adult children and their parents differ considerably in their assessments of the *magnitude* of these problems. In every single category, the children viewed the problems as being more serious than did their parents.

Elderly parents in retirement communities indicated about the same number of concerns as the parents not in retirement communities except with regard to finances. However, the children of parents in retirement communities were considerably more likely to see their parents as having more serious problems, especially health problems. The estimates made by children of parents not in retirement communities much more closely approximated the responses made by their parents.

Why do the children in the second sample perceive their parents' needs as being greater than they are? There are a number of possible explanations. One is that parents who go to retirement communities may do so, in part, to spare their children worry. They might therefore have a tendency to underrepresent their problems. On the other hand, the elderly in retirement communities may be in a better economic position than their nonretirement community counterparts, and actually have somewhat fewer problems in terms of chores, transportation, and finances. The children may assume their parents' concerns to be similar to those of the elderly people who live in the children's own communities—not retirement communities. There is also the possibility that children whose parents are far away have a tendency to fill the void of the unknown with a little more worry or anxiety than is necessary. They may read their parents' letters or hear them talk about various physical problems and exaggerate the level of their parents' concern. It is always important not to assume that you know your parents' concerns, and this may be especially true if you live far from them.

It appears that children who live at a distance from their parents are concerned primarily about their parents' health, and although the concern may be exaggerated, it is true that health is the parents' main concern. Health is also a major concern of elderly parents not in retirement communities. The other major concern of elderly parents involves their emotional needs. It should be mentioned, as well, that although a significant portion of elderly parents live at or below the poverty line (17 percent of women and 10 percent of men over 65), our respondents—both in and outside of retirement communities—were least concerned about financial matters.

The government, from time to time, has attempted to create a policy whereby children would be required to contribute to the support of their elderly parents. In the spring of 1983 the Reagan administration announced that states may under Medicaid legally require children to support their parents financially. This could prove to be a disaster for family relations. Parents want and need to be financially independent, and children want to help in many ways but not always with money. Social security and, to some extent, Medicare and Medicaid are working. When something is working, it might be a good idea to leave it alone. As one older man said, "We [older folks] don't like to take money from our kids. We don't want to be a burden. They don't like giving us money, either. We all get angry at each other if we do that. So we all sign a political contract to deal with what anthropologists would call the 'intergenerational transfer of wealth.' The young people give their money to the government. I get money from the government. That way we can both get mad at the government and keep on loving each other."[6]

Chapter 5_____
The Stress of
Caregiving

A large portion of this book (Chapters 6 through 9) focuses on the emotional, practical, and health concerns of elderly parents. It is intended to help adult children better understand their parents' concerns. However, this chapter will examine the concerns, problems, stresses, and strains of people in mid-life, assess how helping elderly parents may increase stress, and examine the ways in which stress can be reduced.

One of the most positive aspects of helping an elderly parent is that you get the opportunity to see and learn how someone copes with a different stage of life. You can watch and learn as your parent attempts to cope with the problems of late adulthood: declining physical health, retirement, ageism, loss, and the approach of death.

The Life Cycle

The concept of a life cycle is that there are events and experiences throughout life that can be predicted according to one's age. For instance, for infants and children there is an orderly development of motor skills. Most can reach for objects at 5 months, sit alone at 7 months, and walk at about 15 months. The pattern of development in adulthood is not as neat. In fact, some social scientists believe that the age of an adult is a poor predictor of behavior. One well-known developmental psychologist has said, "It no longer surprises me to hear of a 22-year-old mayor or a 29-year-old university president or a 35-year-old grandmother or a retiree of 50. No one blinks at a 70-year-old college student or at the 55-year-old man who becomes a father for the first time."[1] Whereas simple chronological age may no longer be an important predictor of how people live, it is still very clearly related to major life events; and these events do signify major transitions in our lives.

One of the first theorists to suggest the importance of a developmental sequence was Freud. He believed that each phase of life (oral, anal, phallic, genital, and latency) involves needs that must be attended to and problems and dilemmas that must be resolved if the individual is to pass successfully to the next phase. Freud also originated the idea that it was possible to get "stuck" in one phase, or, in Freudian terms, "fixated." In his view if you have problems as an adult, it is because you have been fixated at an earlier stage.

Most psychologists don't agree with Freud's idea that if you pass into adolescence and are able to enjoy healthy heterosexual relationships, you have negotiated all of life's stages. One of Freud's best-known students, Carl Jung, was among the first psychologists to point to the existence of a mid-life transition, or what has been referred to in recent years as the "mid-life crisis." Incidentally, Jung did not think that a transition had necessarily to become a crisis. Transitions become crises if they are avoided or delayed. Issues that are overripe sometimes erupt and can cause a great deal of emotional turmoil. (The point at which middle age ends and old age begins is somewhat arbitrary. According to many psychologists, middle adulthood is roughly from ages 40 to 65. Late adulthood is from 65 on, but there is really very little agreement about how old someone needs to be before he or she is considered middle-aged or old.)

Jung believed that the second half of life, from age 40 on, requires different tasks from the first half. The first half requires expansion, exploration of the outside world, the environment. It involves establishing friendships, intimacy, a family, a career, and so on. A shrinking away from these activities could lead to a psychological disorder like neurosis. The tasks of the second half of life balance the first, according to Jung. Middle age calls for reflection, introspection, self-evaluation, and the recognition that one is moving toward death. These tasks are likely to bring one to more basic and spiritual issues.[2] Jung's view of the second half of life was further refined by Erik Erikson. According to

Erikson, the turning inward described by Jung is really a task for old age, whereas middle age requires a great deal of activity.

Erikson's View of Mid-Life Transitions

Erik Erikson, perhaps the most important psychologist in the area of human development, maintains that the tasks of life are not completed in puberty and that development continues into adulthood and old age. According to Erikson, the major issue for people in middle adulthood is *generativity*.[3] This means the ability to contribute to the world, to be concerned about and to care for other people. For Erikson the task of middle age is to be productive—to support families and run farms, businesses, corporations, professions, and the government. Middle-aged adults tend to have the best jobs, earn the most money, live in the biggest houses, and drive the most expensive cars. Any middle-aged person will tell you, however, that this stage also has a distinctly unpleasant aspect.[4]

The Psychology of Mid-Life

Daniel Levinson, in his book *The Seasons of a Man's Life*, reported that 80 percent of the middle-aged men he studied went through a painful and disorienting struggle, beginning at about age 40 and lasting 2 years. Not only have physical powers diminished, but dreams, hopes, goals, roles, and solutions all have to be reevaluated. Often, in their twenties and thirties, men have fantasies about making it big—writing a best-seller, running for Congress, starring in a Hollywood movie, making partner in a big law firm, developing a lucrative private medical practice, and so on. For most people, it is during middle adulthood that these ambitions should be modified. If you increase the pace, take on more responsibilities, run more laps, diet more strenuously, go out with a younger man or woman, you run the risk of ignoring and refusing to accept inevitable life changes. This is not to say that ambition, eating well, exercise, and romance are bad for you. On the contrary, they can make the middle years much more satisfying. However, when these activities are carried out obsessively and in a manner more suited to a younger age or exaggerated to the point of becoming the center of your life, you are avoiding the opportunity to make an important transition. Accepting and appreciating how far you have come may be a more helpful approach to dealing with the changes of middle adulthood.[5]

Mid-life is a time to stop for a while and reflect on where you have been and where you are going. Since it is such a busy stage, people sometimes need to be forced to slow down and get their bearings. A physical warning sometimes triggers such an evaluation. People in middle adulthood do begin to take seriously the threat of disease and death, and, for men in particular, the concern is not unfounded. The risk of heart disease, which is the primary cause of death for men in the United States, increases after age 30, and the period of highest risk is between the ages of 50 and 60. Similarly, the risk of breast cancer for women is greatest in middle age.

Sex Differences in Mid-Life Transitions

Most of the research that has been done on mid-life transitions has been done on men. It would appear that women do not follow the same developmental pattern. For men, one of the aspects of a successful mid-life transition is that they slow down professionally and attend more to feelings, their inner world, intimate relationships, and caring. These are issues that most women are familiar with earlier in life. Carol Gilligan, in her book, *In a Different Voice*, makes the point that developmental theories have been written by men from a male perspective, with male values. Almost always these theories value independence and autonomy over interdependence and intimacy. In early adulthood, men are taught the importance of being separate, whereas women learn the importance of developing attachments. From the perspective of male psychologists such as Freud, Jung, Erikson, and Levinson, the young adult must first master autonomy and then he is equipped to cope with intimacy and caring. Women are socialized to value caring and relationships more than autonomy. "Thus," notes Gilligan, "males tend to have difficulty with relationships, while females tend to have problems with individuation."[6]

In mid-life in this culture, the task for men changes: successful adaptation to mid-life requires a shift to more nurturing, emotional, intimate, and caring activities. On the other hand, the woman in mid-life whose children are grown and whose husband has reached his highest level of success may be more likely to think about and be involved with her own education or a new business or career. Perhaps researchers will find that as men in mid-life need to move toward interdependence, women need to move toward autonomy. However, the role of women is changing dramatically, with autonomy and independence being valued more by both sexes. Since a greater number of women today are career-oriented, their mid-life transitions may become more like men's.

Although men and women may move in opposite directions in mid-life, perhaps they move toward the same goal—wholeness or completion. As Carl Jung suggested decades ago, the task of mid-life for both sexes is not to move in one particular direction, but to move in a direction that balances or compensates for the one-sidedness of movement in the first half of life.

Helping an elderly parent can be an opportunity for a man who has become one-sided as a result of having followed a traditional masculine path. Men can develop their nurturant sides by helping to care for an elderly parent. Of course, many men resist this change because they feel their independence is threatened. They may feel most comfortable helping financially or with practical tasks. They need to learn that it is possible to care and nurture without relinquishing independence.

Women are expected and are more likely to take on the role of caregiver. For women in mid-life who have just finished raising a family and are thinking about a career, this can be unfortunate. Research indicates that women may too readily give up their autonomy, cutting back on work or their own leisure time in order to assist an elderly parent. It will be interesting to see if sons and daughters begin to share the responsibilities of caring for their parents as husbands and wives have begun to share financial tasks and child care responsibilities. Both sexes should be able to help their parents with the practical tasks as well as offer emotional support. This could help sons and daughters alike to make a more satisfying mid-life transition.

As middle-aged men and women find themselves questioning their goals, their motives, their relationships, their jobs, and their lives, often they are confronted suddenly with a parent who gets sick or needs help. The middle-aged person is thus likely to be under a great deal of stress. Stress can be dangerous.

The Strain of Caregiving

It can be very difficult to care for an aging person, and there is evidence that the most stressful caregiving relationship is between a child and an elderly parent. Marjorie Cantor reported in 1983 that children offered more assistance to frail elderly parents than any other group of potential caregivers, including spouses, other relatives, and friends and neighbors. The children and spouses felt closest to the parent being cared for, but they had the hardest time getting along with them on an everyday basis. Fully 92 percent of friends and neighbors reported that they got along very well with the person they cared for, but only 53 percent of the adult children had the same success. Less than half of the children felt they understood their elderly parent, and only 28 percent felt understood by the parent. One more statistic from this study deserves our attention and points to the difficulty adult children experience when caring for a parent. Only 20 percent of the children, by far the lowest percentage of any caregiving group, felt that they and the elderly persons—their parents—shared similar views on life. Adult children and their elderly parents are at different places in the life cycle. Their issues, concerns, and hassles do not appear to be the same; they are bound together in the same stage of a *family life cycle,* each without sufficient appreciation of what the other generation has to offer.

Of all the caregiving groups, adult children report the highest levels of emotional strain, and the children with the closest bonds to their parents report the most strain. These adult children are in need of help and assistance themselves. They tend to take on the enormous burden of working, housekeeping, and taking care of a parent. They give up socializing, leisure activities, and vacations. Perhaps there would be less stress and strain if there was more of an understanding between the generations. Perhaps adult children would feel more understood if they revealed their concerns honestly to their aging parents.[7]

The "Sandwich" Generation

Eleanor Stoller interviewed hundreds of elderly persons and found that the vast majority were able to take care of themselves. As has been pointed out previously, elderly persons with living mates usually find ways of taking care of themselves and each other. If the parent is married, there is less assistance needed and less given. When one parent dies, the most frequent caregivers (almost half) are children.[8] Researchers have found that somewhere between 16 and 33 percent of the elderly people who live in nonretirement communities need some kind of assistance.

In one study of adults ranging in age from 20 to 70, it was found that of those who had a parent, respondents of all ages were worried about their parents' physical and emotional health. It appears that children in *middle adulthood* worry more about and do more for their aging parents than do *young adults*. Among middle-aged daughters, the older ones—those 50 and over—had more responsibilities than those in their forties. Middle-aged adult children can be so burdened with various responsibilities that they have been called the "patron," "keystone," "caught," "sandwich," and because caregivers tend to be women, the "women in the middle" generation.[9]

One study estimates that middle-aged adult children give an average of 8.6 hours a week of help to their elderly mothers. Unmarried daughters are most likely to be selected by an aging parent to provide support, and such daughters are much more likely to share a household with an elderly parent. There is also evidence that being married or having a career takes some time away from caregiving, but married women with careers may be under the heaviest burden of all when they care for an elderly parent.

Differences in Caregiving Between Sons and Daughters

The research consistently shows that daughters provide many more services to their elderly parents than do sons. Stoller found that daughters assist their parents an average of 30 hours a month, compared with sons' average of 15.1 hours. She also found that employment significantly reduces the hours of assistance only for sons. Men have been socialized to believe that their work role is their major role. A son is therefore not likely to stop working in order to take care of an elderly parent; rather, he is likely to reduce helping when he is employed. There is a discrepancy between what daughters believe and what they actually do. Women believe that a daughter shouldn't quit her job in order to care for an elderly parent. They also believe that children shouldn't adjust their work schedule to assist a parent. Finally, women "believe" that sons should help out as much as daughters; but the daughters provide much more assistance. Where do the adult daughters take the time from in order to help a parent? Being employed does not significantly reduce the hours of help provided by daughters. They take it from their leisure and free time. Women caregivers who are also employed tend to experience more stress than those who are not employed outside the home. There is some evidence that women who are forced to give up working or to cut back on their work hours in order to care for an elderly parent are the most unhappy of any caregiving group.

Although daughters devote significantly more time to assisting parents, sons are frequently very much involved. Yet there is very little research on the helping relationship between sons and elderly parents. While some researchers maintain that daughters-in-law are more likely than sons to assist dependent elderly parents, there is no substantial evidence to support this. In fact, in Stoller's study of 753 elderly people, 24.7 percent listed their first helper as a daughter and 22.3 percent listed a son. Daughters-in-law were indicated as the first helper by less than 2 percent of the 753 elders surveyed.[10]

Stress in Middle Adulthood

Everyone knows what it means to feel stress. Lately, when people experience its symptoms—anxiety, muscle tension, nervousness, fatigue, and exhaustion—they report feeling "stressed out." *Stress* is the accumulated emotional and physical reaction you have to events and the environment. *Stressors* are all the events and stimuli that cause stress. There are innumerable sources of stress, and the effects of too much stress can be devastating. In the 1950s Thomas Holmes discovered that a major life change such as the loss of a job or the loss of a family member often preceded the onset of tuberculosis. This does not mean that major unpleasant life changes cause tuberculosis or other diseases, but it could mean that such changes cause stress, which lowers your immunity to such diseases. Holmes and his colleague Richard Rahe determined how much stress is associated with 43 different major life changes by asking hundreds of people to describe how much readjustment had been required for each. Later research, on 2500 sailors, showed that those who were exposed to the most stress had 90 percent more illness than those who had fewer life changes.

Life-Change Chart

The life-change chart indicates the average amount of stress produced by each kind of life event.[11] Review the chart and ask yourself which of these changes occurred in your life this past year?

Death of a spouse	100	Taking out a big mortgage	
Marital separation	65	on a home	31
Death of a close family		Foreclosure of mortgage	
member	63	or loan	30
Personal injury or illness	53	Change in work respon-	
Marriage	50	sibilities	30
Loss of a job	47	Son or daughter leaving	
Marital reconciliation	45	home	29
Retirement	45	Trouble with in-laws	29
Change in health of a		Outstanding personal	
family member	44	achievement	28
Wife's pregnancy	40	Wife beginning or stopping	
Sex difficulties	39	working	29
Gain of a new family		Revision of personal habits	24
member	39	Trouble with business	
Change in financial status	38	superior	23
Death of a close friend	37	Change in work hours or	
Change to a different		conditions	20
kind of work	36	Change in residence	20
Increase or decrease in		Change in schools	20
arguments with spouse	35	Change in social activities	18

Taking out a small mortgage on your home	17	Change in eating habits	15
		Vacation	13
Change in sleeping habits	16	Minor violations of the law	11
Change in number of family get-togethers	15	Total	_____

Circle and then add up the point values of each event. If your life-change units total 150 to 199, you stand a mild chance of incurring some form of illness in the next year. If the total is 200 to 299, you are at moderate risk. Over 300 points puts you in the group very likely to suffer serious physical or emotional illness.

Interpreting the Results of the Scale

It is important to point out that there are many individuals who score extremely high on the scale but do not get sick or suffer from any kind of distress. Some people seem to thrive in spite of, or perhaps because of, great amounts of life change. It would also be absurd to conclude from the research on life change, stress, and illness that it is always advisable to avoid stress or life change. You may reduce your total life-change score by spending time in a closet, but this would probably not improve your mental or physical health. What the research does suggest is that you may not fully realize all that you are doing and all that has happened to you, and that it may be sensible to think about all of the changes that have recently occurred in your life.

Often you are called upon to help an aging parent at a time in life when you are going through a career change or questioning a relationship, or when your children are in adolescence or in the process of leaving home. It is therefore not surprising that so many adult children feel overwhelmed and "frazzled" when their parents need help.

Hassles

It is possible to score very low on the life-change scale and still experience a high level of stress. This is because major notice-able events are not the only causes of stress. Recent research has disclosed that long commutes to work, traffic jams, noisy neighbors, parking tickets, trouble with the phone company, and the like have at least as strong a correlation to emotional and physical illness as do the major life changes. Researchers have since developed the "hassles scale," which includes items such as "misplacing or losing things," "inconsiderate smokers," "planning meals," and "not getting enough rest," which may more accurately reflect the amount of stress in your life than the life-change scale. The notion that hassles, annoyances, and irritants cause stress, though, does not necessarily contradict the assumptions of the life-change scale, because major life changes almost always involve numerous hassles and annoyances.[12]

What are the hassles most frequently mentioned? Not surprisingly, worries, hassles, and uplifts vary tremendously according to age. College students are most hassled by "troubling thoughts about the future." This hassle doesn't even make the top ten for people in mid-life, who evidently don't have time for worrying about the future.[13]

The ten most frequent hassles of middle age are:

1. Concerns about weight

2. Health of a family member

3. Rising prices of common goods

4. Home maintenance

5. Too many things to do

6. Misplacing or losing things

7. Yard work or outside home maintenance

8. Property, investment, or taxes

9. Crime

10. Physical appearance

When you have to help an elderly parent, this may be considered to be a "change in health of a family member" (44 life-change units). However, such a major life change may also involve the following hassles, all taken from the hassles scale: "troubling thoughts about your parents' health," "more frequent visits," "more frequent phone calls," "caring for your parents' pet," "increased financial responsibilities," "making new decisions," "thoughts about death," "concerns about your parent having an accident," "trouble relaxing," "non-family members living in your house," "not enough money for health care," "fear of confrontation," "concerns about medical treatment," "relatives too far away," "filling out forms," "declining physical abilities," "overloaded with family responsibilities," and finally, "problems with aging parents." Helping an elderly parent is stressful not because it is one major event but because it involves numerous stress-inducing hassles. When a parent needs assistance, you may be involved on a daily basis, depending on the level of impairment of the parent. It is the constant stream of hassles that makes caregiving such a strain.

Effects of Stress

When you are stressed, the body mobilizes itself for action—flight or fight. A signal for danger results in tensed muscles and speeded-up heart rate and breathing, reactions suitable for confronting an enemy or running from it. If your ancestors spied a wild animal, such a reaction was useful. Today the same biological reactions occur when you are tied up in traffic, worried about the bills or a teenage child, or feeling the responsibility to assist an aging parent when you haven't much time. Flight-or-fight reactions are not usually appropriate for twentieth-century stressors. Nonetheless, the body copes with stress by increasing the flow of the hormones epinephrine (adrenaline) and norepinephrine and of the corticosteroids, all of which stops digestion, increases blood-sugar levels, and increases heart rate. The body's reaction is appropriate when you need more energy or need to be more alert in a certain situation. But if you are constantly under stress, the body's reaction will be harmful. Too much stress has been associated with arthritis, asthma, migraine headaches, and ulcers.[14]

Reducing Stress in Middle Adulthood

While it is neither possible nor desirable to eliminate all stress, it is important to make a commitment to bringing stress to a manageable level. Your *attitude* about how much stress you need to tolerate is one important factor. Some people believe that it is not right to feel "comfortable." That is, they feel that they are only living properly if they are suffering or struggling or enduring. Messages from parents and siblings can often lead you into such a trap. There are political, religious, and social traditions which propagandize against ever feeling relaxed or comfortable. It is possible to attempt to rid yourself of such conditioning. I am not suggesting that "working" or "accomplishing" or "doing" are not necessary and valuable. On the contrary, as discussed in Chapter 4, "Guidelines for Helping," taking action and getting results is essential to maintaining a sense of adequacy and well-being. What is not at all necessary is struggle and suffering for its own sake, which may not accomplish anything and often detracts from an effort. Once you understand that it is not desirable or advantageous to be unhappy or miserable, a significant obstacle has already been overcome. *Do less.* Often when people are under the most stress and feel the greatest anxiety, their tendency is to wake up earlier, or go to sleep later, or skip lunch so that they can do all that needs to be done. Often this sequence is self-defeating. You do more and more and then are expected by other people and yourself to continue to do more and more. In business there is a saying: "If you want to get something done, always ask a busy man." This is in fact a very good idea, unless you happen to be the busy man or woman. People often do more or work harder at just the wrong times. If you think about the life-change scale, it should be apparent that it is not advisable to change your residence or job at a time when your parent begins to get sick or really needs you. Some people, in times of difficulty, such as a period of marital disruption, change their appearance or sleeping habits, or redecorate their home. The life-change information suggests that these additional changes will bring on more stress.

Self-Efficacy

Suppose your mother calls and asks if you can take her to the doctor's. You may experience stress if you don't feel you have the time, if you are unsure of your driving ability, or if you are not sure how to get to the doctor's office. You will not experience stress if you feel this is a task that you can easily handle. A situation becomes stressful if a judgment is made that you cannot cope successfully with it. Judgments about your own effectiveness determine how much effort you expend, and how long you persist in the face of obstacles or unpleasant experiences. "Perceived self-efficacy," writes one psychologist, "is concerned with judgments of how well one can execute courses of action required to deal with prospective situations."[15]

You are always making choices about what course of action to pursue and how long you should continue with various undertakings. Your record of past successes and failures helps to determine your sense of efficacy. However, judgments made about your own effectiveness are often faulty, and such faulty judgments alone, especially the negative ones, can help to bring about failure. People who perceive themselves as ineffective think a lot about their personal deficiencies. They tend to imagine potential difficulties as more serious than they really are. While they are preoccupied with their self-doubts, with what can or might go wrong, they could be giving thought to how best to proceed. People with a strong sense of efficacy exert extra effort to persevere and master challenges and pay more attention to how to proceed and cope with the demands of the situation.

There is a whole body of research which indicates that one way to reduce stress is to pay attention to your accomplishments and successes and so be able to think of yourself as someone who can handle and cope with a variety of situations. This proper attitude by itself can help you to do better and feel less stress. There are certain factors which have been shown to undermine your judgment of your own effectiveness. If you dwell on what is new and strange in the field of your endeavor, your performance will be undermined. If you approach a new task by at first paying attention to what is familiar and within range of your capabilities, you will do better. If you are cast in a subordinate role or given an inferior label, you will perform tasks more poorly than you would if you were not so labeled. It has been shown that in a competitive situation, the sight of a formidable opponent can hinder you from performing to the best of your ability.

When caring for an aging parent, you need to define your role as helper in such a way that you feel you can be effective. It will be very stressful if you decide that you and you alone must take care of your parent's health needs or that you must make your parent feel comfortable at all times, or that in the time you spend with her she must be cheerful and pleasant. No matter what you or anyone else can do, your parent's difficulties will not disappear and your actions cannot make her perfectly happy. If your goals are unrealistically high, you will feel you have failed, even when you have done your best and have significantly improved things. Take on tasks that you feel confident you can perform. It is also helpful to think of these tasks as essential and worthwhile. Finally, remember that no matter how self-efficacious you feel, it is important for you to have support.

The Importance of Social Support

If your mother falls and breaks a bone, she will need help and support. If you are raising a family, or working, or both, and if you decide to help her, you will need support from other people. Researchers have shown that your physical and mental well-being is related to the amount and quality of the support you receive.[16] A supportive family has members who help each other and can act openly and express their feelings to one another, even angry and conflicting feelings. A supportive work environment is one in which workers are friendly and supportive of each other, management is supportive of workers and encourages workers to be supportive of each other, and workers are concerned about and committed to their jobs. People in a supportive work environment agree with statements like, "Employees discuss their personal problems with supervisors," and "People take a personal interest in each other." People who have less social support in their families and in their work environments show more depression and more psychosomatic symptoms.[17] It has also been shown that there is an inverse relationship between the number of friends we have and the risk of becoming sick.[18] Friends and relations provide encouragement, advice, information, and affection. This is all necessary, especially in difficult times, when such support can reduce stress and ward off illness.

You should not think that you and you alone can assist your elderly parent. Support systems—family, friends, neighbors, coworkers, professionals, institutions, and even books like this one— can all be seen as possible allies. Your ability to locate and utilize such support systems can be the most important factor in mitigating stress and discomfort. One of your most important tasks in helping an elderly parent is finding the proper support systems. If you are a working mother involved in taking care of your own mother, you have to think about finding help for yourself. Perhaps someone else can clean your house or take the children to after-school music lessons. The person you hire may not do the job with the same care and precision that you do, but it might be helpful to give up some of your perfectionism.

Everyone needs support. If you are feeling burdened by the many responsibilities involved in helping an elderly parent, you may redefine your role so that you can be more of an orchestrator or a director. You can help set up the most beneficial system of supports for your parent. In Chapter 9 I will be discussing some of the *formal systems of support*, such as government programs. It is important for you to think, as well, about your potential *informal support systems* (family, friends, and neighbors). Where can you go for help? Can you ask your children to take a little more responsibility? Children are sometimes very nonjudgmental and can easily spend time with a grandparent who asks the same question over and over again. What about your spouse and siblings? Have you asked directly for the kind of help you want from them? Often there are other relatives who, if asked, are willing to provide money or services.

Daughters of elderly parents may refrain from maximizing support systems for slightly different reasons than sons. Daughters sometimes suffer from delusions of being Florence Nightingale. They feel that there are or should be no limits on their caregiving and are puzzled when they begin to feel anxious or depressed. Sons are more likely to suffer from a macho mentality. They may feel totally exhausted but think that a real man doesn't complain or ask for help.

Relaxation

Find ways to *relax*. It may seem a bit odd to think that people don't know how to relax or need practice relaxing, but this is in fact the case. Many people in mid-adulthood are so busy that they need to cultivate the ability to relax, practicing relaxation the way you would practice a sport or physical exercise. The rewards for such practice are many. There is research which suggests that it is possible to bring down blood pressure by meditating or relaxing for 15 or 20 minutes once or twice a day. All techniques of relaxation, both eastern and western, have certain features in common. They include the following four components.

1. *A quiet environment.* A quiet room with no disturbances or distractions.

2. *A mental device.* Since one of the goals of the relaxation response is to keep the mind from wandering and obsessive thoughts, a mental device is used to still or quiet the mind. Such a device could be saying one word or phrase over and over again. Another common device is to count your breaths up to 10—breathing slowly in and then counting on the out breath. Your eyes can either be closed or open with your gaze fixed on an object or a spot on the floor or wall.

3. *A passive attitude.* When thoughts occur—whether they are memories or thoughts of the future—they should be disregarded and your attention should be redirected to the word or phrase or breathing. It is important that if your mind keeps wandering, you calmly bring it back to your focus and that you not "worry" about how well you are relaxing. Just bring your attention back to the mental device. It is to be expected that your mind will jump around. Don't get upset or self-critical or anxious if you are having difficulty with the technique. Accept what is happening, and as you become aware of the fact that your mind has wandered, simply bring it back.

4. *A comfortable position.* A comfortable position with no unnecessary muscular tension enables you to focus on the mental device and maintain the relaxation response. Various positions, such as kneeling or sitting cross-legged, are thought to be most conducive to meditation. Lying down is not advised because, although you are maintaining a relaxed state, you don't want to fall asleep. Your

mind should be awake and alert, yet passive, with no assignments or tasks, and your body should be relaxed and comfortable yet not slouched or asleep.[19]

Smoking

The most obvious way to reduce stress and prevent illness is not to smoke. About 25 percent of adult women and 35 percent of adult men smoke despite the fact that smoking has been conclusively linked to lung cancer, heart disease, bronchitis, emphysema, pancreatic cancer, and cancer of the larynx. In Chapter 7, "Your Parent as Patient," I will discuss several methods used to stop smoking. Various courses are available to help you or your parent stop smoking if you have difficulty quitting on your own.

Exercise

Some recent studies have indicated that people who exercise regularly are less likely to develop high blood pressure or heart disease and more likely to live longer. There seems to be a combination of physical and psychological factors at work which makes exercise helpful. Exercise helps people of normal weight to keep their weight down and helps overweight people to lose weight. It seems to improve blood levels of cholesterols. It has also been shown to help relieve depression and improve people's sense of well-being.

A Note on "Trying"

Advice about relaxing, smoking, and exercise is probably not new to too many readers. Most people know that they would feel better and be physically healthier if they changed certain habits. Many people "try" to take better care of themselves. They "try" to cut back on smoking, "try" to exercise more regularly, "try" to learn ways to relax or meditate. In other circumstances, people "try" to give up certain drugs, "try" to be on time, or "try" to work on a project that should have been finished long ago. "Trying" can become a way of life, and "trying" is different from "doing." When someone, for example, really tries to lose weight, she often will lose a few pounds and then regain the weight. She then loses more weight only to gain it back again. Such a person could do this for many years and perhaps for a significant part of her life. She could never be accused of not "trying." She has tried mightily. Like the mythical Sisyphus, she has pushed the boulder almost to the very top of the hill. Unfortunately, she couldn't get it to the top, and so it has rolled down. But she will not give up. She will begin the struggle again and push the boulder up the hill—"almost" to the top.

If you are going to change a habit like smoking or overeating or decide to exercise more, it is important that you do it with a sense of commitment or not do it at all. It is bad enough to have unhealthy habits, but it is even worse to torture yourself for having the habit. "Trying" can obviously be a form of self-torture. If Sisyphus had not been cursed he could have gotten help or just walked away.

Chapter 6 _____
Emotional/Psychological Concerns

Other than physical health, the major concerns of the elderly parents we surveyed were of an emotional or psychological nature. Our survey found that although elderly parents have a fear of death, there is just as great a fear of disability and dependency. Some of the elderly surveyed said that at times they felt that they wanted to be "needed," that they wanted to feel more useful. Some said that they didn't think or remember things as well and were worried about losing mental agility and the ability to take care of themselves. Others stated that they experienced isolation, loneliness, and sorrow and loss as a result of the death of close friends, relatives, or spouses. This chapter will focus on the issues that are likely to trouble your aging parent, some possible explanations for these emotional difficulties, and ways in which you can be helpful.

There is no question that adult children are capable of offering emotional and psychological support and that most elderly parents want and appreciate it when it is given and feel a loss when it is not given. One respondent said, "The only kind of support I would like from my children is emotional support. There are times when I could really use it and it's not there." Another said, "I am not satisfied with the help I get from my children. All I want is love, support, and appreciation." Perhaps one of the reasons that parents desire emotional support is the prevalence of ageism in our society.

The Impact of Ageism

A number of elderly parents who responded to our survey said they had problems with self-esteem. Given Americans' widespread negative attitudes toward aging, it is somewhat surprising that this was not a problem for more of our sample.

There are some who have a stereotyped view of older people as the most powerful, influential, advantaged group in society. This view recognizes that many politicians and leaders in entertainment, the arts, business, and the professions are aged. However, the much more prevalent view is that older Americans are sick, alone, forgotten, miserable, and the most disadvantaged group in the country. As one psychiatrist reported,

> In our value system, we believe the elderly are nonproductive, unattractive, useless, garrulous, old-fashioned....When we are young, we absorb these notions on a subconscious level and when we reach that age period we have a built-in system of self-deprecation, causing the elderly themselves to shun the notion of being old. Furthermore, the young in a society that's fashion conscious feel that the elderly are old-fashioned, and everything in our society that's old is to be discarded.[1]

Evidence of the bias against old people—ageism—can be found everywhere in our society. In one psychological study a group of young school children were asked to match a list of adjectives with photographs of either young, middle-aged, or elderly people. The children tended to link adjectives such as "sad," "bad," "ugly," "poor," and "dirty" more with the photos of the elderly than with photos of the young or middle-aged. Even doctors, nurses, and social workers show a tendency to prefer to work with children or young adults as opposed to the elderly. One of the more subtle forms of ageism is revealed when someone pays a compliment to an elderly person by saying, "You are terrific! You certainly don't act like a 70-year-old, you seem years younger." This remark obviously suggests that the typical elderly person cannot possibly look or be terrific.[2]

There is a grain of truth in almost all stereotypes, and this one is no exception. Certainly people in late adulthood are more likely to suffer physical problems than younger people. They also tend to slow down mentally, although, as will be discussed shortly, the mental processes are just as powerful as in youth. And the elderly tend to be more cautious and less flexible. The danger of the stereotype is that it suggests that such characteristics are inevitable and unchangeable. It also suggests that the style and character of youth are distinctly superior to that of age. And perhaps most importantly, as Plato observed, it minimizes individual differences.

> For certainly old age has a great sense of calm and freedom; when the passions relax their hold, then, as Sophocles says, we are freed from the grasp not of one mad master only but of many. The truth is, Socrates, that these regrets, and also the complaints about relations [with older people], are to be attributed to the same cause, which is not old age, but men's characters and tempers; for he who is of a calm and happy nature will hardly feel the pressure of age, but to him who is of opposite disposition youth and age are equally a burden.[3]

Plato's remarks suggest that certain people have a difficult time with old age for the same reasons they had a hard time at any age. This may not be quite true. In this culture, late adulthood represents a more difficult challenge than other stages of development. Look at all the products on the market—creams, dyes, lotions, clothes—that are intended to camouflage or reverse the aging process. Many middle-aged adults don't fully accept that their own aging is inevitable. However, because everyone ages, feelings of dislike or disgust for the elderly are in fact feelings of self-dislike. The elderly are your future—what everyone becomes. Helping and understanding your aging parents will enable you to get acquainted with this stage of life and be better prepared for it when you arrive there. If you show a lack of affection and respect for the elderly, you teach your own children this attitude. The emotions of prejudice—ridicule, disgust, and rejection—are, like most teachings, transmitted from parent to child through modeling and imitation. Ageism in our society is a reflection of a lack of self-acceptance. Many young people don't understand that there is a continuity of personality as aging progresses. The inner person does not change in the way that the body does. The personality of the older person remains intact as he watches his body deteriorate. The best cure for ageism is getting to know older people—especially your parents.

The Effects of Loss—Disengagement

A very controversial but popular theory was developed in 1961 by Elaine Cumming and William Henry, who maintained that "aging is an inevitable mutual withdrawal or disengagement, resulting in decreased interaction between the aging person and others in the social systems he belongs to."[4] There is evidence which suggests that, with age, interactions with other people decline in number, but it is not at all clear what causes the disengagement. Some maintain that the aging process itself is the cause, whereas others maintain that the circumstances surrounding the aging process are responsible. The death of family and friends, the fact that community facilities and transportation are geared toward the young, and, of course, forced retirement, all contribute to less frequent contacts with others.

Many of the jobs, tasks, and daily behaviors engaged in at mid-life are no longer expected of the person in late adulthood. In social-psychological terms, the person in late adulthood fills fewer social *roles* than the person in mid-life.

There are some who think that our identity is the sum total of the roles that we play. This notion is overstated, but it is true that when important roles are relinquished, identities have to be altered to some extent. One role that is significantly changed by the time of late adulthood is that of parent. People over 65 have typically finished the child-rearing process. Another role that often comes to an end at this stage of life is that of spouse. Nearly 90 percent of all persons between the ages of 35 and 44 are married. In contrast, 79 percent of the men but only 50 percent of the women between the ages of 65 and 74 are married. Many thoughts and activities are inextricably intertwined with the role of spouse, and its loss often results in fewer social contacts. For men whose wives had assumed the responsibility for making social arrangements—setting up get-togethers, planning parties and family functions—the loss of a spouse can mean greater social isolation. Similarly, for women, the death of a husband can bring about the loss of many of the social relationships connected with the husband's work and community activities. Of course, the loss of this most intimate of all relationships changes every aspect of daily living. The nature of all contacts, interactions, and involvements changes, requiring years of readjustment. It should not be surprising that the death of a spouse is considered to be the most stressful life event that one can endure.

Retirement

The marker most widely recognized as signaling the beginning of late adulthood is retirement. Over 80 percent of adults over 65 do not work for pay and, as Freud noted in his book *Civilization and Its Discontents,* although people usually object to working, "no other technique for the conduct of life attaches the individual so firmly to reality as laying emphasis on work; for his work at least gives him a secure place in a portion of reality, in the human community."[5] Work not only provides money; it supplies a network of social relationships and a pattern or routine for living. The relationships at work may be troublesome and the schedule may feel stifling, but retirement can mean no one to complain about, no one to commiserate with, and a significant disruption of one's sense of daily time.

Retirement can be especially problematic in cultures like ours which equate making money with personal worth. In a report to the United Nations it was stated that "strongly competitive societies in which too much emphasis is given to an individual's worth in terms of productive work and achievement, in which inactivity is somewhat suspect and leisure is highly commercialized and therefore expensive are not congenial environments in which to grow old."[6]

In our culture there is a great deal of attention and praise given to the elderly who continue to work for money. The doctor or lawyer who continues to go into the office in his seventies and eighties, the aging mom and pop who continue to run the neighborhood store, the elderly writer or painter—these workers seem to get credit in direct proportion to the neglect that the nonworking elderly receive. The vast majority of older Americans do not work for money, but many people are so suspicious of leisure that they tend to be somewhat mistrustful and disapproving of people in late adulthood. For the elderly who continue to work because they want to, it is important to encourage and support their activity. For the 80 percent who are retired, some form of activity is usually helpful. It may be important to help an aging parent adjust to retirement by talking about various activities that he can engage in. It is, however, a mistake to strongly urge your parent to take on activities that he doesn't seem to want to undertake. Everyone has his own dramatically different activity level, and it is not likely that you will help your aging parent find his optimal level by nagging him to find hobbies and the like. Anyone who is forced to be either active or inactive is likely to be unhappy.[7]

Changes in Intelligence and Memory

Intelligence and memory do change in late adulthood, but not in the ways that most people think. Until the mid-twentieth century, it was believed that intelligence increased only until the twenties and thirties and then declined in middle age, and declined more rapidly in late adulthood. This was based on scientific studies which showed that younger people did significantly better on intelligence tests than people in middle adulthood, who in turn did significantly better than people in late adulthood. However, the studies did not take into account the fact that the younger people had enjoyed many more educational opportunities than the older ones. This accounts for more of the difference than does the aging process itself. Studies begun in the late 1950s which followed people from middle to late adulthood show much less decline in intelligence over the years and also show that the declines come much later in life. We now know that intelligence can actually increase, in some respects, into the seventies.[8] We also know that it is helpful to discriminate between two kinds of intelligence—*fluid intelligence* and *crystallized intelligence*. Fluid intelligence is a type of mental dexterity. It helps us to solve mathematical problems, to see old problems in new ways, to solve puzzles like the Rubik's cube or jigsaws, to imagine a problem spatially, and the like. Fluid intelligence does seem to decline in middle adulthood and in old age. However, there is evidence that older people who must use mathematical and similar skills or who practice or are coached in these skills, do quite well on tests of fluid intelligence. It is possible that older people who do less well on these tests are not particularly interested in or never cultivated the skills.

Crystallized intelligence has to do with reading comprehension, vocabulary, the ability to express oneself verbally or in writing, and the ability to process and understand information. This type of intelligence does *not* show a decline in middle or old age, and in fact may even increase as one ages.

One area of mental functioning that does clearly undergo change is memory. People remember things best in their twenties and thirties, and then there is a slow decline in ability. At about age 60 there is a much steeper decline, especially in short-term memory. Older people are likely to clearly remember things about the distant past but will have a hard time remembering the names of people they have just met, or where they put their keys or eyeglasses, or what they were just about to do. If you think that your aging parent underestimates her memory loss and has a harder time remembering things than she thinks, there is research which suggests that you are right. In one study older people predicted that they would do about as well on tests of memory as a group of younger people. The younger people did not do quite as well as they themselves had predicted, but they did do substantially better than those in their sixties and seventies.[9] It may be helpful for older people to realize or admit that their short-term memory has declined, so that they can arrange their lives in such a way as to be less dependent on this type of memory. When he was 78, the well-known psychologist B. F. Skinner wrote that it was helpful to keep a pocket notebook or tape recorder handy for making up-to-date lists of things that he needed to remember.[10] Working out a more organized plan of where to keep things like keys and glasses, and doing things right away, before they are forgotten, are also ways of compensating for the decline in short-term memory. Elderly people sometimes need to be assured that this decline is normal and not a sign of senility or Alzheimer's disease. Although the general pattern of intelligence change has been known to psychologists since the 1950s, the prejudices associated with ageism have prevented this understanding from becoming widely known.

Loneliness

There are three different kinds of loneliness, according to Jeffrey Young, a psychologist at Columbia University. Transient loneliness lasts between a few minutes and a few hours. Situational loneliness, which may have a duration of up to a year, results from a particular event, such as a death or a move to a new community. It may involve unpleasant symptoms like headaches or depression. Finally, there is chronic loneliness. People suffering from chronic loneliness have difficulty making contact with others even when there has been no traumatic event. In 1972 sociologist Robert Weiss did a survey of the U.S. population and concluded that between 50 and 60 million Americans are lonely. One factor in determining loneliness is the number of social contacts. It is clear that elderly people who retire or relocate are at a greater risk of losing social contacts and being lonely. Perhaps one reason the elderly in our retirement community sample reported fewer emotional concerns is that such communities offer the opportunity for many and constant social contacts.

The number of social contacts is not the only factor that determines whether or not someone is lonely. A person's attitude and expectations play a role. For some young people, staying home alone on a weekday night leaves them feeling fine but being by themselves on a Saturday night leaves them feeling lonely. Similarly, an elderly person who expects to be constantly in contact with relatives and friends may feel lonely even though the number of social contacts is high. She may feel perfectly fine being alone on most days but lonely if she is by herself on a holiday. In addition to attitude and the number of social contacts, the quality of the social contacts determines whether someone feels lonely. Just being in a crowd or with large numbers of people does not provide the intimacy or depth of contact that is required to prevent loneliness.

There is some evidence that older people are in fact less lonely than younger people. One survey found that the highest rate of loneliness occurred in people between the ages of 18 and 25, and some researchers believe that adolescents experience the highest rate. Don't assume that your parent is lonely and depressed if she is in fact alone and independent. Alone is not the same thing as lonely. If it is clear that your parent does not wish to have any more social contacts, it probably will not be helpful for you to push her to join a club. However, if you are able to develop a more intimate relationship with your parent, this will help both of you and might make her feel better about seeking other contacts.[11]

The Importance of Contact

There are many ways to offer support. You can help an elderly parent by providing comfortable housing, or arranging for meals to be provided, or mowing the lawn. These practical tasks are all helpful and can give a parent a sense of security and reduce her burden. They can also serve to bring you into close and intimate contact with your parent, which may be the most helpful part of the activity. Everyone needs loving human contact, and although loneliness can be a problem at any age, it is a serious problem for the elderly. What elderly parents may want from their adult children more than any practical advice or assistance is close contact. This may be why the elderly parents we surveyed considered their emotional concerns to be so important. It was not uncommon for parents to make comments like the following:

> "We do not hear from our children often enough—perhaps once a month. Both are busy and involved."

> "We live in two different cities and see each other infrequently. I would like to share their lives more intimately and have them share mine."

> "I am satisfied most of the time with my children, but I would like them to be more considerate and my daughter-in-law to write more."

> "I would like to hear from my daughter at least one time a week."

> "My children live on the west coast and seem to have forgotten me. They call every week or two."

Intimacy

Although there are some parents who desire only a greater frequency of contact with their children, most elderly parents desire more than just contact. They want intimate contact. This kind of contact may be somewhat frightening to adult children and is certainly more difficult to achieve. In one investigation, personal interviews were conducted with 400 elderly women in Los Angeles County in order to determine the factors that contribute to satisfaction in their relationship with their children. The researchers concluded that emotional support is more important than financial support, and that the actual *number* of parent/child contacts is relatively unimportant. "Instead, it is her perception of the general *quality* of her contact with her children and her belief that they will provide for her needs in the future that are of primary importance."[12]

Intimacy means revealing aspects of yourself that are important. Of all intergenerational relationships, that between mother and daughter tends to be the most intimate, because women customarily find it easier to reveal themselves, and self-disclosure is the essence of intimacy. The following is a list of statements that researchers have used to assess degrees of intimacy between elderly parents and their daughters. It may be instructive to examine these to see what may contribute to or detract from your ability to have an intimate relationship with your parent.[13]

1. We want to spend time together.

2. She shows that she loves me.

3. We're honest with each other.

4. We can accept each other's criticism of our faults and mistakes.

5. We like each other.

6. We respect each other.

7. Our lives are better because of each other.

8. We enjoy the relationship.

9. She cares about the way I feel.

10. We feel like we are a unit.

11. There is a great amount of unselfishness in our relationship.

12. She always thinks of my best interest.

13. I'm lucky to have her in my life.

14. She always makes me feel better.

15. She is important to me.

16. We love each other.

17. I'm sure of this relationship.

There are a number of reasons why it is difficult to develop an intimate relationship with an elderly parent. If you would like to improve the intimacy of your relationship, you can locate and overcome these obstacles. Perhaps the most common obstacle to intimacy is a judgmental attitude on the part of a parent or a child. Such an attitude undoubtedly has its roots early in the relationship and continues as the child becomes an adult. Children are likely to avoid their parents when they feel that they are being criticized, evaluated, or judged. Not surprisingly, the urge to criticize or interfere is usually passed on from the parent to the child, who learns to evaluate and judge his parent. One elderly parent we interviewed made it clear that she would like to have a more intimate relationship with her son, who continually urges her to move closer to him even though this is not at all what she wants. Although the son may think he is helping by urging his mother to move so that he can assist her more easily, in fact he is not listening to his mother or accepting her needs. The mother, on the other hand, is not totally satisfied with her son's choice of career, would like to see him pursue other interests, and has even indicated her displeasure with his choice of a marriage partner. Their mutual lack of acceptance leaves both feeling unhappy, and makes it impossible for them to offer each other emotional support. If either one would be willing to be less evaluative and more accepting of the other, they might experience a pleasant revival of intimacy.

One man who returned a questionnaire said that he thought

he could be of most help to his parents by living his life the way they wanted him to, and he wasn't about to do this: "They want me to live my life as they do. They ask for no money. They manage their lives just fine, but they ask that I do more for my needs, as they do for theirs. This is hard for me, because my priorities are not the same as theirs."

Grown children are aware of it when their parents disapprove of the way they bring up their own children, the way they dress or spend money, the kind of work they do, or how selfish or unselfish they are. Children who feel this basic lack of support are hurt and angry, and have mastered the art of returning this hostility by meddling in their parents' lives rather than helping them.

Distance Is Not an Obstacle to Intimacy

Contact, aid, and intimacy are not the same thing. It is perfectly possible to live around the corner from your elderly parent, or in the same house, and *not* have an intimate relationship. It is also possible to have frequent contacts—visits and phone calls—and not be intimate. I suspect that when contact is obligatory, it is not conducive to intimacy. One very recent investigation focusing on the relationships between 132 mothers and their daughters, found that aid and contact are not predictive of intimacy. The researchers concluded that physical closeness can dictate and physical distance can limit the frequency of contacts, but affection is what determines contact at moderate distances.[14] One elderly parent we interviewed said she very much wanted to hear from her grandchildren who lived at the other end of the country. She asked her son to stamp and address postcards to her. The grandchildren could then easily write a few lines about their activities, which their grandmother greatly appreciated. It is possible to make contact at a distance easier by preaddressing postcards or arranging phone conversations when the rates are low.

One way to develop a more intimate relationship with a parent is to participate with him or her in the process of life review. This involves recalling the past, reflecting on previous events, making some evaluations of these events, and trying to develop a new and final sense of self. This process can also be of use to you, by helping you to connect with your own history or roots.

Life Review—An Overview

In late adulthood many important roles are relinquished, and the number of daily contacts is likely to decline. Perhaps this is an appropriate time for slowing down, for reflection and life review. An elderly person who takes the time and trouble to review and analyze her life is not only happier but can, if she shares it with her children, show them how to integrate and think about life experiences, and even prepare for death. For an elderly parent who doesn't feel needed, this sort of teaching role can be very useful. Also remember that crystallized intelligence and long-term memory both tend to function extremely well in late adulthood. These are the faculties that are needed to reminisce and review one's life.

Until recently it was believed that an elderly person who spent time reminiscing was either senile, bogged down in the past, or escaping the realities of today. Middle-aged doctors and scientists, caught up in their busy lives, were convinced that remembering the past was a waste of time. Only in the last 25 years have the positive aspects of reminiscing been understood and appreciated. In 1963, R. N. Butler noted that the elderly tend to reminisce whether it is encouraged or not and found that such activity was very valuable. He defined this "life review" as "a mental process characterized by the progressive return to consciousness of past experience, and, particularly, the resurgence of unresolved conflicts; simultaneously, and normally, these revived experiences and conflicts can be surveyed and reintegrated. Presumably this process is prompted by the realization of approaching dissolution and death, and the inability to maintain one's sense of personal invulnerability."[15] The importance of life review is upheld by the work of Erik Erikson, who theorized that each stage of life requires different tasks. The eighth, or last, stage of development involves the attempt to experience *ego integrity*. This means looking back on one's life and deciding eventually that it was constructive, unique, satisfying, and worthwhile.[16] In one study, involving elderly institutionalized veterans, it was found that those who spent the most time reminiscing were best-adjusted and had the highest degree of ego integrity.

Kathleen King has described the way in which reminiscing can enable an elderly person to review unresolved conflicts and work them through in order to become more peaceful. She offers the following example from her grandmother's journal.

> It's time for a time I had with your mom when she was dating your father. He and his brother John had a big car. So they took turns using it. I think it had a sticker on the back I think it was Amherst college.
>
> Well when Mary had dates I would tell her to be home at 12 or I would lock her out. So one night 12 O'clock and she wasn't home. They would sit in the car in front of forest ave. R.7.Ill. Well I kept on waiting for her to come home and then I went and turned the lights out and locked the doors and went to bed! She came and found the doors locked and Charles was gone. So she went around the back and found the back door open. So she went up basement steps. That door was locked So she sat on the step all night. I was really mean I can't imagine doing such a thing. I wish I didn't write this because I can't imagine me doing such a thing. Mary will you ever forgive me? I thought of it last night wish I could tear it out. But didn't want to spoil the book. So I am sorry and hope that I have done some nice things for you to make up for my meaness that night. And you had to go to work the next day.[17]

In addition to helping her to resolve old conflicts, reminiscing gives an elderly person the opportunity to review positive past experiences and improve her self-esteem. The quote above was taken from a journal. This written document was very helpful to the family as well as to its author. It enabled family members to preserve tradition and gave them a sense of continuity. For many people who engage in life review, late adulthood is the first time that they have had the leisure to actually get to know themselves. Many people find the process of getting to know themselves so interesting that they come to experience time alone as valuable rather than depressing.

How to Help Your Parent with Life Review

Some adult children feel that it is almost impossible to have an intimate relationship with their parents. They feel that their parents are uneducated or fussy, too manipulative, too emotional, or not emotional enough. Some say things like, "If it weren't for the fact that she is my mother, I wouldn't have anything to do with her."

The fact that it is extremely difficult for you to be around a parent is good evidence that she is not an ordinary person who just happens to be related to you. One way of achieving intimacy with a parent and at the same time helping—and being helped—with a life task is to engage your parent in life review.

Ask your parent about the past. Most elderly people need very little encouragement, but if your parent is worried that she is imposing on you, tell her that you want to know more about her past so that you can understand your own roots better. Explain that you are asking about her past not as a favor to her but as a favor to yourself—which is true. One of my clients spontaneously took on the role of a "reporter." She asked her mother about the facts of the past, and took notes. She said it was as if they were playing a game together—a game they both enjoyed and from which they both benefited. It isn't necessary to be this organized or systematic. Your parent does not have to write notes or keep a journal and neither do you. What do you want to know about? Are you interested in the circumstances surrounding your parent's birth and childhood? What about your parent's view of her own parents' marriage? What is your family legacy regarding certain problems and issues? What was your parent's early romantic life like? What initially attracted her to your father, and what were their first years together like? It may also be interesting to ask about your parent's memory of being pregnant and raising children. What are your parent's memories of living through times of great economic and social unrest—the depression years, and World War II? Are you interested in the sorts of foods your mother ate, the clothes and styles of previous eras, the early films, and radio and television shows? Ask especially about how she handled problems and difficulties which you are presently experiencing. If you are having a problem at work or with your own children, it may be interesting to know how your parent or her parents dealt with a similar situation. What was successful for her and what wasn't? By asking, you are likely to be helping your parent and yourself simultaneously. The emotional problems of elderly parents—loneliness, low self-esteem, and the feeling of not being needed—can all be ameliorated through this process. One adult child interviewed his parents and relatives about their past using a video recorder so that he could have a record for *his* children. You can do something that you and your parent can have fun with. Get together and label and organize the hundreds of photographs your family likely has, scattered around in albums, shoe boxes, and closets.

The Benefits of Life Review

Two researchers, A. W. McMahon and P. J. Rhudick, have stated that successful adjustment in late adulthood comes about as "the result of having coped successfully with problems specific to this phase of life, namely the maintenance of self-esteem in the face of declining physical and intellectual capacities; coping with grief and depression resulting from personal losses; finding means to contribute significantly to a society of which they are still members; and retaining a sense of identity in an increasingly estranged environment."[18]

People who are involved or work with elderly people are sometimes astonished to see how they can forget a name or fact they have just learned and yet remember the distant past in rich detail. There is evidence that reminiscing is simply pleasurable for most elderly people, but it also can serve other valuable functions. Through memory, an elderly parent may mourn significant losses. In fact, one may view the process of life review as an elderly person's way of saying a proper good-bye, as well as of preparing herself to make better decisions about what she wants to do with the rest of her life. Your parent can think about past events of which she is still ashamed or embarrassed and attempt to resolve her lingering conflicts. She can also review how she coped with various transitions, problems, and conflicts in the past and use strategies that may have been successful to help solve current problems.

There is evidence that elderly people who reminisce are less depressed, have higher self-esteem, are better able to get over dissatisfactions with the past, have increased enjoyment of social relationships, and are able to preserve a feeling of being worthwhile. As we see in the following case study, sharing the process of life review can lead parent and child to feel mutually enriched, intimate, and helpful and can also enable both to resolve issues regarding how to cope with future difficulties, possible disabilities, and even death.

Maggie—The Development of Intimacy

Maggie, a 47-year-old sociology professor, lives in a large metropolitan city. She is a single woman with many friends and a career that she enjoys. When Maggie's mother, Ellen, became ill, Maggie's older brother disappeared. This was extremely upsetting to Maggie. She describes Ellen as quiet and withdrawn, a dutiful wife and mother. Maggie's father was an unusual man. He made a great deal of money in several business schemes and lost the money in other schemes. Maggie remembers that somehow the feelings in the family remained constant even though there were these upheavals in the family's fortune. Ellen always stood by her husband, whom Maggie remembers as being dominant and quite demanding. Although Maggie's parents never fought, they were never really close, either. Maggie says that Ellen did tell her that once, after her husband had lost a great deal of money, she had noticed him crying as he read the evening paper. This troubled Ellen, but she did not know what to do and so she did nothing. It is Ellen's inability to express her emotions that Maggie finds so difficult. Ellen was never physical with Maggie or either of the other children.

When she was growing up, Maggie was very close to her father, while her older brother, Aaron, was very close to her mother. There is also a younger brother, Howard, who has always been more independent and separated himself from the rest of the family. When Maggie's father died, about 10 years ago, Maggie expected her mother to fall apart, but she didn't. Ellen has been involved in volunteer work with a charitable organization and was doing quite well until she discovered she had breast cancer. She was very upset, confused, and terrified and reached out for her children. Her youngest son called frequently but lived in a distant part of the country and could not really be of too much help. Aaron, who, like Maggie, lived nearby, decided that the situation was not that serious and, even if it turned out to be serious, he had better things to do than to spend a lot of time with a cold, unpleasant woman like his mother. This left Maggie alone to help Ellen every day in the hospital. For several nights after Ellen was first released, the two women shared Ellen's bed. Maggie felt extremely upset and stressed by all of this. She had to miss a good deal of work, and she was absolutely furious with Aaron.

Over time and with some counseling, what seemed like a burden and cause of pain became a very positive experience for Maggie. Today, she feels some resentment toward her older brother. However, her relationships with her mother and younger brother are much improved. Ellen lives in an apartment only 20 minutes away from Maggie. Now mother and daughter speak to each other about every other day. Many aspects of the relationship between them have been totally transformed. In all the time that they have spent together, Maggie has been able to discover a great deal about her mother's past as well as about her own. To finally discover the *truth* about the past is valuable as well as rare. In most families, parents don't tell children about troubling or difficult events. Family secrets are maintained in order to protect children from unpleasantness. When we become adults, the patterns of protection remain intact. Maggie knew that Ellen's parents had separated after 25 years of marriage, but never understood why. Her mother always said, "Certain things happened," and the children always accepted this explanation. When Maggie finally confronted her mother more directly, she discovered that her grandfather, Ellen's father, had left the family because he came home one day and found his wife talking on the front lawn to a young man who was a neighbor. It was clear to everyone that absolutely nothing had happened between the two. However, Ellen's father had been looking for an excuse to leave. This was the kind of excuse that was difficult for Ellen to talk about. She would have had to say to the children, "My father left because he thought my mother was cheating on him." Maggie realized that Ellen had always felt that her father was on the verge of leaving the family, and she also began to consider that perhaps this was why her mother was in such tight control of her emotions. Ellen was always tense and stiff as she prepared herself for the worst. Maggie also came to understand that her mother's coolness was absolutely essential for her own marriage to work. Maggie's father, who won and lost large amounts of money, had required a spouse with the ability to control her emotions while she supported and comforted him. It is not uncommon for an adult child to develop a whole new understanding of a parent and to forgive that parent when the two are brought closer in the helping relationship. Both mother and daughter felt more accepting of Ellen's past as they reviewed and discussed it.

As Ellen began to talk more about her fears regarding her

illness, Maggie saw her mother becoming more open and vulnerable. Not only did Maggie understand and appreciate her mother's past and present situation, she also better understood her own past and her problems today. For the first time in her life she began to tell her mother about her own troubles. Maggie began to realize that she, too, held back in her relationships. Just like her mother and her mother's mother, she was in some sense always prepared for a sudden reversal, for a man to leave or a friend to prove not trustworthy. Now she could examine this quality in herself and decide whether she wanted to make a change in the way she conducted her own relationships.

Intimacy means someone revealing themselves to us while we reveal ourselves to them. Through mutual self-disclosure, thoughts and feelings that had never been shared before were shared when Ellen became more vulnerable and Maggie took the risks that were involved in getting closer to her mother. They have developed such an honest relationship that they have been able to discuss what they will do when Ellen feels that she is no longer able to take care of herself. Ellen does not want to go to a nursing home, nor does she want to live with Maggie or any of her children. They have agreed that if the need arises, Maggie will interview and hire a companion for her mother. Such conversations do not usually take place or go well unless a parent and child have developed trust and intimacy.

Maggie says that in many ways she now asks more of her mother and Ellen "delivers" more than ever before, despite her many physical problems. The helping process works best when there is such reciprocity. Recently Maggie has acknowledged that she should be thankful to Aaron, who by withdrawing allowed Maggie the opportunity to develop a loving relationship with her mother.

Chapter 7_____
Your Parent as Patient

Who should have the responsibility for your parent's health? Your doctor, her doctor, you, your sister, all have some responsibility, but it is important to remember that the ultimate responsibility belongs to your parent. Because people sometimes view going to the doctor or the hospital as a surrendering of responsibility for their own health care to another person or to an institution, loss of autonomy and independence may develop. All of us, especially the elderly, should be encouraged to view doctors as guides for health care. If too much is expected from a physician, disappointment and even anger are almost inevitable. Physicians cannot stop the aging process. It is realistic, however, to expect a physician to help your parent to attain a maximization of function. Your parent is responsible for her health care because she decides which doctor to see and must evaluate medical advice, take her medications, and follow through on "doctor's orders." She is in control of her diet and of whether or not she smokes, drinks, or does exercise. It is important that an adult child not take over this control but rather assist her parent in health care.

There is more to health care than treating disease. In this chapter we will examine two crucial elements of health care that do not receive sufficient attention. The first area involves *interpersonal relations* between physicians, patients, and families. You may not be able to make an accurate diagnosis of your parent's medical problem or prescribe the best treatment, but you can help select a doctor, assist in your parent's preparation for the visit, help her to understand the doctor's explanations and instructions, and help her to understand and follow the reg-

103

imen that has been prescribed. In so doing, you may play an important supporting role in your parent's health care.

The second area is the *prevention* of disease. The most effective and cost-efficient way to treat lung cancer is not with an oncologist, a thoracic surgeon, and a radiation therapist, but by not smoking. In the forthcoming discussions of smoking, exercise, and nutrition, it should be pointed out that it is possible for helping to evolve into nagging, which is not very helpful. You can offer information and suggestions, but if your parent continues to smoke, for example, it would be ill-advised to persist in pushing her to stop. Ultimately someone stops smoking for herself. If you push too hard, your parent will rebel and may not consider her own reservations about smoking. Most people who smoke would like to stop, and by nagging them, you may inadvertently build up their resistance. A more effective way to be helpful is to be sure that if your parent does act to prevent illness, you offer support and encouragement.

Selecting a Physician

If your parent's needs are satisfied by her present physician, her situation is fortunate. For a variety of reasons—dissatisfaction with their present physician, their doctor's retirement, or the need for a specialist—many elderly people find that they must select a new doctor. Under such circumstances a parent may call on you for assistance. You might approach the issue with a few points in mind. A doctor affiliated with a hospital or clinic usually has the most appropriate credentials. You could ask a physician you trust about a recommendation. You can also ask for suggestions from friends and family. There are several aspects of the doctor's reputation that you should consider: success of the treatment, quality of hospital affiliations, and access to up-to-date techniques and equipment. Then there is the matter of the doctor's manner.

Doctors are very powerful people. As can be the case when any discrepancy in power is encountered, a doctor can treat his patient as an object rather than a person. Some doctors treat a medical case or a disease, whereas most people prefer the doctor to recognize that they are people who want and need care. Doctors' attitudes must be understood in the context of American medical education, which may be cold and hostile and encourage students to place more value on science than on the humanity of the patient. In addition, doctors are often overworked and overtired, with limited time for their families, relaxation, and exercise.[1]

If your parent is unhappy because she feels that she doesn't get enough time, attention, sympathy, and concern from her doctor, don't dismiss her feelings. The doctor's personality and manner are very important factors in the success of the treatment. We know, for example, that at least a third of all patients fail to follow their physician's recommendations and that the quality of the relationship between doctor and patient has a role in determining cooperation. It is important to select a doctor whom your parent will like and feel comfortable with, because such a physician is likely to be more effective. Pain and illness are usually accompanied by anxiety, which can have a detrimental effect on health. A trusted physician can allay anxiety and inspire the patient to feel confidence in the treatment. Of course, it is advisable to seek out a physician who is technically competent, but the doctor's manner has an impact on the health of the patient as well.

If you cannot switch from a physician who is personally a dud because either there is no alternative or you can't find one more to your and your parent's liking, there is not much point in undermining his authority and effectiveness by speaking critically of him. This only makes a difficult situation worse. You might as well support the one you are dealing with.

Visiting a Physician

Your level of involvement in this undertaking, as in other aspects of the helping process, may be critical. There are situations in which the best help you can offer is to drive your parent to the doctor's office and to do and say nothing else. Often the best help is the least help. There are other situations which require that you be extremely assertive and a strong advocate in order to be of the most help. One man we interviewed reported having forcefully discouraged a hospital physician from giving his aging mother a series of convulsive shock treatments to alleviate her depression. He believed that his mother didn't fully understand the type of treatment she was about to receive or the possible side effects. He therefore felt that her treatment was inappropriate and became actively involved. In situations where you feel your parent is not getting the right treatment, it is most helpful to proceed assertively but without aggression. You can be very persistent about seeking a second or even a third opinion. You need not be rude or abrasive, as this is likely to alienate the people who are caring for your parent.

Some physicians prefer to talk with and examine the patient alone, others welcome an adult child, another relative, or a friend to assist in the examination and treatment of the patient. If a doctor does not want you present during the preexamination, examination, or postexamination phases of the visit, this does not necessarily mean that he is trying to make things easier for himself; it may be that he feels it is best for your parent to maintain a degree of independence. Many doctors do welcome an adult child before and after the examination phase of the visit.

Even if you do not accompany her at all, you can assist your parent in preparing for a visit. Help her to prepare a medical history beforehand. Make a detailed list of symptoms, complaints, and questions. Visits to the doctor's office can be very anxiety-producing. Patients frequently forget important history and important current information to tell the physician. They are often so distracted or upset that they do not understand or do not remember the doctor's diagnosis or instructions. If you can accompany your parent to the office, be certain that she has communicated all the information about her condition, and that both you and she have enough information when you leave. Sometimes parents and adult children try to be "good patients" and not disturb or trouble anyone. This is not in your parent's best interest. In one study done in 1980, breast cancer patients were asked if they had unanswered questions concerning their treatment. Over 86 percent answered yes. They did not have enough information on the stages of breast cancer, choices of surgery, postoperative therapy, prostheses, reconstructive surgery, or personal counseling. The vast majority of patients (some estimates are about 98 percent) want information on such things as the side effects of the medications they are taking.

One of the most important tasks of the adult child is to help a parent to get such information if she wants it. If the physician offers such information—well and good. If not, you can say that you and your parent want to think about some questions you need to ask. You can write our your list of questions and give them to the doctor or the nurse. Be friendly and understanding but persistent enough so that you get your questions answered.[2] It is best not to be overly intrusive in assisting your parent with a physician. Your parent needs to feel a sense of control. You will not be helpful by charging in and taking over. A way to help nonintrusively is to ask your parent whether she has enough information about the disease and about the plan for treatment. If she doesn't understand aspects of the disease or treatment, ask how she intends to find out more. In this way you help your parent to think and care for herself.

Helping with Medication

Going to a doctor is only a small part of health care. Aside from diet, exercise, and other aspects of life which do not occur in the doctor's office, many elderly people have to coordinate a number of different medications. A high percentage of patients fail to take their prescribed medications, or take them improperly. It is important to know when to take medication. Ask your parent if she knows whether a particular medication should be taken before or after meals. Ask her if she knows whether there are certain foods that should or shouldn't be taken with the medication. It is preferable that you do not take over the responsibility for monitoring your parent's medication schedule, but you can help her to understand and monitor it herself. It may also be helpful to remind your parent to inform her doctor concerning any medications she is already taking. Many elderly people see more than one doctor, each of whom may be prescribing different kinds of medications for different conditions. If your parent informs each physician of precisely what drugs she is taking, the serious problems that can arise from negative interactions between drugs may be avoided. Such problems will also be less likely to occur if your parent has a primary-care physician—a doctor whom she is comfortable with and who coordinates medications and medical care.

If Your Parent Has a Serious Illness

If your parent has a serious illness, she will need professional help and she will also need your help. It is not easy to help someone in such a condition. When people are diagnosed as having an illness such as cancer, they become fearful and uncertain about many things. This is quite understandable. They are afraid of pain, of deterioration, of becoming more and more dependent on others, and of death. If your parent has a serious illness, she will also be faced with a number of decisions—what doctors to consult, what hospital to enter, what to tell family and friends. At a time when she needs to think and act clearly, she will be fearful, perhaps terrified, and will likely have a difficult time communicating any of her concerns to you or anyone else. Often a parent will try two different tacks in order to get the support and attention she needs. She might exaggerate and focus on every problem and difficulty she has, or she might try to hide the fact that she is having problems—adopt a stiff upper lip so that you and other relatives and friends don't get upset and turned off. Both of these strategies are ineffective, but can be inadvertently encouraged by you.

When a parent is seriously ill, many adult children become confused and upset and don't know how to behave with him or her. You might think that although your feelings are profoundly negative you should try to be cheerful and upbeat with your parent as a way of being helpful. You might feel disgust about the illness, or sadness, or guilt, or anger that you have to be involved with someone who is so sick and difficult to be with. Even when you love and care deeply about your parent, it is natural for there to be fear of the illness, a feeling of helplessness, uncertainty about what to say, and distress at your parent's pain. Adult children are often confused about whether they should be outspoken about how they feel or try to cover up their negative feelings and cheer up the parent. With all this ambivalence about how to act, there is considerable evidence that an adult child may try to avoid any unpleasant discussions about the illness, give off mixed messages in a parent's presence, or avoid being with the parent altogether. All of these actions on the part of an adult child can tend to make the parent more confused.

The following are general guidelines to keep in mind if your parent has recently learned that she is seriously ill.

Some Guidelines if Your Parent Is Seriously Ill

Keep in mind that your parent will probably want information and clarification, and most of all needs support. She is typically in a serious dilemma as to how to fulfill these needs. She may feel that she can express her true feelings by complaining a great deal and showing that she is upset, and thereby risk alienating you and others around her, or she can put on a happy face and hope that you and others will spend more time with her, giving her the support she needs. She can vacillate between these two strategies and make it even more difficult for you to know how to respond.

1. Help your parent to get the relevant information about her condition. Find out about the feelings, sensations, and emotions that are likely to be part of the disease or its treatment. It is helpful for both of you to be aware of these factors. If, for example, you are unaware of the side effects of chemotherapy, you will not be understanding when your parent is very tired or feels nauseous.

2. Without pressuring your parent to "open up," invite her to share some of her unpleasant feelings with you. "Gee, Mom, I know it must be very difficult and scary for you." It is important not to pressure your parent, because some people need to maintain control or would prefer to let the feelings out with another relative, a friend, or a member of the hospital staff.

3. As discussed in Chapter 4, it is often very helpful to just pay attention and listen to what your parent is saying. You don't have to say, "How are we doing today?" or "I'm sure you're going to be all right" or "Don't worry, you're in good hands," or give other forms of false reassurance. You may help more by just saying nothing and being there.

4. Be as honest as you can about your feelings. If you feel sad or nervous and you try to cover up your feelings, you may

only confuse your parent. It is also exhausting for you to always wear a mask of optimism and cheerfulness. You are better off saying you feel sad or upset about what is happening or that you feel helpless. This may, in turn, make it easier for your parent to express her feelings, and it may create the kind of atmosphere that is conducive to honest communication. Once both of you are able to acknowledge the unpleasant feelings, you may be able to forget about the illness for a while and talk about other things.

5. Being honest does not mean being hurtful. You may have many negative feelings about your parent's illness. You may find your parent unattractive and downright unpleasant to look at. You may feel resentful and angry that you have to put so much time and effort into being with her. You may also feel guilty about not seeing her often enough or embarrassed about the way she relates to the doctors and nurses. These feelings are understandable but should not be shared with your parent. Honesty does not mean telling someone that her nose is too big or that she has too many wrinkles. You don't have to suppress or ignore these feelings, either, but can share and discuss them with friends, family, and support groups.

6. Take advantage of support groups for yourself and your parent. More hospitals than ever before have support groups for patients and family members of patients with particular diseases, and some groups even exist for the patients and the family members together. Parents in peer support groups can share their problems and feelings with patients in the same situation. They can and often do discuss issues such as how to discuss their physical condition with their children. Patients can compare experiences and understand better what is happening to them and what is normal. It should be pointed out that your parent may resist a peer support group when she first learns she has a disease, because she doesn't want to see herself as someone who is seriously ill. She may be more amenable to a support group later on. Other parents resist support groups because they view discussing problems as a sign of weakness or they view discussing their problems with strangers as inappropriate. In such cases it

could be especially helpful for you to join a family support group, so that you can discuss what it's like to have a parent with this particular disease.

7. If you are having serious problems concerning your parent's illness, you could consult a family therapist. Sometimes families get "stuck" and are unable to resolve the problems that arise with the onset of a particular change. The illness of a parent is the kind of event that family members may have a great deal of difficulty adapting to. A family therapist—usually a social worker, psychiatrist, or psychologist—can sometimes enable family members to communicate in a more straightforward manner or help them in some other way to break the impasse that has occurred. Family therapists have noted that when one member of the family has a serious disease, another member may develop a problem in order to distract everyone from the more difficult problem of the illness. Thus when an aging parent is seriously ill and no one in the family is able to discuss what impact this is having on him or herself, adult children may argue or develop symptoms like headaches, or younger children may have problems in school. Such lesser problems may be attempts at solving the family's dilemma, but a family therapist can often help members to find a better solution.[3]

Helping Your Parent in the Hospital

It's no fun to go into the hospital with an illness. If your parent is concerned or worried or even terrified about going into the hospital and wants to get out as quickly as possible, she is far more normal than someone who wants to stay. A hospital atmosphere does not tend to promote feelings of comfort. Your parent is likely to be met first by a hospital clerk who asks about insurance, money, and other impersonal details. She will then be assigned a strange room with a strange roommate. She will be given strange clothes and subjected to unfamiliar and perhaps painful tests. As many as 30 staff members may pass in and out of your parent's room each day—cleaning, getting information, bringing food, and taking tests. When your parent has questions, she will often not know whom to ask. Sometimes aides ask patients to ask nurses, who ask patients to ask doctors, who then fly into the room and out so fast that your parent won't remember what it was she had meant to ask.

If your parent doesn't know, she will soon find out that a hospital is organized for the convenience of the staff. Her identity as a person becomes less a consideration than the staff's schedule. This is not to say that the hospital staff is uncaring. On the contrary, the great majority of hospital personnel desire what is best for the patient and intend to provide personal and competent care. At the same time, most hospital officials believe that since they are working to save lives, they need to maintain order and efficiency, which they can only do by maintaining total control over their patients. There is no single best way for your parent to cope with this depersonalization.

Some adult children advise their parents to cooperate with the hospital staff, whereas others encourage them to be in conflict with the staff about treatment. Each elderly parent takes on the role of hospital patient differently. Patients who expect to lose freedoms in the hospital and who understand the need for regulation and control in a life-and-death situation are much more likely to accept their lot and be "good patients." People who have been in dependent situations or who have been sick for a long time or who need to please others, especially those in authority, also have a tendency to accept the role of patient. There are problems, however, with the acceptance of this role. Although you shouldn't try to force your parent to change roles, you should be aware of the potential hazards. There is some evidence that the so-called good patient is often confused, anxious, and depressed, but is too timid to say or do anything for fear of displeasing the staff. Be alert to the following dangers if your parent is one of these patients. The cooperative patient often wants to ask questions about her condition but is afraid to. She may also fall into a passive state which is akin to a state of helplessness and depression. It is unfortunate that such a mental state, which is often promoted by a hospital environment, is likely to be inimical to successful treatment. There is also the danger that if your parent becomes too dependent in her role as a hospital patient, she will not take on the responsibilities of taking care of herself when she leaves the hospital. Recovery is commonly thought to be strictly a physical process, but it may also involve getting back one's former identity and a sense of control and independence. Ask your parent to formulate the questions she wants to ask hospital staff members. She can even rehearse them with you. Ask her what she plans to do after she leaves the hospital.

If your parent does not adopt the "good patient" role, what are the alternatives? The most common alternative is the "bad patient" role. The bad patient is a pain for the hospital staff. She walks around the halls at times and in places that are not allowed, complains about the staff and treatment, doesn't eat what she is supposed to, and makes many demands on the staff for attention. Remember that a major issue for all of us, but perhaps especially for older people, is the ability to be in control. When one doesn't feel in control of one's life and choices, helplessness and depression can set in. Anger and "bad" behavior are an obvious reaction to this loss of control and are a desperate attempt to reclaim it. However, it is not helpful to encourage your parent to make problems for the medical staff in order to increase her sense of self-efficacy or decrease her sense of helplessness. She will not improve her situation by alienating the hospital staff or by refusing to take her medications or to follow the prescribed regimen. There is even some evidence that so-called bad patients may be discharged prematurely or given medication so that they will be easier to manage.

The cooperative, compliant patient and the reactive, or "bad," patient are really both attempting to deal with a situation in which they feel themselves to be losing control. Neither approach is perfectly beneficial. If your parent goes too far in either extreme, it may only add to her difficulties if you advise her to act differently. If she is angry, it may not be helpful for you to side with the hospital staff. That may have the effect of finally "defeating" her. On the other hand it may make her feel that much more angry and rebellious. If your parent is overly compliant, it will not be very useful for you to order her to be independent. This is a paradoxical request. How can you advise or push someone to be independent?[4]

The only way out of this dilemma is for your parent to gain a sense of control without having to be either rebellious or passive. If she has questions and concerns, help her to ask the right people so that they are answered. If *you* have questions that are different, she will not be helped by your saying, "Mom, don't you want to know how long the operation is going to be?" This may be your concern and not hers, and it is not helpful to force your concerns on her. Help her to ask the questions she needs to ask. Help her to understand the answers. She may be in such an anxious state that she has trouble listening to the doctor. If a doctor uses a lot of jargon to explain something to your parent, ask him to explain his point in more common terms. If he can't do this, ask some other staff member. Once more it appears that the best course of action is calm persistence. You need not get angry and you need not be resigned. You can help your parent to be determined.

If your parent is in the hospital, it is helpful to visit for several reasons. Of course, your parent will want and need your support and company, but it may also be the case that the hospital staff responds more positively to a patient who has visitors. Patients with visitors are sometimes perceived as being more friendly and deserving than patients without them. Whereas it may be helpful to have a group of visitors, you should have only one visitor who speaks to the hospital staff. If there are too many spokespersons, the staff gets confused and annoyed.

Preparing for an Operation

A major theme throughout this book is that people need to feel that they have control over their lives and over what happens to them. The aging process seems to deprive people of this feeling. In a wide variety of situations, a significant way to help older parents is to provide information that will increase their sense of being in control. This is not easy when your parent faces an operation in a hospital atmosphere, because the situation dictates that the hospital staff is in complete charge, and they often imply that the patient would be better off if she was completely passive.

Find out if your parent knows what she will feel like after the operation. If she has accurate sensory information, she will not be so surprised and the entire experience will be more *predictable* for her. If she will not be anesthetized during the procedure, it might also be helpful, and add to her sense of control, if she knows what she will see, hear, and feel. If your parent doesn't have this information, ask her if she wants it. If she clearly states that she would rather not know because it makes her anxious or upset to hear about such details, then don't force the information on her. There is evidence that some patients aren't benefited by getting too much information. These people cope best by avoiding thinking about a stressful situation.

How should you advise your parent to deal with the discomfort or pain that arises during or after a procedure or operation? Up until now, the point has been made that you should discuss your parent's condition and difficulties directly. However, when a patient is actually *in pain,* she is better off not to focus on it. Research shows, for example, that people can keep their arms immersed in cold water longer if they are distracted. You can be helpful by providing something that your parent is interested in. If your parent is in pain, you can be direct. "Mom, the pain won't be any less if you think about it all the time. Let's talk about something else or do something else to try to make you feel better." It is even more desirable for your parent to provide for her own interests. If she anticipates that a procedure will be painful, you could ask her what she will think about in order to distract herself. She could plan a knitting project, take herself around a golf course, review a particular year in her life, count her breaths, or think about books she has enjoyed.[5]

In summary, to help your parent with an operation so that she can maintain optimal control, keep the following in mind. Before an operation or if your parent is *not* in pain, distractions are not necessary and may even be harmful. Most patients want and need to know the nature of the procedure, and how much and exactly what kind of pain and discomfort they can expect. If they know what to expect, there is more of a sense of control. However, once they are in some kind of pain or discomfort, one way they can exercise control is to know that they can distract themselves from the discomforting feelings.[6]

Stress and Hassles in Late Adulthood

Until recently, it has been overlooked that people in late adulthood experience a wide range of significant life changes and hassles, and that these may be a contributing cause of illness. As was discussed earlier in the book, there is a strong relationship between such life changes and physical and psychological complaints. There is evidence that psychopathology—particularly depression—increases with age.[7]

The current research indicates that chronic daily stresses of a repetitive and stable nature do more to undermine the well-being of an elderly person than any one major stressful event. Such an event, for example, the death of a close family member, is of course very upsetting and is bound to present problems. Of equal significance, however, is the fact that such a change is likely to mean a greater number of chronic daily hassles in the future, and the number of such hassles that an elderly person must endure, with or without major life changes, has been shown to be an excellent predictor of whether she will be agitated, lonely, depressed, and have psychosomatic symptoms, as well as of her attitude regarding her own aging. Some of the most frequently mentioned hassles were: "health related issues such as concerns about health in general, concerns about weight, feeling that physical abilities were declining, and illness of a family member. Concern over economic well-being was reflected in the frequent mention of rising prices. Concern about physical well-being was apparent from the mention of crime, traffic, accidents, and friends being too far away. [Elderly]women reported more hassles than men, especially in regard to rising prices."[8]

Support Systems

Earlier in the book a number of suggestions were offered to help an adult child cope with the stresses and hassles of mid-life. Some of these suggestions will now be discussed in relation to an elderly parent. At every stage in life there are upsetting events and hassles, and at every stage, locating support systems can mitigate some of the stress and discomfort. Family, friends, neighbors, coworkers, professionals, institutions, and even books like this one could be viewed as part of a potential support network. One of the most sigificant losses sustained in the transition to late adulthood is the dwindling of support systems due to retirement, death of friends and family, or relocation. If your parent has recently retired or moved, she has lost the support of her neighbors and coworkers. One of the most important ways in which you can help your parent to cope with the stresses and hassles of late adulthood is to assist her in finding the best and most appropriate new supports. You cannot directly provide even a small part of what your parent needs, but you may be able to help her set up a network of supports that can.

Adults in late adulthood who are single, widowed, or divorced are more likely to develop heart disease and even die than those who are married. For example, it has been found that white males will live 6 years longer if they are married than they would if they were single. One interpretation of these findings is that marriage provides people (especially men) with the support needed to cope with stress and prevent illness. There is a definite inverse relationship between the number of friends people have and the risk of their becoming ill. Especially in times of stress and crisis, friends and relations can help to provide essential emotional and practical support—encouragement, advice, information, affection, and connections.[9]

Encouraging your parent to stay married and to keep in touch with friends and relatives is all usually good advice. If you think your parents' neighborhood is deteriorating, or if you want them to be closer to you, or if for whatever other very good reasons you want them to relocate, it may be inadvisable to suggest such a move. Over the years in their neighborhood, your parents are likely to have developed support systems which they are reluctant to lose.

Reducing Stress Through Self-Efficacy

Just as it is important for you to have a sense of self-efficacy in helping your aging parent, it is also important for your parent to have such a sense. Getting help with daily problems is what coping is all about, but the way one *perceives* problems is also important. Self-efficacy is a concept that comes closest in meaning to the notion of confidence. When some ambiguous trouble comes along—a sore arm muscle and the car doesn't start—what is your parent's judgment about how well she can cope with the situation? Will her reaction be, "Oh, my God, how will I get to the doctor before my arm hurts even more?" or will she be thinking about who to call to get the car fixed? In recent years it has been shown that in the face of stress and hassles, a sense of confidence helps to initiate coping behavior, determines how much coping behavior is exerted, and will help to sustain such behavior in the face of obstacles and adversity. In 1984, researchers concluded that perceptions of low self-efficacy were related to depression and psychosomatic complaints in elderly men and to loneliness in elderly women, "suggesting the significance of self-efficacious thought in coping with events as serious as illness and death."[10]

It is not easy to help promote this kind of confidence and positive thinking in your parents. You cannot force someone to feel self-confident. You can, however, work at being supportive and reinforce whatever self-efficacious statements your parent makes. If she tells you, "I'll try some aspirin for this shoulder," or "Sometimes early in the day the car doesn't start, so I'll try it later," you may not be happy with these solutions, but you should be supportive because they are *her* solutions, her attempts to cope with adversity. This sort of coping behavior must definitely be supported. But although reducing stress and hassles can lessen the chances of your parent becoming ill, there are other, even more obvious ways to prevent illness.

If Your Parent Smokes

Cigarette smoking has been shown to be a major risk factor in heart disease, cancer, and stroke—the three leading causes of death in the United States. People begin to smoke because they are curious, because they are rebellious, because they want to look and feel grown-up, because it gives them self-confidence, because of social pressures, and because cigarettes are available. People continue to smoke because they are addicted to nicotine, because they get an immediate sense of pleasure, because of certain signals and associations in the environment, and because they want to avoid the unpleasant effects of withdrawal.[11]

Everyone knows that it is difficult to quit smoking, but no one seems to know just how difficult it is. Therapists who work with people as they attempt to quit report very low rates of success. However, people who try to stop smoking try on many occasions, and many do eventually succeed. There is good evidence that about 3 out of 4 people who smoke have tried to give it up; half have been successful.[12]

Most people who stop smoking do so on their own. It may be helpful to know the reasons people give for having stopped, if you are trying to assist a parent in quitting. People stop for health reasons, because cigarettes are expensive, because people around them support their stopping, because they want to feel more in control of themselves, because they view smoking as not very attractive, and because they want to set a good example for others.

In clinics and laboratories some methods have been shown to be helpful in enabling people to stop smoking. "Rapid smoking" is a technique used in a clinic where people are instructed to smoke continuously, inhaling every 6 to 8 seconds until they have to stop. The person rests and then continues rapid smoking again. This procedure is similar to "satiation," where the person is encouraged to go home and smoke two or three times what he normally smokes. Both techniques are aversive—they work because under these new conditions smoking becomes downright unpleasant. Another technique involves monitoring the number of cigarettes smoked and the number of puffs taken from each cigarette. People are instructed to pay attention to their tar and nicotine intake and to reduce it gradually. Nicotine chewing gum has been used to enable people to satisfy their need for nicotine while they try to quit. The withdrawal from the gum is dealt with later on. One problem with this method is that with smoking it only takes 7 seconds for nicotine to reach the brain, whereas with chewing it takes 10 to 20 minutes. Other strategies include self-control procedures (such as counting to a certain number before taking a cigarette, or counting between puffs), finding new hobbies, and substituting other, less harmful habits such as chewing sugarless gum or sucking on candy. Another frequently used method is to pay attention to the situations which bring about the desire to smoke and avoid these situations.[13]

Support groups such as Smokenders have been successful in incorporating several of the techniques described above. You can contact the American Lung Association or the American Cancer Society to find out what groups or other treatments are available in your area.

Exercise

There is no longer any controversy about the fact that exercise enhances physical and psychological well-being. In a study of

16,936 Harvard alumni, published in the *Journal of the American Medical Association* in 1984, a strong correlation was revealed between regular exercise and a low heart attack risk. Whether or not you smoke, are overweight, are hypertensive, or have a poor parental disease history, exercise reduces your likelihood of suffering coronary heart disease. The authors concluded that "the current exercise revolution may improve life-style, cardiovascular health, and longevity."[14]

There is not too much evidence that links physical fitness training with improved cognitive ability, or thinking, but there is evidence that among geriatric patients, fitness training may reverse or arrest the physical process of aging and improve overall performance. Exercise improves people's mood states and increases self-esteem. It makes sense that exercise programs which enable elderly people to obtain more motor flexibility and to take care of themselves better and for a longer period of time would enhance self-concept.[15] In one recent and very well controlled study, depressed women did either aerobic exercises, relaxation exercises, or nothing. The women who did the exercise not only developed greater aerobic capacity but also showed a significant decrease in their depression compared with the women in the other groups.[16] If your parent is active and likes to exercise, support and encourage it. If she is sedentary, tell her about the many benefits of exercise. She doesn't have to play rugby or go skiing; a morning walk would be just fine. Find out what sorts of activities your parent enjoys. If she is interested, help her to get started. Remember, though, that it is always advisable for an older person to consult a physician before beginning any kind of exercise program.

Nutrition

We know that nutrition is one of the key elements that contribute to good health, and yet scientists estimate that somewhere between 15 and 50 percent of Americans over the age of 65 consume too few calories, proteins, or essential vitamins and minerals. It appears that many of the diseases that were formerly attributed to the aging process may be the result of malnutrition. Scientists once believed that the body's immune system naturally deteriorates as a consequence of aging. Now, however, many believe that good nutrition can slow or even reverse this decline. When an elderly person is malnourished, her ability to withstand disease is weakened. This lowered resistance can be altered through better eating, which may be one of the simplest and most important ways to improve the lives of older people.

Malnutrition among the elderly may be due to a wide variety of causes. Disease can cause people to lose their appetite. Depression may lead to loss of appetite. A destructive cycle can then ensue: poor eating leading to disease, leading to depression, leading to poor eating, and so on. Some specialists have noted that high-protein items such as meat are expensive and may also be difficult to chew. It is possible to appear well-fed and be eating large quantities of food and still suffer from severe protein deficiencies.

Many elderly people take some sort of medication that may alter taste or make it difficult for the body to absorb the nutrients in a normal diet. Even among the elderly who are neither ill, depressed, nor taking medication, malnutrition is a possibility. This is because in old age, as the senses of smell and taste fade, foods often don't seem as appealing as they once did. This leads to a reduction in appetite and food intake. Given these new findings, it would be sensible to discuss nutrition with your parent and to be aware of the possibility that she may need to pay closer attention to her diet. Studies have indicated that the most common nutritional deficiencies among the elderly are those of iron and of vitamins B-1, B-2, B-9, C, and D.[17] It should also be pointed out that despite the dangers of malnutrition and vitamin shortages among the elderly, it is thought to be dangerous to take large doses of vitamins. Excessive vitamin A can cause bone pain and damage to the liver. Excessive vitamin D can cause kidney damage. Even water-soluble vitamins in excess can cause trouble. Too much vitamin C can cause diarrhea. High doses of vitamin B-6 can cause permanent damage to the nervous system. A vitamin pill may be beneficial, but unsupervised megavitamin therapy is not only not helpful but potentially toxic.[18]

Chapter 8_____
Physiological Problems

Health and health costs are paramount concerns among the elderly. Former Secretary of Health and Human Services Margaret Heckler stated recently that "part of the fear the elderly have about rising medical costs is simply characteristic of the aging process itself."[1] The Secretary's remarks imply that the elderly worry excessively about medical issues and costs because older people tend to be fearful. Is she right? Do older people worry needlessly? Are they hypochondriacal, or do the elderly have a legitimate right to be concerned about health and health costs? The evidence suggests that a person in late adulthood who is not concerned about health and health fees either is enormously wealthy, has more than adequate medical and dental insurance, or is naive. As this chapter indicates, advanced age brings with it a variety of physical problems and diseases. The elderly are concerned about these issues. This chapter focuses on the biological side of health and disease. It summarizes information that may be useful in caring for aging parents.

General Health of the Elderly

According to the United States Senate's Special Committee on Aging, those over 65 experience twice as many days of limited activity because of illness as do younger members of the population. Of those over 85, one-third are in good health, one-third are limited to some degree, and the remaining third need assistance with daily living. Many of these older people in need of daily help are living with relatives other than a spouse. For older Americans, health expenditures are rising faster than increases in income. The expenditures not covered by Medicare equal an average of 13.6 percent of their average income. Concerns about health costs, therefore, are warranted.[2]

Two processes are at work that determine the length and quality of life in old age—primary and secondary aging. Primary aging determines the rate at which we age and our ultimate possible life span. This clock is coded into the genes of each animal species, with slight individual variations. For humans, the ultimate possible life span is somewhere in the early one hundreds. Primary aging is fixed and inevitable. Secondary aging, to be discussed later in this chapter, involves variations in life span due to disease and lifestyle.

Primary Aging

The Senses

Hearing loss occurs with age. By age 60, most people have lost functional hearing of the higher frequencies, and it becomes harder, if not impossible, to discriminate between the sounds *x, z, t, f*, and *g*. Comprehension of speech can be diminished in a noisy room. Elderly people do not interpret rapidly changing stimuli as well as younger people; fine auditory discriminations are hard to make. Older people have difficulty focusing on the relevant and ignoring the irrelevant.

With aging, changes occur in the eyes as well, such as in the lens and ciliary muscles. Almost everyone over age 50 needs corrective lenses for close work and reading. Sharpness of outline and broadness of visual field decline. The eyes do not adjust to the dark as easily and cannot see colors as well.

After age 50, the sense of taste also changes. Some of the taste buds are lost and those remaining are less acute. Because of fewer taste buds and a decline in the sense of smell, it becomes harder to taste all four basic tastes—salt, sour, bitter, and *especially*, sweet.

Suggestions: While these changes are virtually inevitable, their adverse effects can be lessened by awareness of the problems and proper corrective actions. Hearing aids can substantially improve some types of hearing loss. An elderly person should be prepared for a period of adjustment with a hearing aid, since it takes time to learn to use it properly. Remember that it is not helpful to shout at someone who suffers from a hearing loss. Shouting raises the pitch of your voice, thus creating sounds that are more difficult to discriminate. Shouting can also embarrass the person you are addressing. If a hearing aid does not help, an elderly person can learn to become more skilled at watching facial expressions and gestures, since much communication is nonverbal. Some people can learn to compensate for hearing loss without help, but formal training is also available and can be helpful.

Most of our knowledge about the world comes to us through our eyes. Because gradual changes take place in the visual system, it is important for an older person to have regular eye examinations. It is also helpful to make sure that there is proper lighting, and that excessive eyestrain is avoided.

Because of the reduced sense of smell, smoke detectors should be installed and reminders posted to turn off the gas. Unhealthful overuse of salt and sugar should be monitored since it is harder for elderly people to sense these tastes.

Hot-water temperature should be set no higher than 120°F, and checked periodically. Heating pads and hot-water bottles should be used cautiously because of the skin's decreased sensitivity to temperature. The elderly should take care to change position slowly because decreased sensory information can lead to poor judgment and possible falls and fractures.

Sexuality

The good news is that people maintain sexual interest and capability into old age, with a few physical changes. The changes in sexual responses in both men and women can complement one another. Men over 60 may be aroused more slowly than younger men, but they are often able to prolong the erection. Women should welcome this new ability. Barring the loss or illness of a partner, elderly people can look forward to a long and happy sex life.

Suggestions: Adult children sometimes view their aging parents as sexless, and become upset if a parent expresses interest in dating or remarrying. Maintaining sexual activity is important to the old as well as to the young. The following techniques can help to compensate for the changes that occur with age. Regular stimulation through masturbation or intercourse helps to maintain elasticity in women. The use of lubrication or estrogen cream can help to decrease vaginal irritation. Oral and digital manipulation can strengthen responses. It helps to avoid alcohol and medications prior to sex, and to pick a time of day when one is less tired and when preparation time is adequate.

The Nervous, Circulatory, Respiratory, and Digestive Systems

The many individual differences make it hard to generalize about the age-related changes that take place in the nervous system. The changes in the nervous system could account for the increased slowness in the elderly and also for the changes in sleep patterns. The quality of sleep begins to change in the forties and by age 50 the stage of sleep known as deep sleep declines to about half of what it was at age 20. More time is spent awake, and there are more awakenings during the night as a person grows older.

The heart typically has to work harder and delivers less oxygen to the body. The lungs become less elastic and less air is inhaled with each breath. However, respiratory efficiency can be retained well into old age if the individual is physically fit. For the heart and lungs, exercise can help to counteract the impact of aging. Although the digestive process is slower and somewhat less efficient, it is capable of meeting most reasonable demands.

The Skeletal-Muscular System

Muscles atrophy and become less elastic after age 25 or 30. The loss of mobility and the limitations experienced by the elderly are often a result of the muscular and skeletal changes that come with age. The best way to minimize these changes is to maintain good posture and muscle tone, to maintain proper weight, and to do regular exercise. So a sensible diet and regular exercise may be the best medicine for an elderly person, since independence is directly linked to the ability to get around.[3]

While primary aging cannot be stopped, it is possible to exert control over secondary aging. The following are disorders of secondary aging, as well as suggestions that can help to counteract the effects of secondary aging, in order to maintain health.

Secondary Aging

The means for lengthening life and improving the quality of life are at hand. Secondary aging is the key. Secondary aging encompasses all the changeable processes that contribute to a decline in health and fitness, including cell damage due to disease, trauma, and lifestyle. The regulation of diet; of tobacco, alcohol, and drug intake; and of lifestyle offers *some* control over secondary aging. It is possible for more people to get closer to their ultimate life expectancy.

After discussing disorders of the body, we will introduce and examine the most serious problems in old age—disorders of the mind and brain. Although not all of this section is of universal interest, the "Suggestions" provide helpful tips on prevention, and the early warning signs of various disorders.

The Circulatory System

The first and second most common causes of death in those over 65 are heart disease and stroke; both are caused by a dysfunction of the circulatory system. The two together cause 10 times as many deaths as cancer, which is the third leading cause of death.

Elderly people may suffer from *hypertension,* or persistently high blood pressure. Because there are very few symptoms, many people who have hypertension are unaware of their condition. High blood pressure can cause heart failure and further arteriosclerosis, stroke, and/or kidney dysfunction, if left untreated. *Arteriosclerosis,* a thickening of the walls of the coronary arteries, is the most frequent cause of heart disease in older people. It causes the blood supply to the heart to be reduced or blocked. *Myocardial infarction* occurs when complete blockage of a coronary artery causes obstruction of the blood supply to part or all of the heart muscle. Prolonged inadequate oxygen supply to the heart results in heart failure. Symptoms are squeezing pain in the chest, radiating to the shoulder, arm, or neck; sweating; nausea; shortness of breath. In the elderly, the pain can be milder and can be confused with indigestion, gallbladder attacks, and respiratory ailments. *Angina pectoris* is due to an inadequate blood supply to the heart. An attack is characterized by pain radiating from the chest to the left shoulder and down the left arm. One experiences a tight, pressured feeling in the chest and breathing difficulty. Angina attacks can be brought on by excitement, activity, a large meal, or very cold weather. Medication is an effective treatment. *Stroke,* or cerebrovascular accident, causes 200,000 deaths a year in the United States. The most common cause of stroke is a blood clot in the artery of the brain or neck. The blood supply to the brain is reduced or cut off altogether, and brain cells die from lack of oxygen. Other causes are hemorrhage and arteriosclerosis. Small strokes forewarn of a problem with the blood supply to the brain and require prompt medical attention in order to prevent a major stroke.

An *aneurysm* is a dilation in a weakened arterial wall. The "pouch" that has formed fills with blood, and may burst. *Phlebitis,* an inflammation of a vein, most commonly in the leg, is a dangerous condition. Blood clots can form at the site of inflammation, dislodge, then travel through the bloodstream to block a major vessel in the heart, lungs, or brain. Swollen veins in the lower extremities are known as *varicose veins*. These are caused by weakened venous walls and are more common in older women and the obese. *Hemorrhoids* are varicose veins in the lower part of the rectum and anus.

Suggestions: Regular checkups are advisable to monitor blood pressure. An elderly person should participate in a regular exercise program to increase mobility, improve cardiac and pulmonary functioning, and decrease anxiety. Walking, jogging (if one's physician approves), mild calisthenics, and yoga stretches are all recommended activities. Isometrics are not recommended because they raise blood pressure. Over age 50, daily intake should be restricted to 1800 calories for women and 2400 for men. Older people with circulatory problems are often encouraged by physicians not to restrict their activity. You should therefore not interfere with your parent's trying to live as normal a lifestyle as possible, in spite of the presence of circulatory disease.

Attend to the early warning signs of stroke: sudden, temporary weakness or numbness of face, arm, or leg; temporary difficulty in speech; loss of speech, or trouble understanding speech; brief dimness or loss of vision, particularly in one eye; double vision; unexplained headaches or a change in headache pattern; recent change in personality or mental ability; emotional reactions such as depression, confusion, emotional instability, inappropriate emotional responses, and fear.

The Nervous System

The elderly often suffer from a condition commonly called *senile tremor,* the cause of which is unknown. It involves involuntary movements or tremors, primarily in the head, neck, face, and limbs. One may observe head nodding, head shaking, and rhythmic opening and shutting of the jaws. The more serious *Parkinson's disease* is more prevalent in men over 50 than in women. Called the "shaking palsy," its victims experience tremor and muscular rigidity. Symptoms include a masklike facial expression, tremor beginning in hands, muscle rigidity, drooling, difficulty swallowing, proneness to falling, and mood swings. Parkinson's patients need emotional support and understanding. If any of the symptoms are observed, medical advice should be quickly solicited to differentiate senile tremor from Parkinson's disease, which can be treated effectively with medication. *Herpes zoster,* or "shingles," is an inflammatory disease of the cutaneous nerves, caused by a virus. It is extremely painful. The older person with shingles should be cautioned not to transmit the virus to the eyes, by touch. The virus can damage the eyes. Unfortunately, shingles can turn into a long bout of very painful neuritis for an older, debilitated person. *Trigeminal neuralgia,* or *tic douloureux,* occurs when the trigeminal nerve in the face causes fierce pain. The sufferer becomes understandably anxious and apprehensive and may avoid eating or any movement that might precipitate the pain. Drugs and surgery can help to relieve this condition.

The Respiratory System

Lung cancer often coexists with chronic lung disease. If your parent has been a longtime smoker, already has lung tissue damage, or has been exposed to occupational pollutants, he or she is at greater risk for lung cancer. Symptoms to watch for are blood-tinged sputum and/or chronic cough, shortness of breath, wheezing, and repeated respiratory infections or pneumonias. *Bronchitis,* an inflammation of the bronchi, may become chronic in the elderly. Symptoms to be aware of are excess secretion of mucus and difficulty breathing. *Emphysema* results from the breakdown of the alveolar walls; the lungs cannot expand and relax, and remain partially filled with stale, oxygen-poor air. Emphysema is most often caused by smoking. The incidence of this disease, however, increases with age, and, by age 90, most people are likely to have some symptoms. Treatment includes drugs, respiratory therapy, and breathing exercises. *Pneumonia* is a major cause of death among the elderly. *Bronchopneumonia,* an inflammation of the bronchi, is the most common form, and is caused by the aspiration of foreign material, a decrease in lung functioning, poor circulation, or susceptibility to infection. The disease may become advanced before symptoms are recognized. Any persistent cough should be evaluated medically. Treatment consists of antibiotics and respiratory therapy. *Pulmonary tuberculosis* may not be identified until it is in an advanced stage, because the symptoms develop very gradually. Chemotherapy is an effective treatment.

Suggestions: People who have difficulty breathing, understandably often become fearful and demanding. Respiratory diseases leave an individual severely fatigued. These diseases are progressive and debilitating. Your parent should avoid breathing in common irritants such as smoke, dust, pollutants, and dander from household pets. Weight reduction, exercise, and good posture can also be helpful.

The Digestive System

The elderly person may develop lesions in the mouth as a result of poor dental hygiene, decayed teeth, the natural decrease in salivary secretion, poor nutrition, or ill-fitting dentures, partial plates, or bridges. For any of these problems, a dentist should be consulted. *Leukoplakia* are precancerous lesions that appear as white patches on the mucus membranes in the mouth. They are commonly found in older adults. If a parent complains of a sore with irregular edges that bleeds, he or she should be treated immediately. *Hiatus hernia* is common in the elderly, especially in obese older women. In this condition, part of the stomach protrudes through the opening where the esophagus passes through the diaphragm. Symptoms are heartburn, regurgitation, belching, and difficulty swallowing when bending over or lying flat, or after overeating. The chest pain experienced can be confused with a heart attack. The symptom of indigestion is most frequent. Treatment is nonsurgical. *Diverticulitis* results when the abdominal wall weakens and a sac is formed in the intestines (especially the colon), which may become infected and inflamed. Symptoms are pain, nausea, abdominal discomfort, and changes in bowel function. Treatment is usually conservative, and can include bed rest, intravenous fluids, hospitalization, and antibiotics.

Although symptoms and pain are not always present, cancer of the esophagus, stomach, or intestine may be present if there is an obvious weight change, a change in bowel functioning, and a loss of appetite. Cancer of the pancreas is also more frequent past 50 years of age. *Gallstones* are formed when insoluble substances lodge in the bile of the gallbladder. When the stones enter or block the duct, the patient experiences pain as well as nausea, vomiting, and an inability to digest fatty foods. This condition generally worsens and surgery may be required.

Suggestions: Your parent should sit up, rather than nap, right after eating. Defecation habits differ greatly among individuals. Although regular bowel movements are recommended, "regular" does not necessarily mean once a day or even every other day. Dependence on a laxative is not recommended. Exercise, proper diet (high in fiber), drinking plenty of water, and reduced emotional stress are preferred means of preventing constipation.

The Skeletal-Muscular System

The elderly experience more muscle cramping at night, following a day of increased physical activity. Cramps often affect the thigh, calf, foot, hip, or hand. Muscle tension caused by stress may cause pain in the joints and head, and general muscle soreness. *Myasthenia gravis* is a progressive chronic disease in which the nerves' impulses to the muscle cells are defective. It is most common in men over 60 and is characterized by extreme muscle weakness. Symptoms are sagging eyelids, double vision, trouble breathing and swallowing, and general fatigue. Although serious, the disease can often be treated with surgery and/or medication. *Arthritis* affects over 17 million Americans. Its victims experience inflammation of joints, tendons, or muscles. Cartilage degenerates and is replaced by bone, usually in the weight-bearing joints such as the hips, knees, spine, shoulders, or fingers. Symptoms are pain, stiffness upon arising, and creaking joints. There is also a loss of flexibility and range of motion. Arthritis is progressive and can cause the disuse of a joint because of pain, and because degeneration causes restriction of motion and a loss of muscle tone. *Gout* is a condition caused by an increase in uric acid in the blood and a deposition of uric acid crystals in the joints. Attacks are sudden and very painful, lasting five to eight days and incapacitating the victim. The big toe is the common site of affliction. This is a self-limiting disease, but it may become chronic after repeated acute attacks. It can be disabling and deforming. Treatment for gout is generally diet (void of rich foods), increased fluids, and medication. *Bursitis* results from the infection of, calcium deposits on, or trauma to the bursas, which are fluid-filled pockets in the joint. The bursas become inflamed, causing pain upon movement. Common sites are the elbow and the shoulder. Bursitis can be chronic, and response to treatment is usually slow.

Fractures are the leading cause of restricted activity among the elderly. An elderly person who suffers from poor nutrition, muscle weakness, disturbances in balance, reduced reaction time, mental confusion, or limited eyesight is predisposed to fracture. Hip fractures are the most serious. For those over 75, fractures and subsequent complications, such as pneumonia from being bedridden, are a serious threat to life.

Suggestions: There are many new treatment techniques that can enable an elderly person with a fracture to become ambulatory in a relatively short period of time. Preventive measures such as grab rails on bathtubs or near toilets, railings on stairs, and supportive furniture are also helpful. Since most falls happen in the home, it should be accident-proofed adequately, but not so much so that all physical activity is limited. The chance of falling can be reduced by resting between activities, not traveling during peak hours, not going out in inclement weather, avoiding stepladders, and wearing sturdy shoes.[4] A detailed list of safety factors can be found in Chapter 9. An elderly person should also be more careful than others about bending, reaching, stooping, and lifting.

 ## *The Endocrine System*

Diabetes mellitus, or an inability to oxidize carbohydrates, is extremely common among older people. Symptoms are excessive thirst, hunger, and urination; weakness; loss of weight; and decreased wound healing. The elderly can develop arteriosclerosis as a complication of diabetes mellitus, as well as damage to peripheral nerves and lesions in the extremities.

There is a progressive decrease in renal (kidney) function and renal blood supply with age. Obstruction in the lower urinary tract is more likely, as well as increased susceptibility to infection. *Cystitis,* inflammation of the bladder, tends to be common in older women. Symptoms are urgency and frequency of urination, and blood in the urine. *Pyelonephritis* is a severe infection of the urinary tract, which can lead to kidney damage and progressive renal failure. Symptoms are pain in the region of the kidneys, fever, chills, fatigue, weight loss, and gastrointestinal disturbance. Renal insufficiency in the elderly may be due to malfunctioning of the circulatory system or other organs or may be due to kidney disease. It is not considered highly serious until at least two-thirds of the kidneys are destroyed. *Prostate enlargement* crowds the urethra at the neck of the bladder, producing painful urine flow and urinary difficulty. In many cases surgery is the prescribed treatment. Prostate and bladder cancer occur frequently in the elderly.

Suggestions: It is important for the elderly to drink plenty of fluids to prevent constipation or dehydration, unless fluid restriction is ordered by a physician. If they have problems with either urinary incontinence or frequency, they should *not* drink less water. Instead, access to the toilet should be planned and protective clothing worn.

The Eyes and Ears

Specks in the eyes are caused by shadows on the retina from loose cells and tissue floating in the vitreous humor. This is not really a disorder, but it can be a major annoyance. *Cataracts,* common in old age, are the leading cause of blindness in the United States. The lens of the eye becomes increasingly cloudy, and eventually, it can become completely opaque. Cataract surgery helps, and fortunately, age is no deterrent to this type of surgery. After surgery, lens implantation, contact lenses, or special glasses compensate. However, peripheral vision may be restricted and glare bothersome. *Glaucoma,* the second leading cause of blindness in the aged, is a disease of the retina that progresses slowly. Symptoms are headaches, nausea, vomiting, and seeing halos around lights. Glaucoma is caused by increased ocular fluid or decreased drainage, which results in intraocular pressure and leads to blindness if the pressure gets too high. Periodic glaucoma testing is advised. Glaucoma can be treated with medications and surgery. *Macular degeneration* is another major cause of visual impairment in the elderly, involving decreased blood supply to the macula, which is the spot in the retina responsible for distant or fine vision. This condition causes the loss of central vision, though peripheral vision remains intact. Magnifiers help those with vision problems due to macular degeneration. *Otosclerosis* results from bones in the middle ear, the ossicles, becoming rigid and dysfunctional. These are age-related changes and can lead to deafness unless there is surgical intervention. *Tinnitus* is a condition in which ringing, whistling, or buzzing occurs in the ears. It adds to the distortion in communication that some elderly people experience. *Ménière's disease,* found mostly in older men, is a dysfunction of the inner ear. Symptoms are severe dizziness, hearing loss, and buzzing. The condition is chronic and can be treated surgically.

Suggestions: Regular examination by an ophthalmologist can detect vision problems when they start. Increasing the intensity of lighting and using large-print materials can make reading easier for elderly eyes. Using matte finishes, shades, frosted bulbs, and sun-glasses helps to reduce glare. Using night-lights and fluorescent tape on switches can prevent accidents at night due to weakened night vision.

Adults should have early audiometry testing to establish a baseline so that hearing loss can be measured when it occurs. Periodic examinations can handle wax buildup and removal as needed. Many elderly people have found that attending to non-verbal cues can help. Hearing-aids are sometimes resisted, but can be extremely helpful. Elderly parents should also be encouraged not to hesitate to ask other people to speak more slowly. The elderly who suffer from hearing loss should take extreme care when driving or crossing streets.

The Skin

Because their skin is thinner, dryer, and more sensitive as a result of age, the elderly suffer from *pruritus,* or itching of the skin, most commonly on the legs. Prolonged, chronic itching may also be a symptom of liver disease, cancer, leukemia, diabetes, uremia, thyroid problems, or mental disorders, so it should be attended to by a physician.

The incidence of skin cancer increases with age, becoming especially prevalent after age 70. It is caused by overexposure to the sun or by chronic irritants to the skin. Basal-cell and squamous-cell cancers are most common in the elderly. *Basal-cell cancer* looks like small, flat, smooth, or solid elevated lesions with scales or crusts that bleed easily. It usually occurs on the face and does not spread to other parts of the body. *Squamous-cell cancer* are solid, elevated lesions on the face. These grow rapidly and spread quickly to the lymph nodes. *Malignant melanoma,* which is highly malignant and develops slowly, is dangerous. Be on the lookout for flat or elevated lesions with irregular margins that are colored blue, black, tan, brown, white, or pink. Look for a change in the size or coloration of a mole or the beginning of itching or bleeding. Seek immediate medical care. This form of cancer is only curable as a primary lesion, in which case the rate of cure is excellent (95 percent). *Keratosis,* another skin disorder, comes in two forms. *Seborrheic keratosis* resembles a yellow or brown wart. This form seldom becomes malignant. *Senile keratosis* is raised brown or gray scaly areas that should be removed because they can become malignant.

A *stasis ulcer* is caused by varicose veins and poor venous return of the blood to the heart. The lower leg is the common site for this itchy ulcer, characterized by edema and swelling. Scratching the ulcer can cause infection. Obesity, sedentariness, and tight socks, especially knee-high socks or stockings, contribute to this condition.

Older people's skin is thin, with less subcutaneous fat. Prolonged pressure on bony areas of the body breaks down the skin and causes *decubital ulcers,* also known as bedsores.

Suggestions: The elderly can use lubricants and moisturizers to help prevent cracking and peeling of the skin. Only mild soap should be used. Bathing less frequently is helpful. Avoid heavily perfumed cosmetics, use gloves for housework, and apply a sunscreen, because older skin tans more easily. Older persons should use caution in trimming nails and calluses on the feet and should dry carefully between the toes to prevent blisters.

The Reproductive System

Older women are more likely to experience several disorders of the reproductive system. They may suffer inflammation or infection of the vagina and more painful intercourse. This can be treated with locally applied or orally taken estrogen, if caused by estrogen depletion. A *cystocele* is a herniation of the bladder into the anterior vaginal wall. A *rectocele* is a herniation of the rectum into the posterior vaginal wall. Both cause difficulty for older women, and are usually caused by childbirth. Symptoms are heaviness in the pelvic area and difficulty urinating or defecating. *Prolapse of the uterus* is the downward displacement of the uterus into the vagina, caused by stretching from childbirth. Surgery can successfully treat all of these conditions.

Cancer of the vulva is most common in elderly women. In half of the cases of this type of cancer, the victims reported first noticing thick, white, shiny patches on the vulva, and two-thirds experienced vulvar itching. Women of any age should have suspicious-looking vulvar lesions promptly evaluated.

Suggestions: Regular gynecologic exams should continue into old age, especially in cases of vaginal discharge or bleeding. Breast cancer is a leading cause of death in older women, which makes it very important to have regular gynecologic exams.[5] Because monthly examination by a physician is impractical, a monthly self-examination is recommended along with yearly checkups by a doctor including mammograms. If there is a family history of breast cancer, yearly mammograms should begin at age 35. If there is no such history, yearly mammograms should begin between the ages of 35 and 40. Treatment for breast cancer is a combination of surgery, chemotherapy, radiotherapy, and hormone therapy.

Senile Dementia

Senile dementia may be the most tragic disorder suffered by the elderly. Dementia refers to a group of symptoms with a variety of causes that involve a progressive impairment of memory and other cognitive abilities. At the present time some dementias are irreversible, while some are potentially treatable. The most common irreversible dementias are *Alzheimer's disease* and *multi-infarct dementia* (caused by multiple small strokes). Senile dementia afflicts 1 to 4 million people, roughly 15 to 20 percent of the over-65 population and 30 percent of the over-80 population. As life span increases, these figures are expected to rise.[6] More than 50 percent of the cases of senile dementia are attributable to Alzheimer's disease; 17 percent are due to a series of small strokes that incapacitate more and more brain tissue; and the rest are due to other potentially treatable or preventable conditions that cause mental confusion.

At age 75, the brain weighs only about 55 percent of the weight of the brain of a young adult because of the loss of neurons. This is normal, and the majority of elderly people are not senile. Pathology arises when the loss of neurons exceeds the normal rate, and when atrophy and other kinds of cellular changes occur.

Remember that mental impairment may be due to any number of causes, *most of which are treatable*. Older people may be misdiagnosed as having irreversible dementia or Alzheimer's disease (for which there is no cure), when in fact their symptoms may be explained by any of the following reasons:

1. A reaction to medications can bring about confusion and disorientation.

2. Nutritional deficiencies can cause mental confusion.

3. Diseases such as hypothyroidism, Parkinson's disease, and others may exhibit the symptoms of dementia, but can be diagnosed and treated.

4. Depression is caused by feelings of helplessness and the experience of many losses. A significant number of people *diagnosed* as having Alzheimer's disease are in fact suffering from depression. People who actually complain about memory loss are more likely to be going through the normal aging process or suffering depression than to be suffering from irreversible dementia.

Alzheimer's Disease

Senile dementia of the Alzheimer's type (SDAT), or Alzheimer's disease, involves the deterioration of memory, cognitive functioning, and personality, and has been called the "most devastating infirmity of age."[7] Alzheimer's is the major chronic illness requiring long-term care, and, therefore, it is our most costly illness. Up to 3 million Americans suffer from the disease, approximately 7 percent of the 27 million over 65. It kills over 120,000 a year, making it the fourth leading cause of death among the elderly, after heart disease, cancer, and stroke; and fills a third or more of the nursing-home beds in the country.[8]

One of the most tragic aspects of this situation, however, is that many people are misdiagnosed. *Do not accept a diagnosis of Alzheimer's disease or irreversible dementia until and unless every other possible disease is ruled out.* Many patients thought by themselves or their family to have Alzheimer's disease, do not. Just because your parent has lost memory and/or control, don't assume that he or she has the disease.

Researchers are attempting to develop a direct test to determine whether a patient has Alzheimer's disease. At the present time there is no simple laboratory test for senile dementia of the

Alzheimer's type. A CAT scan can help to detect brain atrophy, but is quite expensive. The procedure usually involves a $500 medical evaluation, (the CAT scan accounts for half of the cost). The tests most often done are those that eliminate other possible causes of symptoms: blood tests to detect anemia, thyroid abnormalities, or vitamin B-12 deficiencies; and tests for detecting strokes or tumors. Often a battery of tests for memory, attention span, language, spatial ability, and abstract reasoning is conducted. The only absolutely positive diagnosis of Alzheimer's would be from a biopsy of the brain, showing "neurofibrillary tangles"; this is rarely done.

Dr. Barry Reisberg of New York University Medical Center, a specialist in treating patients with Alzheimer's, is quoted as saying that of the patients referred to him, up to one-half are suffering from some other illness or are simply experiencing normal aging.[9] It is important to remember that those who have some forgetfulness may be experiencing normal age-related memory loss.

Causes: In 1906, Alois Alzheimer, a German neurologist, had a patient with severe dementia, though she was only 51. After her death, upon autopsy, he discovered that her brain contained neurofibrillary tangles, or clumps of twisted nerve-cell fibers. Because the syndrome seemed rare and confined to people younger than those who usually suffer from dementia, it was named "presenile dementia." When in the 1960s researchers discovered the same tangles in the autopsied brains of elderly patients, who had suffered from dementia, they became aware that they were dealing with one disease process. It is now known that the onset of Alzheimer's can occur as early as the forties or fifties. The average age of onset is 54 years.

Alzheimer patients' brains are smaller than the brains of unafflicted people of the same age, because of cortical atrophy of the frontal and temporal lobes. The loss of neurons in these brains is hard to assess because neurons are reduced by approximately 50 percent in the cerebral cortex in normal aging. There is a sevenfold increase in aluminum in the brain of patients with Alzheimer's disease. It is not known whether this is a cause or a secondary phenomenon.

Scientists have become particularly interested in the connection between Down's syndrome and Alzheimer's disease, because practically all Down's syndrome patients over 50 develop Alzheimer's. Scientists think that understanding the connection will give some clue as to how to treat Alzheimer's.[10]

Research conducted with families of patients who suffer from Alzheimer's indicates that there is an added likelihood of developing the disease if a "first-degree relative" is a sufferer. About 10 to 15 percent of the cases involve patients in families in which at least one other member is also a victim. Just as a history of early heart disease or breast cancer in a parent or sibling can increase an individual's risk of contracting either heart disease or breast cancer, so is early-onset Alzheimer's in a close relative a cause for concern.[11]

Effects: At the onset of the disease, memory loss starts to affect one's social life and to interfere with work responsibilities. During this phase, victims tend to deny or minimize the problem. As memory continues to fade, trouble with language may occur and some personality changes may be noted. Changes of mood can be accompanied by depression and the collapse of social relationships. The outstanding symptom is incipient intellectual deterioration, involving loss of judgment and spatial orientation, defective perception and comprehension of abstract material, and the narrowing of the ability to do several things at once. Some patients—experiencing difficulty reading words across a page—complain of eye trouble. Others begin to find it difficult to perform rote gestures. This latter difficulty is called "apraxia." Loss of memory of recent events is a signal symptom of the disease, as are alterations of the speech mechanism: words are forgotten, pronunciation is difficult and faulty, and comprehension of spoken language is poor.[12]

As the disease progresses, the person becomes irritable, anxious, and agitated, sometimes exhibiting antisocial behavior and paranoia. Seriously impaired judgment may result in self-injury. Speech is lost and intellectual impairment is obvious in every mental performance. Mood is deeply altered; patients become depressed, apprehensive, and distressed. There is hyperactivity, becoming more futile and aimless with the advance of dementia. A crisis in care usually occurs at this stage, leading to institutionalization.[13]

In the last stage of the disease, there is apathy, incontinence, and the loss of response to most stimuli. This is a terminal illness, ending in atrophy, seizures, difficulty swallowing, and susceptibility to infectious disease. Death may result from pneumonia caused by food inhaled into the lungs. It appears that if onset is slow, progress is slow, but if onset is fast, the decline is rapid. Duration of the disease is usually 6 to 8 years, but some may endure as long as 20.

The cost of caring for individuals in the late stages of Alzheimer's disease is monumental. It costs over $6 billion a year to provide nursing-home care in the United States for patients whose primary condition is dementia. This takes on alarming proportions given that the number of Americans suffering from dementia is projected to triple within 75 years. The cost of Alzheimer's is not fully covered by either Medicare or most private health insurance policies. A family must have exhausted all its resources in order to be accepted for federal-state Medicaid. It may cost $20,000 or more a year for hospitalization, *if a hospital will accept the patient, who is often considered too troublesome.*[14]

Caring for the Patient: As is the case with any other illness, the best approach to treatment is to enable the patient to maintain a maximum amount of dignity and comfort. Yet, with Alzheimer's disease, this is a most difficult goal to accomplish. Caregivers are likely to experience guilt, anger, and sadness as well as embarrassment, frustration, fear, and confusion. Symptoms vary, but it is not uncommon for an Alzheimer's patient to ask the same question several times in a span of minutes, to forget the names of friends and relatives, to masturbate in public, to wander away and get lost, or to become angry and accusatory. A list follows of suggestions for coping with this most difficult of disorders.

1. Get as much information as possible about the disease. Poor or partial information can create many problems. For example, some families believe that if they strenuously exercise the patient's memory with quizzes, memory will improve. This is not so and may increase the patient's and the caregivers' frustration and anger. There must be a balance achieved between allowing your parent to function to the best of his or her ability and not expecting too much. To obtain relevant information, ask your physician and/or write for the brochure "Questions and Answers: Alzheimer's Disease," published by the National Institutes of Mental Health (Publication #81-1646).

2. Your parent's memory loss is not designed to cause you pain. If your parent asks you the same questions repeatedly, he or she is not trying to annoy you. Also, if your parent denies the memory loss, he or she is not trying to fool you. If your parent accuses you of stealing or being manipulative, he or she is not trying to embarrass or hurt you, but rather, to deal with the insecurity of not being able to remember. If your parent is unable to control him- or herself and gets angry or disrobes or masturbates in public, remember that he or she is suffering from brain damage.

3. Make use of labels and signs in the house to enable your parent to function safely. You can place notes on closets, drawers, and even on doors so that your parent knows what he or she will find within: "Kitchen Utensils—Forks and Spoons," "Coat Closet," "Front Door—Do Not Leave Open," "Bathroom."

4. Let your parent go out for walks and shopping. Your parent can wear an identification bracelet with name, address, phone number, and medical information. You can alert neighbors or the police of your parent's condition, or hire someone to escort him or her on walks. If you take your parent out shopping or dining, find out when the store or restaurant is less crowded and go at quiet times.

5. Try to distract rather than confront your parent when he or she engages in inappropriate behavior. Some Alzheimer's patients pack and unpack their suitcases several times a day, because they are disoriented. Don't try to argue or reason. Say, for example, "When you finish packing, let's have a snack." Alzheimer's patients usually for-

get what they are doing in a very short period of time. If your parent acts inappropriately in public, try to interest him or her in something else and handle the situation as quietly as you can.

6. Treat your parent like an adult. If possible, encourage him or her to make the labels for the drawers and cabinets. Don't ridicule your parent's forgetfulness. Be sure to include him or her in conversations and activities. Ask your parent for help with chores.

7. Get help. You should consider hiring someone to help at home. Many adult children feel that no one other than themselves can help a parent with Alzheimer's. People with Alzheimer's are often resistant to hiring household help. Keep in mind that these patients usually feel anxious and insecure with any new person, place, or situation. If you hire household help, be prepared for a decidedly negative reaction. However, keep in mind that most patients will adjust to a new routine if you allow them enough time.[15]

Recent Developments

New research is exploring several phenomena, one of which is that Alzheimer's patients have significantly less of an enzyme that produces the neurotransmitter acetylcholine. As such, lowered levels of acetylcholine can be a key in the diagnosis of Alzheimer's. Research is also being directed at finding out if there is a gene that causes Alzheimer's.

Whereas in the past, treatment of Alzheimer's disease was very limited, research has fostered the development of new treatments. Scientists are hopeful that research will eventually lead to prevention and cure of the disease. Under study are drugs that enhance the function of the brain's cholinergic system, the effects of increasing oxygen flow to the brain, and the effects of anticonvulsants and local anesthesias.[16] Currently, conventional antidepressants are used to alleviate the depression that is a dominant symptom in the early phase of Alzheimer's disease. This therapy may allow the patient to remain independent longer.

Behavior therapy is used in the form of "memory crutches" such as lists, reminder calls, and signs posted around the living area.

Doctors recommend such preventive measures as the reduction of psychosocial stress; a decrease in the intake of tobacco, caffeine-containing beverages, and alcohol; and improved nutrition. As elevated aluminum levels have been implicated in Alzheimer's, it has been suggested that people not use aluminum cookware, and underarm deodorants and antacid pills that contain aluminum. Scientists note that 15 years ago heart disease was thought to be an unavoidable part of aging; now it can be successfully treated with drugs and diet. The same may someday be true of Alzheimer's.[17]

Support for the Caregivers

Caring for a parent with Alzheimer's disease may be one of the most stressful undertakings that an adult can experience. Chapter 10 describes a family living with a parent in the early stages of Alzheimer's. Chapter 11 assesses the psychological and practical issues that arise when placing a parent in a nursing home.

Sources of support are developing all over the country for those with a relative or friend suffering from Alzheimer's disease. Alzheimer's Disease and Related Disorders Association (ADRDA) has one hundred and twenty chapters nationwide, and sponsors three hundred self-help groups. New kinds of facilities are being developed to cope with the problem. For example, there is a center in San Diego that costs $25 a day and cares for patients Monday through Friday. The center helps with basic physical care and provides companionship. Entertainment is also provided: current events classes, old movies, and dances to the music of the old big bands, which, as a bonus, may help stimulate the memory.

In the Respite Care Program, located in Portland, Oregon, volunteers make home visits to relieve the families of Alzheimer's patients. The volunteers learn to develop empathy for the patient by experiencing simulated handicaps; for example, threading a needle while wearing vision-distorting glasses, or shuffling cards while wearing gloves.

Charwell House, a 124-bed home in Norwood, Massachusetts, is one of the 24-hour nursing homes needed in end-phase Alzheimer's disease. This facility uses a process called "patterning," in which the patient follows a schedule to eat, bathe, and dress, in the same pattern he or she was used to at home. This is a structured setting requiring a lot of activity and "memory sessions," in which patients are reminded of familiar environmental stimuli.[18]

A number of books have been written recently to help the families of patients with Alzheimer's disease. They offer emotional support and many practical suggestions.

The 36-Hour Day: A family guide to caring for persons with Alzheimer's disease and memory loss in later life by Peter Rabins, M.D., and Nancy Mace. Johns Hopkins University Press, Baltimore, Maryland, 1981.

Alzheimer's Disease: A Guide for Families by Lenore Powell and Katie Courtice. Addison-Wesley, Reading, Massachusetts, 1983.

The Hidden Victims of Alzheimer's Disease: Families under Stress by Steven Zarit, Nancy Orr, and Judy Zarit. New York University Press, New York, 1985.

Chapter 9_____

Practical Concerns

The combination of retirement, loss of income, loss of family and friends, and, of course, physical deterioration makes it hard for many elderly people to care for themselves as well as they used to. Your central goal in helping your parents should be to enable them to maintain as much self-sufficiency and autonomy as possible. The vast majority of adult children do not want to live with their parents (see Chapter 10, "When a Parent Moves In"), nor do they wish to place them in a nursing home (see Chapter 11, "Nursing Homes"). Most want their parents to live independently for as long as they can, and this is precisely what most elderly people hope for themselves. Experts agree that, in general, parents who are patients "heal faster, feel better and may even live longer in a home setting."[1] But what if your parent can no longer manage routine chores? Who will shop and prepare the meals? Who will do the laundry? Who will take your parent to the doctor and help with medical and other bills? Fortunately there are a great many local, state, federal, nonprofit, church, and private agencies that can help with these and many other problems.

It may seem ironic that this chapter focuses on providing you with the information you need to help your parent get information, services, and assistance, but in fact, the most self-sufficient people are at the same time involved in a network of mutually supporting relationships. Here is practical information that can be used to allow your parent to live independently for as long as possible. Some of it could also be useful if your parent lives with you.

In many localities there are doctors who will make house

calls; there are senior centers that provide a variety of programs (only about 7 percent of the elderly population in New York City takes advantage of the 300 senior centers there); there are home-care workers who are both competent and compassionate. Often, just giving your parent a phone number can be helpful. You may need to spend some time with a phone book, and even more time on the phone, tracking down the information and services that you need. There is no national clearinghouse that can refer you to the most appropriate agency. Every state and locality offers different services and has different eligibility requirements. In Appendix A is a listing of the names and addresses of each of the state agencies or departments on aging. What follows is a list of programs and services that can help keep your parent at home and self-sufficient.

Basic Federal Programs

Social Security

All wage earners pay into this compulsory retirement and dis-ability insurance program in order to receive benefits at retire-ment age. Payment levels are based mainly on the level of income of the individual, or of the individual's spouse or parent, during the working years, and the age at which the individual begins receiving payments. Living arrangement does not affect pay-ment level. A spouse does affect payment level, whether or not the spouse lives in the same household. A wage earner and his or her nonworking spouse receive a benefit that is one-and-one-half times that received by a single wage earner. A widow or wid-ower of a wage earner receives a benefit even if she or he never worked. If both spouses worked, they are each entitled to his or her own benefits or one-half of the spouse's, whichever is greater.

Medicare

Generally those who are eligible for social security are also eli-gible for Medicare. There are no income or eligibility tests. This program of health insurance covers some expenses for hospital care, doctors' bills, and some (but very little) skilled nursing-home care and skilled nursing care in the home. For a monthly premium, any person over 65 can purchase additional coverage, which helps to pay for diagnostic tests, ambulances, certain drugs, medical equipment, and prostheses.

Some recent changes in Medicare regulations have had an impact on elderly parents and their caregivers, and some additional changes may be on the way. Under the new regulations, hospitals receive a flat fee from Medicare for a particular diagnostic category or surgical procedure. The hospital receives the same amount of money whether the person receives care for 4 days or 12. The hospital thus has an economic incentive to discharge patients more quickly and to not readmit the patient for the same illness. Elderly people are now said to be leaving hospitals "quicker but sicker." According to hospital social workers, because of the new policies, family caregivers are under more stress than ever before.

Supplemental Security Income

Supplementary security income (SSI) provides anyone over 65, as well as blind or disabled persons, with the necessary income for daily living. Your parent's eligibility for this program, as for Medicaid—discussed below—depends on her living arrangement and sources of support. If an individual lives with others and receives some amount of food or shelter, the federal payment will be proportionally reduced.

Medicaid

This is a program of medical assistance for the poor. Medicaid will provide necessary health care in a home, outpatient clinic, or institutional setting. If an elderly person lives with a spouse, their combined income is considered in determining eligibility for Medicaid. However, if an elderly person lives apart from the spouse or lives with children, only the income of the elderly individual is considered in determining Medicaid eligibility. If a family member provides income to his or her elderly parent, this is considered part of the resources of the elderly individual, but the children do not have a legal obligation to provide for a parent's care.[2]

Elderly parents can be faced with the prospect of losing life savings before they become eligible for Medicaid. If large medical expenses appear to be coming up, some give their money to children or other family members before it is all spent. An unfortunate side effect of this structure of medical coverage is that it encourages parents to part with their money and thus a certain degree of control and independence.

State and Area Agencies on Aging

Community services for the elderly are increasing throughout the country. The best place to begin to get information about what services are available in your community is through your local area agency on aging. Under the Older Americans Act, each state has established an office on aging and most states have designated area agencies on aging to serve older people in specific communities. The programs administered by these agencies were created to provide older Americans with an array of social and human services, which include nutrition and supportive services, senior center facilities, and public service employment programs. Millions of older Americans benefit from these programs each year. For example, in 1984 approximately 213 million meals were provided to the elderly with 60 million home-delivered. Your local area agency on aging can make referrals and provide information regarding services available in the community and how to apply for them. Two major legislative goals of the Area Agencies on Aging (3As) are to help older Americans maintain independence and dignity at home and to prevent unnecessary nursing home placement. For more information about the programs described throughout this chapter, contact your area agency on aging. If you have trouble locating your local 3A, contact your state agency on aging. Addresses and phone numbers can be found in Appendix A.

Other Government Programs

Direct-Deposit Banking

Direct deposit is a free government service that enables individuals to have their government payments sent directly to a checking or savings account. Anyone receiving social security, SSI, railroad retirement, civil service retirement, or veterans administration compensation and pension may use this service. Payments are made by electronic funds transfer, thereby eliminating the need to print or mail checks.

There are numerous advantages to this service, particularly for those who are homebound or have difficulty with transportation. Lost or stolen checks are no longer a concern, and the money is available the day the check would normally arrive in the mail, without a trip to the bank. Anyone interested in utilizing this service may do so by taking her next check to her commercial bank, savings bank, or credit union. After completion of a form, the payments will be directed to the personal account. Implementation of this service takes about 60 to 90 days.

Heat/Energy Assistance Program (HEAP)

This service provides financial assistance with heating costs and fuel bills to those who meet certain financial eligibility requirements. More information can be provided by the local office of the aging or social service department.

Section 8 Housing Assistance Program

The Section 8 housing assistance program is a federally funded program that assists families and individuals of low to moderate income who live in rental housing. The agency evaluates and inspects the rental units to assure specific quality standards for safe, decent, and sanitary housing. In addition, the agency provides monthly stipends to property owners to defray a percentage of the rental costs of qualified families or individuals. Inquiries regarding eligibility can be made by calling your local housing authority. Interested individuals must complete an application. The amount of assistance varies, depending on the situation, but generally the program provides help to offset rent exceeding 30 percent of the household monthly income.

Social and Recreational Programs

Congregate Meals

Congregate meals began as a result of a federally funded nutrition program designed to provide low-cost, nourishing meals for elderly people. The congregate meals program provides two important services. It improves the daily nutrition of older people by assuring at least one hot, nourishing meal per day, and it enables many individuals to escape the isolation of their home. The company of others is often more important than the meal. Many senior citizens living alone do not want to go to the trouble of cooking, because they have no one to share their meal with.

Congregate meal sites are centrally located in many communities throughout the United States. They are usually in operation 5 days a week, and there are no financial eligibility requirements.

Retired Senior Volunteer Program

Retired Senior Volunteer Programs (RSVP) utilize the talents of older people interested in volunteering their time and services through nonprofit private and public community organizations. The assistance provided by these volunteers covers a vast array of support and advocacy services, including fixed-income counseling, tax relief and legal rights assistance, and nutrition counseling. The volunteers serve in hospitals, nursing homes, crisis centers, schools, day-care centers, correctional facilities, and the like. The programs provide senior citizens with an opportunity to share their experience and expertise with others. They provide members of the community with a wealth of services they could not afford to buy.

Anyone aged 60 or over is eligible to become an RSVP volunteer. There are no restrictions based on education, income, or experience. More information can be obtained by contacting the ACTION regional office or the ACTION toll-free number (800-424-8580) or by calling the local office of the aging.

Senior and Community Centers

Many communities have developed senior citizen programs to meet the recreational needs of older people. With more leisure time, many senior citizens welcome the activities offered and the companionship they find at the community centers. Programs vary according to the locality and are in part dependent on available funding and the degree of participation of the area residents.

Centers may have exercise programs, craft classes, volunteer programs, sponsored trips, bridge clubs and/or classes, and so forth. To encourage participation, some of the better-funded, more sophisticated programs provide transportation (sometimes in their own "senior citizen van") to and from the senior center, as well as to shopping malls and health-care facilities. Guest speakers are brought in to discuss pertinent topics, and discussion groups provide stimulation and a learning experience. Local hospitals and physicians may volunteer services such as blood pressure monitoring and medical screening.

Generally, these programs hire specially trained program directors who are aware of the needs of older people and have a thorough knowledge of community programs and services. These directors are a valuable source of information and assistance. More information regarding available services in a specific locality can be obtained by contacting your parent's community recreation office, senior citizen center, or office of the aging.

Other Community Services

Chore Service

Chore Service was established to assist elderly or infirm people with the care and maintenance of their homes. It is usually provided through the same private agencies that provide homemaker and personal-care aide services, although in some communities it is provided by volunteers. Services include interior and exterior repairs, yard work, and heavy cleaning. Rates are usually determined by income but may vary depending on the funding source. The service is generally available to anyone 55 or over.

Meals on Wheels

Meals on Wheels is a nutrition program supported by federal, private, and community funds. It is designed to serve homebound elderly and disabled people. A nutritious meal is delivered to the home 5 days a week. The cost is generally minimal and depends in part on local funding levels. The volunteer delivering the meal may be the subscriber's most—or only—regular source of contact with the "outside world." He or she may stay for a brief chat, providing friendly support and serving as a vital link between the subscriber and the community.

Transportation Services

Many elderly people become shut-ins long before any physical injury or illness has limited their mobility. The public transit systems in many communities pose such insurmountable hazards for older persons that it is easier and safer for them to stay at home. Changes are being made, but not fast enough to help the current population of senior citizens. Many communities are cognizant of the need to provide transportation for elderly people. Some have volunteer organizations which provide transportation services as well as an escort. More advanced communities have shuttles which provide free transportation to all residents 60 years or older. Often a parent becomes dependent on an adult child when no other means of transportation is available. When this is the case, it is important for the adult child and the parent to discuss their respective needs and agree on a solution that will be helpful to the parent without creating undue hardship for the child.

If a parent is on Medicaid, transportation to and from medical facilities may be provided and paid for by Medicaid funds. This can be enormously helpful, particularly when a great number of doctor's visits are required on a regular basis. The agency administering Medicaid can provide more information regarding the availability of this service in a given locality.

If Your Parent Is Considering a Move

Remember that only a small percentage of the elderly population in the United States live in retirement communities, nursing homes, or with children. Some 30 percent of Americans over 65 do move, for a variety of reasons. Some find their house too expensive, too large, too difficult to maintain, or too inconvenient. Others move because the neighborhood offers too few activities or is too far from shopping centers, too noisy, or too dilapidated. Still others move because the weather is too severe or because their children and friends have moved away and they want to be closer to companionship. A good source of information on this subject is the American Association of Retired Persons, 1909 K Street N.W., Washington, DC 20049. It publishes a booklet called *Housing Options for Older Americans,* which contains information on owning a home, owning a duplex, renting an apartment, mobile manufactured homes, condominiums, cooperatives, retirement communities, home-equity conversions, accessory apartments, echo housing (a separate, self-contained unit designed for temporary installation in the side or backyard of an adult child's home), home-matching programs in which would-be home or apartment sharers are introduced to home or apartment seekers, shared housing, and federal programs and senior housing. If your parent is interested in making a move or in getting the kind of security via an accessory apartment that makes it unnecessary to move, the booklet has a wealth of information. Most elderly persons, though, want to stay put. They are near close friends and familiar stores. They know and feel secure in their neighborhood. Only 4 percent of the elderly population move out of the state where they lived when they turned 65, and only 3 percent buy new homes; 70 percent don't move at all.[3]

Safety in the Home

There are now three federal agencies that have taken steps to reduce the number of accidents (3 million annually) suffered by elderly Americans in their homes every year. It has been estimated that 70 percent of all people who die from clothing fires are over 65 years of age.[4] Many of these deaths could have been prevented by such measures as wearing short or close-fitting sleeves while cooking. The following checklist can be used to spot potential safety problems in your parent's home. Go over the list with your parent, remedy any hazards or deficiencies, and you can both feel more secure.

1. Are lamp, extension, and telephone cords placed out of the flow of traffic?

2. Are cords out from beneath furniture and rugs or carpeting?

3. Are cords attached to the walls, baseboards, etc. with nails or staples?

4. Are electrical cords in good condition, not frayed or cracked?

5. Do extension cords carry no more than their proper load, as indicated by the ratings labeled on the cord and the appliance?

6. Are all small rugs and runners slip-resistant?

7. Are emergency numbers posted on or near the telephone?

8. Does your parent have access to a telephone in the event that she falls or experiences some other emergency which prevents her from standing and reaching a wall phone?

9. Are smoke detectors properly located?

10. Are smoke detectors working properly?

11. Are any outlets and switches unusually warm or hot to the touch?

12. Do all outlets and switches have cover plates, so that no wiring is exposed?

13. Is the light bulb in each lamp or fixture the appropriate size and type?

14. Are heaters which come with a three-prong plug being used in a three-hole outlet or with a properly attached adapter?

15. Are small stoves and heaters placed where they cannot be knocked over, and away from furnishings and flammable materials such as curtains or rugs?

16. If your parent's home has space-heating equipment, such as a kerosene heater, a gas heater, or an LP gas heater, does she understand the installation and operating instructions thoroughly?

17. Is wood-burning equipment installed properly?

18. Is there an emergency exit plan and an alternate emergency exit plan in case of fire?

19. Are towels, curtains, and other things that might catch fire located away from the range?

20. Does your parent wear clothing with short or close-fitting sleeves while she is cooking?

21. Are kitchen ventilation systems or range exhausts functioning properly, and are they in use while your parent is cooking?

22. Are all extension cords and appliance cords located away from the sink or range area?

23. Does good, even lighting exist over the stove, sink, and countertop work areas, especially where food is prepared?

24. Is there a step stool which is stable and in good repair?

25. Are chimneys clear of accumulations of leaves or other debris that can clog them?

26. Has the chimney been cleaned within the past year?

27. Are hallways, passageways between rooms, and other heavy traffic areas well-lighted?

28. Are exits and passageways kept clear?

29. Are bathtubs and showers equipped with nonskid mats, abrasive strips, or surfaces that are not slippery?

30. Do bathtubs and showers have at least one (preferably two) grab bars?

31. Is water temperature on the hot-water heater set at "low"—120°F or below?

32. Is a light switch located near the entrance to the bathroom?

33. Are small electrical appliances such as hair dryers, shavers, and curling irons unplugged when not in use?

34. Are all medicines stored in the containers that they came in, and are they clearly marked?

35. Are lamps or light switches within reach of each bed?

36. Are ashtrays, smoking materials, or other fire sources (heaters, hot plates, teapots, etc.) located away from beds or bedding?

37. Is your parent's electric blanket free of all coverings when it is in use?

38. Does your parent avoid "tucking in" the sides or ends of her electric blanket?

39. Is your parent careful never to go to sleep with a heating pad which is turned on?

40. Is there a telephone close to your parent's bed?

41. Does your parent check lighting, fuse boxes or circuit breakers, appliances and power tools, electrical cords and flammable liquids in the basement, garage, workshop, and storage areas?

42. Are stairways well-lighted?

43. Are light switches located at both the top and the bottom of inside stairways?

44. Are sturdy handrails fastened securely on both sides of the stairways?

45. Do the handrails run continuously from the top to the bottom of each flight of stairs?

46. Do the steps allow secure footing?

47. Are steps even and of uniform size and height?

48. Are the coverings on the steps in good condition?

49. Can your parent clearly see the edges of the steps?

50. Is anything stored on the stairway, even temporarily?

Safety in the Streets—Crime Prevention

Crime and the fear of crime create special problems for elderly people. According to one office of crime prevention, your parent should follow these common-sense guidelines.

Walking

- Plan your route and stay alert to your surroundings. Walk confidently.

- Have a companion accompany you.

- Stay away from buildings and doorways; walk in well-lighted areas.

- Have your key ready when approaching your front door.

- Don't dangle your purse away from your body (12 percent of all crimes against the elderly are purse snatchings and street robberies).

- Don't carry large, bulky shoulder bags; carry only what you need. Better yet, sew a small pocket inside your jacket or coat. If you don't have a purse, no one will try to snatch it.

In Stores

- Don't display large sums of cash.

- Never leave your purse unattended.

- Use checks where possible.

In Your Car

- Always keep your car doors locked, whether you are in or out of your car.

- At stop signs and traffic lights, keep the car in gear.

- Travel well-lighted and busy streets. Plan your route.

- Don't leave your purse on the seat beside you; put it on the floor, where it is more difficult for someone to grab.

- Lock bundles or bags in the trunk. If interesting packages are out of sight, a thief will be less tempted to break in and steal them.

- When returning to your car, check the front seat, back seat, and floor before entering.

- Never pick up hitchhikers.

- If your car breaks down, get far enough off the road, turn on your emergency flashers, raise the hood, get back into the car, lock the door, and wait for help.

Banking

- Many criminals know exactly when government checks arrive each month, and may pick that day to burglarize your home or mailbox. Avoid this by using direct deposit, which sends your money directly from the government to the bank of your choice. And, at many banks, free checking accounts are available to senior citizens. Your bank has the information.

- Store your valuables in a safe-deposit box.

- Never give your money to someone who calls on you identifying himself as a bank official. A bank will never ask to remove your money.

- When someone approaches you with a get-rich-quick scheme involving some or all of *your* savings, it is *his* get-rich-quick scheme. If it is a legitimate investment, the opportunity to contribute will still be there tomorrow—after you have had time to research and consider it.

At Your Door/Home

- Never open your door automatically. Use an optical viewer first.

- Draw your blinds or draperies at night.

- Lock your doors and windows. (Three-quarters of the burglaries committed against older persons involve unlocked doors and windows—and less than half of these burglaries are reported.) Keep your garage doors locked.

- Vary your daily routine.

- Join Neighborhood Watch. Concerned neighbors are often the best protection against crime, because suspicious persons and activities are noticed and reported to police promptly.

- Don't leave notes on the door when going out.

- Leave lights on when going out at night; use a timer to turn lights on and off when you are away for an extended period.

- Don't place keys under mats, in mailboxes, or in other receptacles outside your door.

- Notify neighbors and the police when going away on a trip.

- Cancel deliveries of newspapers, etc. and arrange for someone—a neighbor's child, perhaps—to mow the lawn if need be. Arrange for your mail to be held by the post office, or ask a neighbor to collect it for you.

- Be wary of unsolicited offers to make repairs to your home. Deal only with reputable businesses.

- Keep an inventory, with serial numbers and photographs, of resalable appliances, antiques, and furniture. Leave copies in a safe place.

- Don't hesitate to report crime or suspicious activities.

Home Health-Care Services

The health-care system in this country now provides support services which enable elderly people to remain in their own homes without creating unnecessary hardship for themselves or their families. Knowing what services are available and how to obtain them is essential when formulating a plan for the care of a disabled parent. Frequently, adult children make the mistake of taking total responsibility for the care of a parent. This is not only impractical, but may be unfair to everyone involved. A parent in this situation often feels like a burden and loses her vital sense of autonomy, and hence her self-esteem. The adult child who hastily takes on this responsibility without researching the supports available in the community is a likely candidate for burnout if the illness is long-term. The typical course of a disabling illness used to involve hospitalization followed by discharge to a skilled nursing home, a health-related facility, or home. Prior to the advent of support-service delivery for the homebound patient, many families were forced to choose between attempting to care for their disabled parent at home and placing them in a facility which could provide the required supervision and care. Now, thanks to advances in health-care services, there are many choices available.

If your parent becomes ill or disabled and requires hospitalization, the *hospital discharge planner,* most often a social worker or nurse, can formulate a discharge plan, taking into consideration your parent's specific needs. This is usually the easiest route to obtaining help for your parent. Because of their special training and familiarity with the services available in the community, discharge planners can lend a family invaluable assistance in determining eligibility and obtaining needed services for a parent. Discharge planners are often very busy, and you may need to persist in making your needs known to them. You should also be involved and encourage your parent to be involved in assessing needs and services. Don't leave all decisions to the discharge planner.

If your parent becomes ill or disabled without requiring hospitalization, you can still get information on home health care by contacting a local hospital discharge worker. In the event that a caregiving spouse dies, leaving the other spouse needing care, your parent's doctor may also be able to direct her to the appropriate agencies. In addition, most areas now have an office of the aging which can make referrals and provide information regarding the services available in the community and how to apply for them. When looking for good home care you should shop around just as carefully as you would when selecting a doctor, as described in Chapter 7, "Your Parent as Patient." Friends, neighbors, your own doctor, local clergy, and elected officials are also potential sources of information for finding good home care.

Assessing Your Parent's Needs

Talk with your parent about what services she needs. Live-in help is usually unnecessary. Home-care agencies offer the services of registered nurses, licensed practical nurses, physical therapists, occupational therapists and their assistants, social workers, homemakers, and home health aides. Each type of home-care worker contributes a different expertise and service. For example, occupational therapists, often underused in home care, can reveal to your parent many strategies and devices for making household chores easier. You, your parent, your parent's doctor, hospital personnel, concerned family, and friends should assess your parent's home-care needs. Many professional agencies offer a free in-home assessment of such needs. Janet Zhun Nassif, in her book, *The Home Health Care Solution,* suggests that if you need home care, you should be a shrewd consumer. Ask questions. Does the agency conduct an in-home assessment before developing a care plan and providing service? Does the agency consult with appropriate doctors and other professionals? Is there a policy for personnel to be properly screened, trained, and supervised, and so forth.[5]

Visiting Nurses

Upon referral by a physician, the public health department in most localities will provide visiting nurse services to patients confined to their homes because of illness or disability. The services provided range from short-term care following discharge from a hospital to long-term services to delay or prevent institutionalization. Services may include professional nursing care, medical social work, physical therapy, speech and occupational therapy, home health aide service, and supervision of personal-care aides. The range of services available depends, in part, on the area and can be determined by contacting the local health department.

Home Health Aides and Homemakers

Home health aides and *homemakers* are generally provided by private agencies. Services may be coordinated with the public health department and area social service agency or be purchased privately, depending on the circumstances of the patient. The purpose of the home health aide (also called a *personal-care service worker*) is to enable a disabled person to function within her home. There are three levels of care provided:

Level 1 provides assistance with the care of the environment, including such tasks as dusting, cleaning, and cooking.

Level 2 provides personal care—bathing, dressing, and the like—as well as assistance with the environment.

Level 3 provides level 1 and level 2 care plus assistance with the administration of medication, changing of dressings, and so forth.

Health aides at all levels usually work under the supervision of a trained registered nurse, but level 2 and level 3 care providers require standardized training. The level of care provided is determined by the patient's needs, and the cost may vary accordingly.

The personal-care and homemaker services have enabled many individuals, suffering from a variety of infirmities or disabilities, to continue to enjoy the comfort of home. It should also be mentioned that this service can be used to assist a parent living with an adult child, when additional support is required.

You should be acquainted with the problems that occur most frequently with homemakers and home health aides so that you can anticipate and remedy them. First, the quality of care varies and is in part dependent on the care provider. It is important to maintain an open line of communication with your parent regarding how she feels about the care. Even a simple personality incompatibility between the aide and your parent can be unsettling. Remember, this person is providing "personal care." It may be the first time in your parent's adult life that she has been placed in such a dependent role. Second, aides have emergencies, and there may be times when they are not able to care for your parent. Agencies are aware of this and usually make every attempt to provide a substitute. However, there may be times when this does not work out. Depending on the severity of the situation, backup plans should be made so that your parent feels secure in the knowledge that somebody will be available. Third, circumstances change. Your parent may need more (or less) assistance than was originally provided. If you feel this is the case, it should be brought to the attention of the doctor, agency, or visiting nurse so that adjustments can be made.

The Cost of Personal Care

The cost of personal care may be assessed on a sliding scale or be offset by assistance from agencies such as the office of the aging, or it may be covered by private insurance, Medicare, or Medicaid. Since the cost of home health care can be high, it is important to be knowledgeable about income eligibility for government assistance programs such as Medicaid. Information gleaned from telephone inquiries regarding eligibility may be misleading. Although a ceiling income is often quoted, the agency may consider many factors, such as indebtedness, living expenses, valuable assets such as real estate, and savings accounts in making its final determination. Therefore, it is usually worthwhile to complete an application for Medicaid. To further complicate matters, it may be determined that an individual is ineligible because of a small overage in monthly income. But don't be discouraged. An overage of, for example, $50 may be satisfied by paying the first $50 of each month's medical expenses, according to Medicaid's "spend-down" requirement. All other expenses would then be covered under Medicaid. When a personal-care aide is prescribed by a physician, Medicaid considers the fee for such service to be an eligible medical expense. A personal-care aide might easily cost $50 or much more per week. A patient with a $50 monthly overage would therefore pay the first $50 toward the personal-care expense, and all remaining medical expenses—doctor's visits, prescriptions, hospital care, home health care—would be picked up by Medicaid for that month and every month thereafter that the overage is satisfied. An example might be helpful to illustrate this point.

Mary Jones recently injured her hip. Her doctor did not feel that she required hospitalization but ordered a personal-care aide to assist her for 5 hours per day, Monday through Friday, for the duration of her convalescence. Mary's daughter works full-time and was able to assist her mother only in the evenings and on weekends. The total monthly cost of the personal-care aide was approximately $600, computed at $6 per hour for 100 hours of care. Mary's monthly income is $450. She does not own her own home or any valuable assets. In Mary's locality the Medicaid income eligibility cutoff is $400 per month. This means Mary Jones is over the cutoff by $50 per month. There are several avenues Mary could pursue. She should first determine what coverage her Medicare and/or other medical insurance might provide. She could then contact her local office of the aging to determine how they might assist her. She might also inquire whether the agency providing care can arrange for her to pay a sliding-scale fee. If this is not successful, Mary might then make a decision to apply for Medicaid. Because of her $50 monthly income overage, she would, under the "spend-down" stipulation, be required to pay $50 of her income per month toward her medical expenses. It is safe to assume that Mary has other medical expenses as a result of her injury. How she satisfies the $50 is up to her. Once it is satisfied, however, Mary Jones becomes eligible for Medicaid and all further medical expenses will be paid by her Medicaid insurance each and every month that she satisfies the "spend-down" requirement.

Long-Term Health-Care Programs

Nursing Homes without Walls

If Mary Jones had been seriously disabled with little possibility of improvement, her personal-care needs would have been much greater. The severity and projected duration of your parent's illness will partly determine what direction she goes in to obtain financial aid. A fairly new concept which is gaining popularity is sometimes referred to as "nursing home without walls." Essentially, this program relies on the home-care system to enable a patient who might formerly have been institutionalized to remain at home. To qualify for this program a patient must have her health assessed to determine whether or not she meets the criteria for nursing-home placement. If these criteria are met, the patient and her family have the option of choosing nursing-home placement or a system of long-term home health care.

Social service agencies, public health agencies, and personal-care providers participating in the program work together to enable those patients who might previously have been placed in a nursing home to remain home when they want to. However, there are problems with this system. Your parent's Medicare or private health insurance may have payment restrictions. This should be carefully reviewed before a plan is established. There are also restrictions regarding the number of hours that care is provided each day. Because of these problems, long-term home health care is most successful when a patient needs a good deal of care but has a strong family support system that can take over when the personal-care aide is not present. This type of care has the advantage of enabling an elderly parent to remain in a familiar environment with the support of family and friends.

Geriatric-Care Agencies

A growing number of health-care professionals are leaving non-profit agencies and setting up private geriatric-care practices. These professionals are often hired by adult children who pay approximately $200 to $500 for an initial consultation and an average of $50 per hour thereafter. A *geriatric-care manager* will assign someone to be or will personally serve as a companion to your elderly parent. This person may help with tasks such as hiring a plumber or arranging trips to the doctor or beauty salon.[6] Such care arrangements are especially helpful when distance separates a parent from her adult children. For example, grown children outside of New York can ensure that a parent who lives in New York City is cared for by Elderlink, a new program run by the nonprofit social-care agency Selfhelp. There is no charge for an initial consultation. The development of a service plan by a geriatric social worker costs $150. A service package for elderly parents living at home costs $125 per month. This includes an evaluation of benefits, a weekly check-in phone call, and a monthly consultatiton with the children. If an elderly parent requires hospitalization, an Elderlink social worker will consult with doctors, coordinate discharge plans, and visit the patient for a weekly fee of $175.[7] Similarly, Elder Concern, a geriatric-care agency in Florida, is intended to help families with elderly parents who live in Florida and adult children who do not. An Elder Concern worker will visit the parent to assess her situation, write an evaluation, suggest local resources, determine if the parent needs homemaker services, provide such services ifneeded, and make recommendations regarding transportation, social activities, and financial and legal counseling. The worker will also determine if a visit by the child or children is needed and make recommendations about such things as nursing homes. Elder Concern will help on a one-time basis or develop an ongoing agreement.[8]

Whether you live far from or close to your parent, you should be sure to get the maximum advantage from public programs and services. The private agencies described above may help to get you started on the right track, but you should take advantage of the public ones. Your local social service agency or office of the aging can direct you to public, nonprofit organizations that can provide all the services that the private agencies do. As Senator Claude Pepper has stated concerning the private care services, "in theory these services may be a good idea, but if people turn to them instead of to the public services we have worked so hard to put in place, we may lose those public services. The public also has to keep in mind that there is no watchdog for this group. I think most often, the elderly will reach out to a nonprofit group. It's their children who want them to have a $50-per-hour friend."[9]

Day Care for Adults

Adult day-care programs were created to meet the needs of adults aged 60 or older who have some infirmity or are dependent or isolated. They were designed to provide a respite for caregivers and to delay institutionalization while improving or maintaining the physical, intellectual, and emotional functioning of the participants. Information regarding their availability and location can be obtained by contacting the local office of the aging or homemaker service agency.

Adult day-care programs usually operate 8 hours a day several days per week. Eligibility requirements may vary according to the program. Generally, however, any adult who is able to function in an ambulatory care setting and to participate in group activities is a good candidate for day care. Adults who are extremely mentally impaired, violent and physically abusive, chronically incontinent, or in need of one-to-one supervision are not accepted into the program.

Adults enrolled in these programs have an opportunity to spend time with other adults in similar circumstances. They also benefit from the change in their surroundings and can participate in a variety of activities including arts and crafts, music, exercise, and discussion groups. These activities provide both physical and mental stimulation and encourage social interaction.

Some programs provide more sophisticated supports such as physical, speech, and occupational therapy. Most facilities are staffed by a registered nurse and an activities director with some specialized training. Meals are provided during the day-care hours, and transportation is arranged.

Emergency Medical Systems

Lifeline

Your parent may find the support services of a personal-care aide adequate to enable her to remain in her own home. However, circumstances may make it necessary for her to have immediate access to emergency help during the hours the aide is not present. Lifeline is an emergency response system designed to assist the elderly, handicapped, or disabled person who may be in need of emergency help. The system has three components:

1. A small wireless pushbutton unit designed to hook into any standard telephone.

2. A communications unit that connects to the telephone and automatically dials a 24-hour response center when activated.

3. The response center, located in the emergency unit of a cooperating hospital and staffed by highly trained professionals.

Individuals participating in this service wear the pushbutton unit and are able to activate it anytime they need help. A built-in timer signal may also activate the unit, if an individual is unable to push the button. Once a call is received at the response center, a staff member reads the subscriber code from the unit and retrieves the subscriber's file. The file contains the name and number of the subscriber, medical and health information, and the names of relatives, friends, and neighbors who are to be contacted in the event of an emergency. The response center first attempts to contact the subscriber. If this is not successful, the staff member evaluates the level of help needed, contacts the emergency responders, and continues to monitor the situation until help arrives.

Potential subscribers to Lifeline or other emergency response systems may obtain information regarding the availability of this service, as well as an application, by contacting the local office of the aging, public health department, or hospital. Preference is given to those individuals who have the most serious health problems. There is a minimal charge—to defray the cost of the equipment and operation of the service—which may be covered by health insurance if the service is judged to be a medical necessity.

Medic Alert

Medic Alert is an emergency medical identification system. A Medic Alert emblem is worn as a bracelet or necklace and is engraved on the back with the wearer's special medical condition. In addition there is a special "call collect" number that provides instant access to medical records, physicians, the names of relatives or friends to be contacted in case of emergency. A membership card, to be carried in a wallet or purse, contains additional personal and medical information and is updated annually.

Membership costs are minimal (approximately $15 for life), with a nominal fee for updating records. More information may be obtained by contacting the Medic Alert Foundation International, P.O. Box 1009, Turlock, CA 953881-1009.

Protective Services for Adults

Protective Services for Adults (PSA) provides social services for any adult who can no longer protect his own interests, who is threatened with harm by his own actions or the actions of others, who needs help with daily living activities, or who is unable to provide for his basic needs and has no one able or willing to assist him. Many adult children care deeply for their parent and want to assist him but are unable to provide the help and assistance he needs. They may be restricted because they live far away and have little opportunity to visit, or because their parent resists attempts on their part to lend assistance. When a parent is in a situation that threatens his basic safety and well-being and an adult child is unable to intervene in a way that is effective and useful, Protective Services may be the solution.

Any concerned person or agency may make a referral, or a person in need may call directly. There is no charge for Protective Services, and eligibility is not affected by income. Services include identification of needs, provision of homemaker and housekeeper, counseling, money management, and assistance in obtaining necessary benefits and services. The following situation illustrates how PSA may help a parent.

John Brady's mother, Jane, died suddenly of a heart attack approximately 1 year ago. John was an only child and very concerned about his father, David, who had diabetes and a heart condition and at times suffered from mental confusion. John did not feel his father could adequately care for himself. In recent years David had relied on Jane for a great deal of assistance and support. Now that Jane was gone, John worried about his father. David Brady lived on the east coast and John on the west coast. John was married and had two children and a job that precluded a move back to the east coast. John, after much difficulty, convinced his father to move out west and reside with his family.

David Brady hated the move. He disliked the weather, missed his friends, and felt John was meddling in his life. He became increasingly irritable and intolerant of his grandchildren. Finally, it was agreed that David would return home. David harbored resentment toward John. He blamed him for upsetting his life and felt his son had forced the move out west upon him. John's attempts to provide help and keep in touch with his father were rejected. John maintained contact with David's neighbor, who was also concerned. David's confusion was getting worse, and his personal hygiene was deteriorating. He was also becoming more reclusive and would not accept any help or suggestions from friends or neighbors.

The situation continued to deteriorate, with John feeling more and more frustrated by his inability to assist his father. One night, while cooking, David Brady had an accident which resulted in a small fire. It was uncertain whether he had passed out from diabetic shock or merely been careless. This frightened John. After several inquiries he was directed to the PSA unit in his father's county. John explained the situation to a social worker, who made immediate contact with John's father. David Brady had also been frightened by the fire incident and was able to talk to the social worker without feeling a loss of pride. The social worker encouraged David to have a complete medical checkup. She also convinced him to accept the services of a homemaker recommended by his physician as well as regular visits from the public health nurse. In addition, the social worker set up a plan to help David Brady handle his finances. His mental confusion was getting worse, and he had difficulty keeping track of his income and bills. John felt better knowing he had made a connection with someone who could maintain regular contact with his father and assist him whenever he needed help.

Sometimes, an adult child must accept the fact that he or she is not the best person to assist a parent. In the case of David Brady, his pride and John's location made it impossible for his son to provide the help and support required.

Financial Management

Often, adult children have difficulty deciding what to do when they feel their parents no longer have the capacity to handle their own financial affairs. This is a tricky situation at best and requires great tact and sensitivity. First, there is the issue of personal rights. When does an adult child have the right to intervene and make a decision regarding how a parent "should" manage her money? Second, assuming there is reason for an adult child to be concerned, how and when does she or he intervene? Operating on the presumption that intervention is necessary, it is always best to discuss this with a parent, sharing your concerns and asking her help in finding a solution. A parent may react to this conversation with a sense of relief and have definite ideas as to how you can help her. If this is the case, there are various ways in which you may proceed, but it is always a good idea to legalize whatever plan you formulate. This is for your protection as well as your parent's.

Since laws differ from state to state, it is important to obtain the services of a lawyer to help you take appropriate legal steps. For example, you might file for *joint tenancy*, in which both parties have total control over the assets involved, or for *power of attorney*, in which another person, usually an adult child, is given power to manage a parent's assets and funds. Both of these procedures require your parent to be sufficiently alert to enter into contract. In addition, power of attorney is null and void if the parent is judged to be legally incompetent, unless the original agreement stipulates the power of attorney should continue in the event of incompetency. These are just two of many possibilities, and many complications can occur. Therefore, it is a good idea for you and your parent to discuss and plan in advance the course of action she would like you to take in the event she is no longer able to manage her finances owing to physical illness or mental impairment.

Sometimes, as was the case with John Brady, an adult child is unable to assist a parent in the handling of personal finances. When this happens, the protective services unit or a private agency in your parent's area can provide financial management. A worker can visit your parent on a regular basis to go over the bills with her and write the necessary checks. This system is most useful when a parent is still alert and wants to participate in her financial affairs. Sometimes this is not the case and it is necessary for the agency providing financial services to be named the payee. When this happens, the client's checks, and all bills, are sent directly to the agency providing financial management. The agency is then responsible for all financial affairs including the payment of bills. Government agencies that perform these functions are scrupulously checked.

Alternatives to Home Care

There are alternatives to home care. When evaluating or selecting an adult foster home or domiciliary care facility, you and your parent should follow the same guidelines that you would in searching for a suitable nursing home (see Chapter 11, "Nursing Homes"). Many of the emotional issues involved are similar as well.

Foster Care for Adults

Sometimes, for a variety of reasons, the personal-care or day-care services described in this chapter cannot adequately meet the needs of an elderly parent. Yet, hospitalization or a skilled nursing home may not be appropriate or indicated. If an adult child is involved in helping a parent but the child's living circumstances are not conducive to a parent's moving in, or the adult child does not have the freedom to be consistently available, adult foster care may be the answer to an otherwise unsolvable dilemma.

Essentially, adult foster homes take the place of a nursing home but do not provide the medical care. In addition, residents have more freedom and mobility, and weekend visits with family members are not uncommon.

Foster homes are licensed by government agencies and must follow the guidelines imposed by the licensing agency. Care providers are investigated and must meet stringent requirements before a license is granted. In addition, the physical structure must pass certain safety standards which are consistent with the needs of the elderly, disabled, or infirm residents. Supervision must be provided by a caregiver 24 hours a day. This means at least two caregivers must be involved, to assure backup supervision at all times. Furthermore, licensees are allowed to care only for a limited number of people, usually not more than four, to assure quality care.

Often, the atmosphere of the home will replicate that of a family setting. The care providers are responsible for meal preparation, cleaning, laundry, and so forth. They can be very supportive, and some are willing to provide transportation and assist with shopping. Set fees for care are established, and payment arrangements are made with the client. Usually the care provider will use the client's funds to provide for clothing, entertainment, and personal needs. Accurate financial records are kept and are periodically audited by the licensing agency. Like everything else, the quality of homes may vary. In the case of adult foster care, the quality of the home will determine the success of this arrangement. More specific information regarding foster care in a given locality can be obtained by contacting a representative in the area social service agency, office of the aging, or social security office.

Adult Homes or Domiciliary Care Facility

The adult home is very similar to the family foster care home but is larger in size and in most localities does not require supervision by a government agency. Generally, there is a considerable difference in cost, with adult homes running substantially higher than foster care homes. Again, the quality of homes differs and an on-site visit plus investigative work is always a good idea before considering such an arrangement. With both adult homes and family foster care, supplemental social insurance will cover part of the cost if need is established. The prospective client should apply to the social security office for assistance once the cost of the home has been determined.

Chapter 10_____

When a Parent Moves In

It has become a circumstance that can and often does create excessive family tension: elderly parents, more usually one elderly parent, after some years of independence and living apart from their child, move into the home of that child who now is an adult.

Fred Ferretti
The New York Times, July 8, 1985

When a parent shares a household with an adult child, it is not necessarily because the parent needs assistance. In some cases it is the child who needs assistance. In other cases the child simply never left home. In situations where the family has already been living together for a long period of time when the parent begins to need more help, it is often easier. There is an understanding in such families that members are mutually supportive. If someone gets sick or needs help, other members of the household are available.

When a parent becomes sick or impaired and only then moves in with a child, the situation is much more difficult. This is the more typical situation. Daughters who share households with their mothers provide the most help of any adult child caregiving group. One study revealed that 40 percent of adult children caring for an elderly parent in their home devote as much time to the parent as they would to a full-time job! Most often when an elderly parent moves in with an adult child, the parent is alone, has lost a spouse, and is significantly impaired. Obviously, this can be a very difficult situation for all family members. No matter how close and loving a relationship has been or is, there is always physical strain and emotional stress when a parent moves back in.

Characteristics of the Adult Child Caregiver

When a parent moves in with an adult child, the parent is most likely to be a woman and the child most likely to be her daughter. Older middle-aged women are more likely to have an elderly mother living with them than are younger middle-aged women. In an analysis of 23 million women between the ages of 40 and 59, only 5.5 percent shared a household with an older relative. The percentage grew to 16.6 percent for women between the ages of 55 and 59. Often the child feels she has no alternative. She feels herself to be the last line of defense against institutionalization, which tends to be avoided strenuously by both elderly parents and their children.[1] Research shows that adult children who live in the same household as an aging parent are stressed. They are frustrated in trying to find community programs and feel isolated themselves, anxious that there will not be backup help if there is a crisis, and exhausted from endless nights of interrupted sleep.[2]

Adult children who care for a parent in their own home tend to get very little help from siblings with either daily care or decision making. According to the caregiving child, the uninvolvement of the other siblings with the parent is frequently a continuation of a relationship long characterized by distance and/or conflict. This, however, does not mean that the caregiving child tends to have a good relationship with the elderly parent. Some do, and describe the parent/child relationship as perennially close or say that they are good friends. Other children take on caregiving duties not because of a positive past relationship, but because they believe that family members have a *responsibility* to take care of one another. Although a sense of responsibility is the principal reason why most children take on these caregiving duties, they also offer other reasons, such as the wish to reciprocate the assistance they received in the past, the sense of satisfaction that comes with helping someone, the need to fill a void in their life, and a desire to avoid placing the parent in a nursing home.

Adult children whose parents move in to be cared for feel more accepting of the situation when there has been a history of mutual caregiving or there is the sense that taking care of the parent helps to fill a void. Children who take care of their parents simply because they feel it is their duty feel much more tension, and some cannot mention even one satisfying aspect of caregiving. There are other factors that make a difference in how the adult child feels. One is the family. If the adult child anticipates that the situation will promote conflicts within his or her own nuclear family, he or she feels much more apprehension. Another involves timing. If the elderly parent experiences a gradual intensification of need, as opposed to a sudden onset of extreme neediness, this will give the child—and other family members— time to adapt. Some family members have stated that the experience of caring for an elderly parent has brought them together and resulted in a feeling of greater unity. This, of course, is only true when other family members "come through" and support the adult child.[3]

Level of Impairment and Caregiver Satisfaction

As is most often the case in helping aging parents, the level of impairment of the parent is a crucial determinant of how the adult child feels. Of all adult child caregivers, those whose elderly parents require a great deal of care report the lowest levels of satisfaction. However, even a parent who requires little care can cause stress and conflict when she moves in. If you haven't lived with a parent in 20 or 30 years, you will probably have an enormous adjustment to make. Styles and habits of living may clash: the way you and your parent eat, sleep, and decorate a room, the music you listen to, how often or what you watch on television, how many lights you leave on, and so forth. Even if your parent needs no care at all and is completely independent, the forging of a new family structure is likely to be very difficult. In the two case studies presented in this chapter we will see two families, each consisting of three generations. The first—the Suttor family—with an elderly parent who is not in very much need of assistance, exemplifies some of the difficulties inherent in this type of arrangement. The second family—the Browns—represents a family that must cope with a more serious level of impairment.

Helping an Independent Parent at Home

The Suttor family is made up of a grandmother, Rose Evans, her daughter, Sarah, who is 37, Sarah's husband, Peter, who is 36, and their two children, 7-year-old Jesse and 3-year-old Jeff. Sarah spoke about the circumstances surrounding her mother's moving in with them and what it is like for her now.

The Suttor Family: Sarah's Perspective

"My mother was living in Florida when her sister and brother-in-law decided to move to Texas. Then she called me and it all came out. Every time she was about to leave after visiting us, she would get very depressed. She missed my two children very much—especially the youngest, Jeff, who is 3. I had thought that my mother was pretty happy and very much valued her independence, but she said, "I need to come up and live with you; I miss you all and I am very lonely." That was it. I cried because I hadn't realized how lonely she was and hadn't been perceptive or sensitive enough to realize how much she needed us. She also started getting all these minor ailments—one cold after another that just seemed to hang on month after month.

"There was such a strong bond between her and Jeff. I think she missed that more than anything else. Down in Florida she was never kissed or hugged. Jeff is a very affectionate little boy and he totally loves his grandma. It's funny because my mother and myself are not great huggers and kissers, but she and Jeff have a very innocent, natural, and direct way of showing affection for each other. So Peter and I talked it over, and in 3 weeks she was up north with us. There was no real discussion or planning. We just knew it was going to happen. I told Peter a long time ago that I was my mother's only child and that we didn't really have any other choices. I couldn't shift the burden of responsibility to a brother or sister or aunt or uncle. Peter's parents, on the other hand, have six children! He understands his commitments and responsibilities. One problem, though, is whether or not he can get emotionally involved in his responsibilities. That's another story.

"Financially there is no problem. She gives me money for the groceries. If she makes any phone calls, she pays for them. She doesn't pay anything toward the utilities, but she does take us out to dinner on occasion and she buys clothes for the kids. One big problem is that she doesn't have enough space for all her things. She used to have her own large apartment, and now she is just in one room. Another problem, and the biggest inconvenience for me, is that she doesn't drive, and we live in the country. This means that I have to take her to the doctor, to the hairdresser's, shopping, and just about anywhere she needs to go. We are trying to work out a way for her to go out with other people, but we haven't yet. In the meantime I don't want to upset her, so I take her wherever she needs to go. Another problem is that she likes very different food than Peter and I. We eat a lot of very spicy foods—garlic, chilis, hot peppers, and so on. Mother won't eat any of this. She also likes to have plenty of sweets in the house—brownies, candies, and lots of ice cream. She has lost weight since she's moved in, because she doesn't eat big meals with us, and I've gained 10 pounds because we never kept sweets in the house and I can't resist them when they're here.

"She watches the children for us, but Peter and I haven't gone out once by ourselves for several months. She encourages us to go, but I feel that we should take her. I guess it's guilt. She loves to go out for dinner, and the thought of Peter and me going out by ourselves is just appalling. It makes me uncomfortable to leave her at home just to babysit the kids. Mother and I are close, but we can't really discuss anything too important or meaningful. She has problems and concerns that she doesn't discuss with me. We both have a great deal of pride. She doesn't let her guard down and I don't do much prying. Maybe I should give her more of a chance. Our lack of real contact may be as much my fault as hers.

"There seems to be no question about who is in charge of the house or children. I try to be considerate and ask her opinion, but it's my house and I want it run my way. This must bother her, since she was the authority in her own house for 30 years. There is a bit of a problem with Jeff. Just the other night he and I had a confrontation. I had to discipline him, and when I did he ran to Grandma. Sometimes I wonder if he is confused about who his main source of love and support is. I mean, Grandma spoils him all day long, and then Mommy comes home and makes him clean up his room, wear certain clothes, and do certain chores. When he needs comforting and calls "Grandma," I cry. For a few minutes I cry and then I realize that it's natural and that he knows that I am his mother. Mostly, any resentments or difficulties I have with my mother are out in the open, blow up, and are quickly resolved.

"My husband, Peter, and my mother are a different story. They are not the same kind of person. She is a very emotional person and he is very logical. As a result he just won't talk to her. When they get into any sort of argument I feel awful—right in the middle. I don't want to take sides, but most of the time I think Peter is right. One night Peter came to the dinner table without a shirt, and Mother was shocked and appalled. They got into quite a tiff about it. His attitude was that it was his house, but I said, 'You are offending my mother.' Finally he went and put a shirt on. I think Mother's presence inhibits him and us a little. For a while she was sleeping in a room right below us. I made sure the television was on very loud when we wanted to be close.

"Sometimes I guess Mother thinks Peter is too logical, and she gets annoyed with him. I sit down and beg and plead for him to talk with her. I tell him that he talks to strangers and others who aren't so pleasant or easy to be with, why can't he talk to Mother? It breaks my heart and he knows it, but he won't change.

"Overall, Mother definitely feels better now that she is here. She now has a purpose. She said the other day that she didn't know how I did the laundry and cleaned the house and worked and took care of two kids. She very much likes to keep busy. She needs to feel useful and she is. She helps tremendously. She also knows that she is needed, and I think this has contributed to her feeling better physically."

The Suttor Family: Peter's Perspective

"I think Sarah's mother just expressed a desire to be with the kids. She was not happy in Florida. I felt compassion for her. Sarah and I never discussed Mother's move, although it wasn't a complete surprise. I think it was already a foregone conclusion. Sarah had always said she was the only one who could help out her mother. Mother hardly ever asks me anything. She always asks Sarah, who then asks me. Sarah did say before Mother moved in that there would be free babysitting, but we pay her $50 a week, so it's not really free.

"One problem is that since we live way out in the country, it's hard for Mother to have people over. I would imagine that she would want to have people in to give her some company, but she never invites anyone out here. Maybe if she had her own small place next door to us she would be less hesitant about having people over, but in the meantime she devotes all her social attention to Sarah, which isn't very good for Mother—she should be more extroverted. When we go shopping it's always Mother talking to Sarah, Mother doing this with Sarah, and me shopping by myself. Usually I try not to end up with both kids, although there have been occasions when they have tried to pawn them both off on me and go off by themselves. I don't allow that to happen too often. Another related problem is that it's harder for us to have friends come over. Mother doesn't always fit in. She has different interests, and sometimes when our friends come over Mother goes into another room and watches television. I really don't want to ostracize her or anything like that.

"Mother gives us $15 a week for food, which is really not enough. Otherwise we pay for everything. It was never really discussed, and frankly it doesn't make a difference to me because it's my house and I figure that I will pay for whoever is in my house. They are here only with my approval, so I'm willing to pay. Since there is someone here during the day, I have to load the wood stove twice as much as I normally would, but that's the biggest sacrifice.

"Sarah gets home from work before I do, so by the time I'm home, Mother has already told Sarah everything that has happened during the day. If anything unusual happened, at the dinner table, Mother will say to Sarah, 'You say what happened.' Mother uses Sarah as her spokesperson. Mother doesn't like hearing or dealing with my opinions, so she uses Sarah. If Sarah happens to disagree with something that I think or feel, Mother will *always* take Sarah's side. Whether she's right or wrong doesn't make a difference. Sarah and I are usually able to have fights or disagreements and then get back on track with the relationship and usually grow and benefit from the exchange by both changing a little. Somehow Mother makes that more difficult by always siding with Sarah. It makes us both a little more standoffish. Mostly, though, Sarah and I can reason with one another and come to some kind of resolution, so it's all right.

"I know one thing, though, that if Mother was causing a tension between Sarah and me to the point that our relationship was beginning to fail, I would put a stop to it. Someone would have to leave, and it wouldn't be me and it wouldn't be Sarah. It would be Sarah's mother."

Discussion of the Suttor Family

The Suttors are coping with their problems in a fairly good and straightforward manner. The family is making plans to build separate quarters on their property for the grandmother, which will allow them all an increased amount of independence. This will also separate Sarah from her mother a bit more, which should be good for all concerned. In a basic sense all the members of this family are trying very hard to deal with each other with patience, caring, support, and love. The elderly mother is not impaired, there is no real shortage of money, there is a fair amount of space, and yet it is obvious that substantial tension arose when the parent moved in with her adult child. Fortunately, although she will take her mother's opinion into account, Sarah recognizes that she and Peter are the authorities in the house. She also tends to ally herself with Peter more than with her mother. Not doing this would be a recipe for disaster. The tensions and difficulties that this family experiences are minimal but typical of those that all families consisting of three generations must face. Their situation might be eased if they did a few things differently.

Sarah and Peter leave a few too many things unsaid. There should have been a much more extensive discussion about whether and how the move would take place. Peter and Sarah did not quite take joint responsibility for the mother's presence. They mutually, implicitly "arranged" for Sarah to take the responsibility for the decision to have her mother move in. This allows Peter to remain on the outside, feeling somewhat unhappy—annoyed or alienated—and Sarah to remain in the middle, feeling somewhat unhappy, or guilty. They both feel burdened, although in different ways.

Although both Sarah and Peter feel that Sarah is in the middle, it is more likely that Sarah's mother is in the middle. In this family, marital conflicts which are normal and expected get obscured by the mother's presence. Peter obviously gets more annoyed with his mother-in-law than he does with Sarah, and Sarah feels bad or sad or guilty in relation to her mother rather than in relation to herself or Peter. Sarah may need to convince her mother that she can take care of herself, and that she doesn't need her mother to take her side in the arguments she has with Peter. Mother might be better off if she kept away from marital conflicts; she can only be blamed and resented if she gets involved in any way. This is terribly unfair to her. When Mother sees Peter simmering, Peter needs to make an effort to show her that she needn't be concerned for her daughter, and that their normal domestic quarrels don't get out of hand and do get resolved.

Sarah should not, of course, continue to operate as Mother's mouthpiece in relation to Peter. She should simply decline this role. Mother can speak for herself. She doesn't need Sarah to do this. Sarah has a tendency to treat her mother as less capable than she really is. If Sarah refrained from chauffeuring Mother around, Mother would be more likely to make other arrangements, Sarah would feel less taxed, and Peter might feel less jealous. They might also do better if Peter and Sarah could *agree* on how much money Mother should contribute for utilities, wood, food, and even rent or upkeep. This is best to do at the very beginning, so that they are living together with a contract. Such an agreement certainly doesn't have to be written, but it should be understood. As things now stand, Peter unquestionably has some problems with their arrangement that he does not voice, but which leave him feeling quietly resentful.

Helping a Dependent Parent at Home

The services that adult children provide to aging parents who share their household are legendary. They do ironing, washing, and shopping, prepare meals and clean, bathe them, sit up with them at night, take them out for fresh air, provide transportation, and handle their financial responsibilities. As will be discussed in the following case study, one common problem in families of three generations in which the aging parent is frail is that, although the children are loving, it is possible to do too much for a parent.

Edith Todd is 84 and her children believe that she has Alzheimer's disease. She now lives with her daughter, Kim, who is 43, Kim's husband, Greg, 48, and their five children, aged 12 to 21.

The Brown Family: Kim's Perspective

"My sister and I grew up in this house, and I moved back in here with my family about 5 years ago specifically to take care of my mother. She was always very dependent on my father. She had been an alcoholic for part of her life, and he helped to control her drinking by not letting her out of his sight. When he died she started drinking again and she began going downhill pretty fast. Three years after my father's death, my husband and I started to plan to move here. It took us a while to sell our house and for Greg to open a business down here. We chose to live here rather than move Mother up with us because at her age we didn't want to move her away from the place she had lived all her life and away from all her friends.

"My sister, Lucy, and my mother had a pretty combative relationship when we were growing up, and I think I get along with my mother a lot better than Lucy ever did. The other reason *I* am taking care of my mother and not Lucy, is that my father took me aside one time and said, 'If anything happens to me, I really want you to take care of your mother.' At the time Lucy was living in the city and she didn't want to live here. There was never any discussion. It was just sort of assumed that it was something I would do.

"At first we thought we'd buy or build a house nearby, but everything was so expensive. Then we thought we'd find an apartment for Mother and we'd live in the house, but when we looked around she got upset and anxious. Then we thought: this house has 14 rooms; Mother is funny, easygoing, accommodating, not interfering; why not all live together? For a long time it worked out real well. She got along great with the kids; in fact, she was really very helpful. Then the drinking became more of a problem and her nasty side came out. For the last year she has been real bad, so bad that we can't leave her alone, we can't even go away.

"There was a period when she became very angry with me. At the time she couldn't articulate that well. She went through a real stage of paranoia. She would be sitting there and all of a sudden she would say, 'You did it!' and I would say, 'What did I do?' And she would say, 'You know what you did. You know.' Then later she would take a small amount of her social security money out of the bank for the week's spending money, and that was fine. But we began to notice that she had large amounts of money one day and nothing the next, so we guessed that she was giving it away. There was then a transition period when I had to take over the money, which was very difficult. She was very angry that I was handling her money. She thought I was stealing it. I tried to give her $25 a week, but even that didn't work out. She would spend it so fast. So now I give her a few dollars a day. All during that time she would be visiting neighbors and saying just awful things about me. It was a really awful period. She also started losing everything. She lost her teeth, her glasses. We had to go through the garbage every night because she started throwing out the dish towels. She must have thrown out about 25 of my dish towels. She also threw out my father's letters, and his pictures—he was an amateur photographer. Then it got to the point where she would "wash" the dishes and they would be in the cabinet totally filthy. So we put up a sign saying, 'Please don't do the dishes.' Just this morning she put on her coat three times and I asked her to hang it up and she got very angry. After 2 years of this we decided to get some help.

"There doesn't seem to be any lack of people who want to help take care of an elderly person. We started paying about $4 per hour, and now we have someone in 5 hours a day. This has made a big difference. One of the reasons we came down here was so that she could be with her friends. She used to be a great card player. I remember the last time she was supposed to have a group of friends over to the house. She became very agitated. Just before they arrived she turned the heat up to 90° and then she opened up all the windows. Finally I had to call the members of the card group and tell them that Mother couldn't be a member anymore. Mother was relieved. She had really been faking it for a number of years. She wasn't able to hold her cards. Someone had to help her. None of them ever calls or comes by anymore. I tell you this really hurts me. It hurts a lot.

"Mother doesn't seem to be aware of any of this. She seems happy. She really does, and she isn't suffering at all physically. Tonight she was sitting watching me make the cookie batter, and when I was done I gave her the spoon to lick just like she gave it to me. She gave me a lot of spoons to lick, and now I'm giving them to her.

"Before we had help, my sister, Lucy, would come up once in a while and take Mother out. Then, when Mother began really deteriorating, she took Mother every other weekend, and that's the way it continues to be. At first, Lucy would take Mother into town and wine her and dine her, and Mother decided Lucy was the wonderful daughter and I was the witch. But now my mother is really out of it and has a memory span of about 3 minutes, so she doesn't even remember what anyone does with her. There is a little resentment that I feel toward Lucy. Her weekends with Mother are very short, and if she is doing something on the weekend, she will say she can't take her. But *we* can't do that, we have no choice. When I went to the hospital for a while I said to Lucy, 'You take Mother, she isn't Greg's responsibility.' But somehow it worked out that Greg had Mom. I realize that some of these things should be talked out, but it's not easy. Lucy will come sweeping in and start criticizing everything, and that really upsets me. I feel like saying, 'If you want her, you take her and see if you can do a better job.' But I don't say anything. I guess I feel like the good daughter. It's funny, though, I find it very difficult to do things like give Mother a bath and wash her hair. One time I steeled myself and washed her hair and dried it, but I just can't do things like cut her toenails. Lucy can do those things, but I can't. I'm not affectionate with her. I mean, if I go in and say good night, I'll bend down to kiss her, but it comes from a feeling that it's what I should do. Lucy isn't like that, though. She'll come in and hug her and kiss her. I do do a lot with her, though. And Greg has been very supportive.

"Sometimes I feel guilty about the money area. We have had pretty free access to Mother's money. We borrowed quite a bit of money after Father died, because we were in bad financial shape. Since then, things have been equalized by Lucy borrowing. However, over the past 5 years, while caring for my mother, if I couldn't make a payment some way, I would go into the estate money. This has been an underlying problem for me. Greg's feeling is that whenever we need extra we have every right to use the money because we are taking care of her. I have to say that I have never discussed this with Lucy, but I have kind of hinted at it. We have decided this year that we would have my mother pay us $300 a month for all the expenses we incur by her being with us. When I think of that…It's $10 a day—it's nothing really, but still sometimes I feel guilty."

The Brown Family: Greg's Perspective

"Initially I was worried about making a living down here, but it's worked out pretty well. We don't get much help from Lucy. She doesn't come first thing in the morning on Saturday, and Mother is back by Sunday evening. Lucy gets defensive if you say anything about it, so there's not much point. Before we moved in here we did discuss things with the children, but they weren't part of the decision making. Mostly they were excited about it. They had been down here visiting the grandparents, they knew the town, and everyone was going to have their own room. Our middle daughter was a junior in high school, and she was afraid that she wouldn't fit in, but she didn't say anything about it until after we got here. After a time she adjusted.

"There was an increased heating cost because Mother couldn't take the house being so cool, but there were tremendous economic advantages, there's no doubt about it. The hardest part is her inability to take care of herself. Actually she is in extremely good physical health. I wish I had her blood pressure. She has none of the usual diseases of old age—no cataracts, no arthritis, and so on. It was during a two-year period that she began to get harder and harder to take care of—losing things, forgetting everything, and being very paranoid and angry. There was a tremendous emotional strain. For me the hardest part was the reversal of roles. Mother is like another child but you can't deal with her or handle her like you would a child. Becoming a caretaker or provider when it has always been the other way around is hard. Kim's mother and I always got along real well. I mean we've always liked each other, but she was always a kind of distant person. This is the reason why Kim isn't very physical with her mother. Her mother was never really very physical with her. Kim reads to her a lot, sings songs to her, but very little touching.

"Of course, Kim gets most upset. I am always telling her not to be so upset, that Mother doesn't really mean what she is saying. Also, Mother has had a couple of accidents. Once she fell and broke her wrist. Every time we took her to the doctor she tried to hug him. She has gotten very sexual in her old age. Just before we moved up here she would tell us stories about picking up men, etc. We were never really sure how much was fabrication and how much was real. On occasion, even when the kids' friends are here, she will come out naked. Lucy thought we should put her in a home, but after a time we decided to get someone in to help take care of her. We talked a lot about the alternatives, but none of them seemed better. Once it was suggested to hire someone to come in, Kim seized on the idea. At first I thought since Kim wasn't working it wasn't necessary, but now I realize that with someone in, Kim has a choice about being able to leave the house or do some things that she wants to do."

Discussion of the Brown Family

The motivations of children living with a disabled elderly parent are somewhat different from those of children who are living with a parent who is unimpaired. Children of disabled parents do not get into this situation because they want Grandmother to babysit for the kids. There is no sense of a reciprocal arrangement that has been worked out or understood. Some children do it because they feel it is an obligation to which there are no alternatives: "It is a tremendous burden, but what other choice is there?" Others feel that because they were helped out when they were young, they owe a weakened parent their assistance. Many feel that to place their parent in a nursing home would be intolerable. Their feelings of shame and misery at the thought of doing this reflect the very strong anti-nursing home sentiment that prevails in this country.[4] Others say that they feel an obligation but that their primary motivation is love and caring. These adult children recognize that they can't deny the connection between themselves and their parents. One man we interviewed said, "I really care about my mother. If she is unhappy, I feel pain. By taking care of her, I am therefore also taking care of myself."

The Brown family is also typical in that there tend to be expressions of support and caring between spouses and shared resentment toward the less-involved sibling. Both Kim and Greg take pride in the fact that Kim is the "good" daughter. Even Kim's father recognized this by confirming in advance her role as caregiver in the event that something happened to him. Kim has accepted this role, but she is annoyed with Lucy. Why doesn't Kim feel resentful toward her father or mother, who helped put her in this position? We don't really know enough about the situation to be certain. Perhaps the reason Lucy is able to be more affectionate and physical with her mother is that she is allowed to remain relatively free of responsibility. On the other hand, it may be that by allowing Kim to take care of her mother, Lucy helps Kim to view herself in a positive light, enables Kim and Greg to bond as they support each other and complain about Lucy, and, at the same time, keeps her mother from being resented.

The fact that the family moved in with Edith Todd before she began to need a great deal of help allowed them to make many major adjustments before they were called on to make the further adjustments involved in more active caregiving. The family considered alternatives but felt they had little choice. The Browns, like most families, share this household with their parent because they want to avoid placing her in a nursing home. Although the problems Edith Todd presents to her family are greater than those posed by Rose Evans, Edith is not totally disabled. Some families care for elderly parents who cannot see, cannot walk, cannot move by themselves, cannot remain in a sitting position, cannot remember anything, and cannot control their bladder. At the present time Edith Todd is in good physical health, although her mental state is rapidly deteriorating. When, over time, her health begins to diminish, the family's resources and patience will be further strained. At that point the family will have to choose between increasing the hours of hired help and placing her in a nursing home. Families in which there is a more sudden deterioration and less preparation experience more of a sense of being overwhelmed and are consequently more likely to choose nursing home placement.

The Brown family made a very sensible decision to hire a professional "homemaker." When there is a need for continuous supervision or companionship, the family will need more help. Some elderly parents do not like the idea of being taken care of by a "professional." They may feel somewhat humiliated by the idea that the family cannot provide all the necessary assistance. One elderly woman we spoke with reported that she used to think that to be seen in her neighborhood walking with a professional caregiver would be the most humiliating experience of her life. Once her children helped her to get over these fears by allowing her to participate in the hiring process, and by allowing the caregiver to be hired on an experimental basis, the elderly woman became fast friends with her caregiver.

For dual-career families, the possibility of live-in help could be considered. Emily Wiggins, an extension family life specialist at Clemson University, described a situation in which she and her husband had demanding jobs and two sons attending the local university. When her husband's mother, who was living independently just 17 miles away, became frail, they put an advertisement in the newspaper which read, "Dual-career family needs a live-in household manager for a family of five, including one young-at-heart 85-year-old elderly lady. Call for an interview Saturday or Sunday."[5] There was enough room in the house, and the elder Mrs. Wiggins had enough money to pay for the services. The adult children supplied room and board. All seemed to go well for a while, but Emily Wiggins reported that her mother-in-law became angry and upset when the children didn't give her enough time and attention. "We knew Mother was a proud and stong-willed individual all along. However, we didn't count on her giving dependency such a hard fight. She resented her body giving out on her, and she resented our offers of help with such personal tasks as bathing. We suffered as we watched her struggle to continue doing for herself as long as she could. Yet we admired her for her strong will and determination."[6] The Wiggins family, like the Browns, may be of just as much help by allowing their elderly parents their fierce independence, their anger, their desire to take care of themselves. When people become overly dependent, they "give up."

Although the Browns are a very caring family and Greg and Kim have sacrificed much for Kim's mother, it may be that they would be helping more by doing less. Edith Todd may be suffering from Alzheimer's disease, although this hasn't yet been officially diagnosed. We do know with certainty that she is deteriorating and that she is angry and suspicious. Greg and Kim should consider the possibility that they are doing too much for Edith. It is usually more helpful to an elderly parent to allow her to do as much as she possibly can for herself. Kim called her mother's friends to stop the card game, and she gives her the spoon of batter to lick. An elderly parent should not be so infantilized. There is memory loss, to be sure, but memory loss can be minimized if the memory is used. It may have taken Edith hours to do the dishes, or days to arrange for her friends to come in and play cards, but this is preferable to restricting her functions, which tends to make her less able to function at all. Kim and Greg were not sure if Edith was giving away her money, but by giving her only a few dollars a day they are further undermining her freedom and independence. Edith's anger, although inappropriate, may be the result of her unhappiness over her loss of independence. Anger is often an assertion of autonomy and independence, of a desire to take care of oneself. Elderly parents often do better if the children are patient and allow them to operate at their own pace. Memory, skills, and abilities are more likely to deteriorate if they are not used. This is not to say that a parent who is incapacitated and unable to get around physically should not be cared for because such caring will make her overly dependent; but every effort should be made to allow the parent living with you to bear as much responsibility for herself as is possible.

Knowing how much care to provide a frail elderly parent is one of the most difficult dilemmas facing adult children. There are some diseases, like pneumonia, which can leave a parent weak and dependent. In this case, it is best to care for the parent but to eventually work toward helping her to regain her independence. Other diseases, like Alzheimer's, eventually lead to almost total deterioration, and helping a parent toward independence is therefore impossible. If you are unsure about how much care is best for your parent, you should certainly consult with physicians, social workers, psychologists, or other professionals.

Points to Remember Before Your Parent Moves In

1. Honest communication with all relevant family members is the most important ingredient for a workable situation. If you know what the potential difficulties are, they can more easily be avoided.

2. Talk with your spouse. Find out his or her feelings, opinions, and concerns. Can your spouse's concerns be alleviated and coped with? Be clear that your primary allegiance is to your current family. If you take in an elderly parent, it should not be the decision of one spouse. It should be a joint decision. If your spouse says, "I don't want to have your mother live with us, but if you insist, I guess I have no choice," you would probably be making a big mistake to go ahead and invite her to live with you. You would undoubtedly find yourself unfairly but constantly in the middle, always dealing with your spouse's resentments. The decision should be one that "we," the couple, make.

3. Talk with your own children. You and your spouse should find out their feelings and concerns. Each child should be handled differently, depending on his or her age. Younger children have fewer rights and responsibilities. If a 5-year-old says that he doesn't want grandma to move in because there might be less cookies, he deserves reassurance. An older child might have more realistic concerns, about losing space or privacy, which should be discussed. Again, it must be emphasized that if you are a single parent, the decision is yours, and if you are married, the decision should be made by you and your spouse.

4. Talk with your siblings. Make your expectations and desires explicit. When there is annoyance and resentment toward a sibling, it is often because arrangements and understandings are not explicit.

In the case previously described, Lucy was supposed to care for her mother every other weekend. She picked up her mother on Saturday morning and dropped her off on Sunday night. The Browns needn't regard 2 days as such a short time. They might get more cooperation from Lucy if they told her explicitly what they wanted or needed from her, and they would feel less guilty if they explained what they were doing with the finances, instead of "hinting at it." In some cases, no matter how explicit you are, a sibling may well refuse to help out at all. If your sibling adopts such a position, you may experience any number of legitimate reactions and feelings. You have every reason to be angry and not accepting of an irresponsible sibling. You could also take the attitude that none of you *must* help a parent. If you choose to help, it doesn't mean that your sibling must. If you care about your parent, you help her because her discomfort and unhappiness bring you pain. You therefore are helping yourself as you help her. If your sibling doesn't get involved, it may be because he cannot allow himself to care because when he cares about someone he feels pain. The only way for your sibling to block out the pain of watching or knowing that your parent is distressed may be to pretend not to care. This is the heavy price that an uninvolved sibling often pays. As noted already, an uninvolved sibling also gives you the opportunity to be the responsible, caring, and good child.

5. Talk with your parent. What are her needs and expectations? Since if you are married it should be a joint decision, you should tell her that this is something that you and your spouse decided together. If you anticipate some problems because one of the children is less than enthusiastic about the move, it is better to say, "Look, Mom, Joe isn't wild about you moving in with us, but we think that he'll get over it." This way your mother will be more prepared for an icy look from Joe, and there needn't be a lot of whispering. Similarly, if you and your spouse are both working and your parent

expects that she will have your full-time attention, it is best that she knows before she moves in that this will not be the case.

6. Be prepared for a significant transition period. The point was made earlier in the book that the most stressful times in any organization are when someone enters or leaves it. Since a family is a type of organization, everyone in the family goes through a period of adjustment when someone enters or leaves it. When a parent moves in, there will be the tumult that comes with reorganization.

Points to Remember When Your Parent Moves In

1. If you move into your parent's home or she moves into yours, will there be struggles or uncertainty about who is in charge? Organizations function best when everyone has a say and everyone's opinion is considered and taken seriously but everyone knows who is ultimately in charge. You should certainly be respectful of your parent and take his or her advice seriously, but you have to make decisions for yourself and your children.

2. Families can get into trouble when there are coalitions across generational lines. This means that if one spouse consistently takes sides with the grandparent against the other spouse, problems will arise. Similarly, if a grandparent consistently sides with a grandchild against a parent, problems can arise. There should be an understanding from the very beginning that although a grandparent can support, care for, and love a grandchild, she should not undermine the parents' authority.

3. You and your spouse should be the primary parents to your child. But if you have a child and you decide to allocate some responsibility for child care to your parent, you should not undermine that responsibility. A grandparent cannot be effective if you tell your children to "listen to Grandma" when you leave the house,

but then imply that, when you're home, Grandma is silly or not quite competent.

4. Find out what assistance is available. Today, with more women in the work force, caring for family members requires more assistance from formal support systems. Adults today depend on good day-care centers, camps, schools, after-school programs, and the like for help in parenting their children. Homemakers, senior centers, and other support options are becoming increasingly available (see Chapter 9, "Practical Concerns"). When the informal, or family, support systems are stretched, you must take advantage of these other means of assistance.

5. Allow for the possibility of change or escape. Today, when people marry, they often write prenuptial agreements because they know that one out of two marriages ends in divorce. Of course, when people get married they hope and expect to be able to fulfill a commitment, but realistically they know that everything in life is precarious and subject to change. If your parent moves in, it is probably not the best idea to think of it as an experiment. It should be well thought out, and you should be prepared for a long-term commitment. However, if everyone is unhappy over a significant period of time, you should be able to discuss alternative solutions and arrangements. When a parent is extremely impaired, nursing home placement is an option that should be considered. The factors that should play a part in your considerations are discussed in the next chapter.

Chapter 11 _____
Nursing Homes

As aging progresses and the requirements of care become greater, the unyielding burdens of everyday living may make continuing care for an elderly parent a commitment that is beyond reason. The elderly parent who last year needed only weekly help with household chores may now require daily assistance in a greater number of areas. The parent who several months ago got by with part-time nursing may now require constant attention. If the burden of guilt prevents you from recognizing the limits of your capacity and care is continued beyond reason, there may be a spiral of resentment. This pattern can seriously reduce the quality of care which the parent receives and may lead to depression in the adult child. In such situations, a heavy price is levied against both parent and child.

There may come a time when reexamination of care plans is needed. It is important to realize that the idea of relinquishing some aspects of care is not incompatible with a steadfast love of child for parent. Sometimes the newfound freedom that comes with having substantial help with the care of your parent is just the impetus needed for a stronger and more positive relationship.

Considering the Nursing Home Option

Although a universal formula does not exist, there are a few general points to keep in mind. It has been found that mental impairment or debilitating senility on the part of the parent induces far more stress in caregiving families than physical impairments. This factor is further complicated when sleep disturbances or incontinence are part of your parent's problem. Under circumstances such as these, the effects of strain tend to spill over into other relationships, often creating resentment and even rejection of the elderly parent, and indicating the need for a reconsideration of care plans.

At some point, there may be a noticeable decline in your parent's ability to carry on everyday tasks without risk of injury. Careless habits in the kitchen, misuse of prescription drugs, difficulty with personal hygiene, a tendency to become disoriented, and resultant wanderings are often due to changes in mental functioning that are difficult to monitor, whether the elderly person lives alone or with family members. These factors also may provoke consideration of nursing home placement.[1]

Placement may also be sought when less severe mental or physical conditions are present. Nursing homes are designed to serve a wide variety of needs, so it is not simply a matter of meeting the negative criteria for a particular degree of disability. In some circumstances, in answer to social needs as well as physical ones, an elderly person may prefer nursing home residency, especially if living with a child is likely to cause stress for all involved. In fact, the nursing home environment may allow an elderly person greater independence than an overly solicitous family caregiver. One 95-year-old woman moved in with her daughter when she broke her hip. After some time, the family established a routine whereby the elderly woman would ring a bell when she wanted something from her daughter or son-in-law. No one in the family felt satisfied with the situation. The adult children were stressed to their limits and the mother was deteriorating. The mother was finally placed in a nursing home, where, after a period of adjustment, she regained a great deal of the independence she had lost while living with her daughter.

The population of elderly people in nursing homes consists of individuals with different levels of functioning. It is not possible to say that consideration of nursing home placement should only be undertaken when a particular point of degeneration is reached. Instead, the key criterion should be *the needs of your parent— physical, mental, social, and emotional—weighed against the availability and desirability of other options.*

You may protest that your deep-rooted sense of loyalty stirs feelings of obligation and, in turn, guilt at the thought of assigning primary care of your parent to strangers. Before allowing yourself to become a victim of unyielding guilt, consider realistically the mechanics and specifics of your situation. If you are already over-burdened with the combined obligations of family and career, you will be negating the value of your positive intentions by allowing your mental health and the emotional well-being of those around you to bear the brunt of increased expectations. Keep in mind that your parent needs you. If assuming too great a burden destroys your strength and your capacity to carry on, if it creates resentment or weakens relations between you and your parent, you both will have lost a very vital link. You can best serve the obligation that you feel by preserving yourself.

If you feel willing and able to manage the care of your parent at home, at least for the time being, it is certainly appropriate to do so. Along with this, however, it would be a good idea to acknowledge to yourself, as well as to your parent and other family members, that *periodic reassessment* of your parent's condition and of your coping abilities needs to be made. Avoid closing off consideration of other possibilities which might alle-viate the feeling of being trapped. In this feeling may be a mes-sage that is important to all concerned.

Your Feelings about Nursing Homes

The decision-making process is often fraught with confusion and anxiety. "Is this the right thing to do?" and later in the process, "How should I go about looking for the right place?" Certainly, the answers to these questions are never simple. Good nursing home placement requires thought and adjustment. Your search requires not only consumer awareness but careful consideration, so that the decision "feels right" on a personal level.

This consideration can begin with an exploration of the feel-ings that you have about nursing homes in general. It is helpful to start here because these feelings may be a stumbling block in your decision-making process. They can cause you to delay think-ing about the problem, or can leave you with feelings of guilt once a decision has been made.

It can happen that the decision is taken out of the family's hands by the occurrence of an emergency requiring hospitalization, with health professionals supporting and encouraging a quick placement decision. This may not seem bad, and certainly may be appropriate, but it can also deny family members—including your parent—the opportunity to work through existing feelings, and to have a role in making the decision. As will be discussed, active participation, by your elderly parent and all family members, is important to successful later adjustment.

Some families can make the decision to seek nursing home admittance only by bullying past their own negative feelings. In these cases, adult children may feel a continuing sense of guilt for having disappointed and failed the parent. These difficult feelings can express themselves in different and sometimes unpredictable ways. It is best that you explore your underlying feelings about nursing homes first. Then, certainly, you and your parent will have a sounder base for viewing your own circumstances realistically.

Apart from your unique experiences and views, or those of your parent, there seems to be a general feeling that we, as a nation, harbor toward nursing homes. This feeling is, for the most part, negative. For a variety of reasons, we generally think of nursing homes as a last resort, as a step which signals hopelessness, denoting finality, the end of growth and potential. In this view, the nursing home is a long-term, medically oriented holding place, strictly custodial in nature, where real living and progressing ceases, and where sterility and efficiency, the "nursing" components, take precedence over warmth and caring, the "home" components. Understandably, then, while it may bring you relief to think of your parent receiving more efficient and constant care than you could offer, the prospect of life in such a place may leave you feeling disturbed.

The reality of many nursing homes is not as bleak as people may think. Although it is true that a nursing home does not provide comfort in the same way as home, it is not necessarily a cold, lifeless place, either. The fear of many adult children that nursing home residents are left to a slow and inevitable wasting away is largely unfounded. A recent study has shown that when populations of nursing homes are broken down into shorter and longer-term residents, the two are not easily distinguished in terms of social and emotional functioning.[2]

The critical factor that determines satisfaction in a nursing home is health, most notably mental health. Senility, as it approaches a severe level, is the primary culprit in causing deterioration and pain in older people, including those residing in nursing homes. In other words, deterioration is not a function of residency itself but of an individual's overall level of mental functioning.

Your parent's reaction to the move and her adaptability to the nursing home environment is largely dependent on the very physical conditions that prompted consideration of such a move in the first place. These factors are beyond your control. What is in your control, as a first step, however, is the way in which the decision-making process and the preadmittance period are handled. This has been shown to be important to the elderly person's, and the family's, later adjustment.

The Decision-Making Process

Consideration of nursing home care for an elderly parent brings families to a point of transition and stress. Regardless of your parent's level of functioning, nursing home placement forces you to accept the undeniable evidence of your parent's dependency. With this comes an inevitable and deep realization that your position must change accordingly. It is not unusual for this chain of events to provoke a sense of loss and even mourning for what was. It is likely that you will not be alone in this. Other family members will probably be experiencing similar emotions. At the same time, it is likely that relationships among family members will be stirred, and feelings heightened.

Frequently, families need to reach joint decisions on such things as power of attorney and sale of the family home. When family members work together to resolve these issues, the transition becomes smoother, and the benefits of this harmony are shared by the parent. However, such harmony does not always come easily. A wide array of factors may get in the way. For example, many families have difficulty agreeing on whether every opinion should have equal weight. If one child had primary responsibility for the care of your parent prior to consideration of nursing home placement, it is possible that longstanding resentments and differences will now come to the fore. It may be that the caregiving child, feeling exhausted by his or her dutifulness, is resentful of siblings or others who may have avoided responsibility. Perhaps the caregiving child has become possessive of his or her primary position and is resentful of interference and of pressure to let others in on the decision-making process. Or it may be that such resistance is based on the feeling that others do not really understand the situation.

In making a decision, you need to weigh your own commitments and tolerance against the demands of caregiving. How much care does your parent really need? Her difficulty in preparing meals is a different matter, with a greater number of possible solutions, from her difficulty in feeding and dressing herself. As her disability increases, the range of solutions becomes more limited. Be careful not to be edged into accepting responsibilities that you are uncomfortable with. It may happen that a caregiving child is praised for good deeds and encouraged to continue by others in the family, without being helped in any real way. If you find yourself in these circumstances, make your feelings known. When the burden becomes too great, the key is to find out if others are willing to share it. If no one is willing or able to provide substantial help, the decision to seek other arrangements will have to be made—but not by you alone. Others' refusal or inability to step in and share responsibility is a vote in itself. It is important to not "slide" into any situation. If you fail to express your feelings and ideas clearly, the result is likely to be pain. If you accept caregiving responsibilities that are too much for you, you will soon feel anxious or depressed.

A Family Meeting

Earlier in the book, I emphasized the importance of family meetings, in which members take the opportunity to discuss feelings and make plans. If nursing home placement is being considered, such a meeting should certainly be held. Strong differences between family members may make absolute agreement on all matters an unrealistic goal. You can, however, at least generate momentum toward such efforts. Family meetings at this point can be useful in allowing each member to air his or her opinions and feelings.

You may be reluctant to "open up" at such meetings because of past difficulties in family relationships. This reluctance can get in the way of decision making and delay transitions. It may be helpful to realize that, at crisis times, as immediate needs take precedence, old differences sometimes dissolve. Family members, now faced with the task of resolving issues, often find great comfort in rallying together and drawing from their common ties. The following case illustrates this turnabout.

One woman we interviewed had been living with her elderly mother when a stroke brought on severe disability. The woman panicked. Because she had barely been able to maintain her career and care for her mother before the stroke, the new situation seemed impossible. Although she had a brother who visited regularly, she felt that she was alone in the dilemma because her brother had never offered substantial help. The woman resolved that care in a nearby nursing home was the answer and that she would simply inform her brother of the decision. The surprise came when the brother said he had never realized that his sister was under stress. The two of them were able to communicate honestly and arrive at a solution. In this case, they agreed to try a mutual caregiving arrangement, and to leave the possibility of nursing home placement open for the time being.

Friction between siblings is not the only type of conflict that may surface as you explore alternative care arrangements. It is not uncommon for conflicts to arise between parent and child, with the elderly parent resisting discussion of such a change and giving messages that induce guilt in her child. This can be a very uncomfortable situation. On one hand, the adult child has carefully considered and knows the bounds of his or her capabilities, as well as those of the situation. On the other hand, such messages from a parent have great power. As a child, you sought your parents' approval and feared their rejection. Now, with a reversal in positions, any suggestion that you may be rejecting your parent is likely to induce an overwhelming sense of guilt. This factor is probably the most potent in arresting the decision-making process. Rational discussion of options and possibilities as well as honest discussion of feelings are the only foundations for making decisions not strictly motivated by emotions of guilt or anger.

Your Parent as Participant

Regardless of the limitations of the situation, your elderly parent's feelings and ideas must be considered. This may seem obvious to you if your parent is functioning at a rational level and may seem less necessary if your parent seems unable to understand and communicate. But as the following illustrates, you cannot always read with precision a person's level of understanding.

After Ed Wood had been hospitalized with advanced senile dementia, his family sought out professional facilitation of their meetings. The purpose of these meetings was to help Ed's wife and children accept his rapid deterioration and their own shift in roles, and to guide them in a decision about what to do next. Because of the severity of his condition, family members saw no value in including Ed in the discussions. However, when encouraged to do so, they expressed no objections and Ed was routinely brought in to join the group. During the initial sessions, he sat in a slumped position and did not respond to their conversation. When spoken to, he made no reply. Given this, his wife and children went through the sessions as if he wasn't there. Later in their series of talks, however, Ed began to make some eye contact, and after 6 weeks, he told his family that he wanted to leave the hospital and be settled into a nursing home.[3]

The series of meetings helped this family to go through a difficult period of transition, and the fact that this man was able to contribute to a decision about his care was significant. A parent who is not included in the decision-making process is likely to feel manipulated, and to have greater difficulty in adapting to his new situation. In that case, the move may become a custodial one, and one that is not likely to be accepted.

As already mentioned, it is not always the case that a leisurely approach to the decision-making process can be taken. Frequently, placement in a nursing home is recommended following a crisis, such as a stroke, and initiated from an acute-care environment. Regardless of the circumstances, however, nothing needs to be done in such a hurry that you, other family members, and your parent miss out on participating in this important decision. You should not be pushed, panicked, or impelled into a decision.

Shopping Around in Advance

Many nursing homes have waiting lists. This basic fact often comes as a surprise to families who make a decision to seek immediate placement, only to be disappointed. If you think there is even a possibility that you might seek placement, you should look around before the situation feels desperate. Begin with the goal of finding and contacting several nursing homes that would suit your needs, instead of just one. In addition to increasing the likelihood of successfully gaining admittance, establishing contact in advance will give you the opportunity to be selective as openings come up.

Whether you target one or several homes, the task of shopping around is a matter of understanding your parent's circumstances, knowing what she needs, and being able to evaluate a home in light of these factors. Nursing homes are not all the same. Although the task of finding the right nursing home is easier when you have advance information about what to expect, you and your parent are the only ones who can decide what factors you will finally place the most emphasis on.

Categories of Nursing Homes

Your parent's level of functioning, more than any other factor, dictates the level of care that is required. The nursing home must be able to provide the specific care which your parent needs. If full care is not needed, you should not jeopardize your parent's sense of independence by placing her in a home where full care is the norm; nor is it sensible to pay for more services than you really need. There are three major categories of nursing homes, corresponding to the three levels of care: residential, intermediate, and skilled nursing.

Residential-Care Facilities

Here the emphasis is on providing a structured and safe home environment for individuals who are reasonably healthy and capable of functioning semi-independently. Dietary and housekeeping services are provided, and medical care is monitored so that residents will be "kept on track" in following care plans. Social and recreational opportunities are also emphasized, and residents tend to be active. The goal of these facilities is to relieve the worries and anxieties of old age so that residents can simply enjoy life more fully.

Intermediate-Care Facilities

These homes, sometimes called *health-related facilities,* are intended for individuals who retain some aspects of independent functioning, but who are not able to meet all of their regular care needs. The intermediate-care facility will provide the same services as residential-care facilities, as well as regular medical and nursing services. The emphasis, however, changes with the addition of these services. In intermediate-care facilities, there is an attempt to balance residents' dependencies with their need for autonomy, but certainly a good deal more direct care is given.

Skilled Nursing Facilities

This is the type of facility that most often comes to mind when people think of nursing homes. Although individual residents differ in their needs and capabilities, there is a general emphasis on providing full nursing care. Registered or licensed practical nurses are available on a 24-hour-basis to administer medication, injections, and other procedures which have been ordered by a physician. Patients in the rehabilitative stages of traumas, such as heart attacks or strokes, can be given the care that they require as well as receive specific therapeutic services. Dental and diagnostic laboratory work, including x-ray services, are frequently available as well. The skilled nursing facility provides a medically oriented environment while attempting to maintain a balance between the physical and social needs of the resident.[4]

To the visitor, each type of facility "feels" vastly different. These differences are primarily a function of the residents' varying levels of medical needs. Residential-care facilities are quite homelike in quality, whereas the skilled-care environment feels more like that of a hospital.

If you have doubts regarding which type of facility would best suit your parent's needs, consult your family doctor, as well as the social worker in the homes that you visit. Your family doctor should also be able to give you leads on particular homes you might consider. Other sources of help in locating homes within your area are your local health department and your state's affiliate of the American Health Care Association. (See Appendix B for the addresses and telephone numbers of these state affiliates.)

Meeting the Costs

The cost of nursing home care is high. An average room may run about $90 a day, with possible extra charges for nonstandard services (get specifics when visiting each home). With a figure like that in mind, it is easy to see that financial planning will need to be done beforehand. In fact, the nursing home to which you apply will review your parent's financial situation early in the process.

There are some designated insurance policies that cover nursing home care, and we might expect to see this option become more readily available in the future. As it stands right now, though, such coverage is unusual, since insurance companies generally classify nursing home services as custodial rather than acute care. You should check your parent's policy to be sure.

Medicare offers limited nursing home benefits if certain conditions are met. Your parent must be admitted to the nursing home within a restricted period of time following a hospital stay, and must be diagnosed by a physician as being in need of skilled nursing care.[5] In this case, benefits will be paid for up to 21 days of care. Benefits can be extended to 100 days, however, if the condition for which the patient initially required hospitalization persists beyond the hospital stay.

The nursing home will carefully scrutinize your parent's assets in order to determine her ability to pay. If those assets are below a certain level (the criterion varies from state to state), Medicaid will pick up the costs. If her assets exceed Medicaid's stated level, payment is expected privately. In other words, your parent will be expected to utilize personal funds until her resources are depleted to the stated level. Only when that occurs will Medicaid accept financial responsibility for your parent's nursing home care. Some parents give their life savings to children or other family members if they anticipate being placed in a nursing home, so that Medicaid will pay the expenses. If a parent files for Medicaid assistance too soon after making these gifts, she will be ruled ineligible. You should consult a lawyer to determine what the laws are in your state, and to get advice on the best possible course of action.

Touring and Evaluating the Facilities

Once you have compiled your list of possible homes, make arrangements to tour each one and to talk with staff members—especially the administrator, the social worker, and the director of nursing services. These individuals will be able to answer your questions about the services that are provided as well as give you an idea of how things are run in that home. Even your feelings about these staff members and the attitude that they communicate will provide information about the atmosphere of the home.

If your list includes more than three or four homes, it may be helpful to keep track of your impressions by jotting down notes after each visit. That way you will be able to keep the distinctions clear and make comparisons afterward. As a starting point, you might check out the basics: Does the facility have a current state operating license? And does the nursing home administrator also hold a current state license? These items in themselves don't guarantee that the facility and its operation will suit your parent's needs, and, of course, state requirements for both types of licenses vary.

Location and Setting

As you begin your series of visits, you might first take into account the type of setting that your parent is most comfortable in. One elderly woman who had spent a good part of her life on a farm in a small New England town was transferred by her children to a midtown nursing home. Her family did not think that the outdoor setting mattered since the woman was unable to go out alone and in fact seemed to have no interest in leaving the building. However, their mother was unhappy with the location. It is a good idea to consider the type of location that would most please your parent. Even if your parent does not go outside, the view from her window will be a continuous reminder of her setting; a view that she feels comfortable with may go a long way toward giving her a sense of security.

Most often, elderly residents are able to leave the building for outings, either as part of a resident group or with visitors. Given the features that nursing homes are expected to provide (elevators, ramps, automatic doors) to make access to the environment easier, your parent may be less of a prisoner in the nursing home than she was in her previous location. Therefore, the area surrounding the nursing home is important. Your parent may enjoy having access to such places as shopping malls, movie theaters, or libraries. He or she might enjoy visiting a nearby park, or being able to observe animals in a nearby field. When evaluating a nursing home, check the surroundings, both on and outside of its grounds, for sights and sounds that might stimulate your parent's interest. After she has moved encourage her to make outings.

The Public Spaces

As you approach the building itself, your first impression will be of the lobby. Is it a warm, welcoming lounge that can be used by both residents and guests? A comfortable lobby, sometimes present in an intermediate-care or residential-care facility, allows residents and visitors to mix and encourages residents to greet their visitors as they enter the home.

Find out where the visiting areas of the home are. Unless your parent is bedridden all of the time, it is important that she have a pleasant lounge for meeting with fellow residents and visiting with guests. This will be the number one public spot, similar to your living room. The quality and atmosphere of such an area, including its decor, is of great importance. Keep your parent's personal tastes and probable reactions in mind as you tour the home. For example, contemporary furnishings may give the room a fresh look, yet not appeal to your parent.

If, having made your way through the hospital-like halls of a skilled nursing facility, you find the visiting lounge to be a large interior room into which a dozen or so patients have simply been wheeled and left—to do nothing more than stare at walls or at each other, or sleep—you are not likely to feel comfortable in your visits.

Studies have shown that health status or level of functioning is the best predictor of the ways in which residents will use space within the nursing home. Patients who have not suffered mental impairment due to stroke or brain deterioration continue to differentiate between public and private space. In a public area, such as a lounge, these individuals refrain from normally private behaviors and actively engage in social contacts with others. In contrast, elderly patients who have suffered mental deterioration tend to show little change in their behavior as they move from private to public areas. Hallways, dining rooms, and lounge areas are just as likely as bedroom areas to be the site of typically private behaviors. These patients talk to themselves openly, sleep in hallways, and generally fail to exercise the self-control that healthier residents do.[6] When you visit skilled nursing facilities, you are likely to see some discomforting sights. Patients in advanced stages of senility are not consistently able to function with the social graces which make us feel comfortable. However, even persons at this level of disability are capable of social interactions. It has been generally noted that all but the most severely disoriented patients can periodically be induced to establish contact with others.[7]

Meals in the nursing home should be regarded as a social event as well as a physical necessity, and as such are worth observing for yourself. Unlike hospitals, where meals are taken individually, nursing homes have dining rooms, designed to stimulate social interaction. You might ask yourself if the dining room looks attractive. Remember that a sea of wheelchairs and walkers might look forbidding to you as an outsider, but not necessarily to one who is part of the group. Stick around at mealtime and observe the routine. Does the food smell good? Does it look attractive? These factors will obviously be important to your parent. Is enough time allotted for slow eaters to finish? And what about assistance in eating? Does the home have help available, but to be used only when needed? Residents who have limited but workable skills are best served by staff who believe in fostering self-reliance.

Cleanliness Counts

Possibly the number one factor that is considered and discussed in selecting a nursing home is cleanliness. In general, this can be evaluated by visual inspection. The second criterion by which cleanliness is most often measured is smell.

You will undoubtedly have a sense of whether the home lives up to your own and your parent's standards of cleanliness. However, although cleanliness is certainly important and indicative of the overall level of care that is taken, you need to approach it with some flexibility. Consider the business of running your own home. The state of your home probably differs depending on the time of day. Typically, after the morning rush or after a flurry of activities in the evening, there is a period of time when cleaning is called for. If you tour a nursing home in the morning, when sheets are being changed, and when incontinent patients are being dressed, it is likely that you will notice odors. The key to determining whether or not your concern is justified is the persistence of the odor. Check back later in the day and make note of changes. Odors that are evident throughout the day cannot be innocently attributed to daily routines, and are a sign of trouble. If, however, traces of odor disappear along with the soiled sheets, they need not be cause for concern.

Safety and Services

The regulations governing safety features as well as those dictating the amount and type of services that must be offered in nursing homes vary greatly from state to state. Do not assume that the state will regulate safety features. What is stringently controlled in one state may be loosely controlled—and hence surprisingly below grade—in another.

Consider the following questions: Are all areas of the nursing home well-lighted? Are the handrails in the halls and bathrooms securely installed and at the proper height for your parent? Are chairs sturdy and easy for your parent to get into and out of? Are signs large enough for residents to read? Are exit signs well-marked, and stairwells closed off by doors? Is a cooperating hospital close by, with transportation easily available? These safety features are imperative.

In evaluating services, consider whether the hygienic needs of patients unable to care for themselves are quickly tended to. Are physicians and other service personnel (for example, pharmacist, dentist, physical therapist, dietician, beautician, barbers) available? Check further to see if private physicians are allowed, and if medical records are kept daily and care plans reviewed periodically.

These provisions will often be spelled out for you at the time of your initial inquiry. Press for specific answers that will leave no doubt in your mind about the amount, type, and quality of care which your parent can expect to receive.

Private Space

Going from public areas of the nursing home to private areas such as bedrooms introduces a new set of considerations. Private space and privacy in general are at a premium in skilled nursing facilities, and their availability at residential- and intermediate-care facilities varies.

Privacy in a nursing home setting can be thought of as having two dimensions: physical space and staff courtesy. In terms of space, you might consider what areas within the home have designated quiet times or are located away from the bustle of active areas such as the nurses' station and the dining room. In terms of courtesy, observe staff members as they go about their rounds. Are closed doors respected? Do staff members knock before entering a room? Arrange to be present just before mealtime. At some homes, staff members begin to bring wheelchair-bound residents into the dining room well before the meal is served, leaving them to wait for long periods of time.

In many skilled nursing facilities, intrusions and a resulting lack of privacy have probably come to be viewed as necessary and acceptable, because of the disabilities that are often present. Typically, the more able and mentally alert a resident is, the more privacy she can expect to be given.

Independence and Dependency

A recent study of the perceptions of staff members in skilled nursing facilities revealed that staff members tend to view newly admitted residents as emotionally well-adjusted and intellectually intact provided that they show an initial degree of self-reliance and an ability to maintain a distinction between public and private behaviors. Yet, indications are that as time goes on, a different set of behaviors are viewed as emotionally healthy.

Staff members tend to rate longer-term residents as well-adjusted if they have become oriented to the nursing home routine and are *agreeable* to staff members as they go about caring for residents' personal needs. In other words, although independence is viewed as desirable in a newly admitted resident, an elderly person's adaptability to the realities of the nursing home environment may be the quality most appreciated by staff as time goes on.[8]

These conclusions may seem to indicate that the nursing home environment is detrimental to your parent's mental health—that over a period of time, it requires a submissive, dependent attitude. Although this view may be valid to some extent, it should be noted that the transition toward greater dependency can occur in any elderly or infirm person whether she is living in a group situation such as this or with a member of her family. A delicate balance needs to be found between independence and dependence. Inappropriately forcing dependency on your parent, whether in major or minor areas of daily living, will demoralize her and undermine her sense of personal dignity.

Good morale, on the other hand, is likely to be an outgrowth of feelings of competence. Situations that permit an elderly person to demonstrate and reaffirm her capabilities, and to take responsibility for herself—to whatever degree possible—will enhance her emotional well-being and increase the likelihood of further rehabilitative gains. Studies of nursing home populations have clearly shown that elderly patients who are given opportunities to make decisions, to exercise control over aspects of daily living, and to play an active part in the nursing home community show evidence of improvements.[9] Specifically, these gains have been reflected in residents' own estimates of their level of happiness and hopefulness, as well as in their increased participation in nursing home activities and social interactions.[10]

It has been shown that patients benefit not only from opportunities to assert competencies but also from being able to predict from day to day what will happen in their surroundings.[11] Inconsistency, or a feeling that one's activities might be unexpectedly intruded upon, probably results in the feeling that one has little control and is in a subordinate position. These two variables, then— *opportunities for control and responsibility*, along with *consistency and predictability*—are likely to be intertwined and should provide standards by which to evaluate the homes that you visit.

Seemingly minor details, like being asked which shirt or dress is preferred that day, what vegetable should be served at lunchtime, or at what time of day a bath should be given, are meaningful. Even small decisions are representative of continuing control over one's life.

Needs for independence, then, must be balanced with needs for custodial care, with neither being seen as excluding consideration of the other. For example, if it is realistically assessed that your parent is not able to be self-reliant in dressing, it is still important for her to be asked to choose her clothes on a daily basis. Capabilities which are present should be accentuated, and areas of dysfunction should be periodically reassessed in the hope of sparking improvement. In an atmosphere of respect for continuing capabilities, it is likely that your parent's self-image will improve and that her resistance and anger will thereby diminish.

The Program of Activities

It is important to examine and evaluate the program of activities that a nursing home offers. Although many people tend to view recreation programs in nursing homes with skepticism, imagining that such programs begin and end with busywork, the actual picture can be quite a bit brighter. Many nursing homes are attempting to become more attuned to the ongoing needs of their residents, and to offer opportunities directed to fill these needs.

Even if your parent does not initially seem able to participate, the activities program warrants your consideration. It is good to know that the nursing home will be able to serve your parent's changing needs and to offer meaningful activities in conjunction with rehabilitation. Equally, however, the general atmosphere of the home is brightened when residents are challenged and stimulated. One woman whose severely disabled father had entered a skilled nursing facility commented that the enthusiasm of some of the more active residents was a comfort to her as she made her way to her father's room, and had occasionally sparked her father's interest.

In addition, the range and type of activities that are offered is a good indicator of the overall attitude of the home's administrators. If all that is offered to residents, besides the routines of daily living, is sessions of bingo or basket weaving, you would be justified in questioning the attitude that the administrators of the home hold toward its residents. Much more encouraging is an emphasis on meaningful living.

There are several functions that may be served by meaningful activities.[12] First, they may be useful as part of the *restorative process,* by allowing residents to redirect their attention—from despair and self-pity to enjoyment of the present. Activities can also create an opportunity for residents to release some of the tensions that infirmity and dependence must bring, and provide a chance to reassert capabilities. This in itself is an important goal, since decreases in function will probably have led to a dramatic decline in your parent's view of her remaining abilities.

Recreational programs can also be thought of as *preventive* in nature. The loss of functions that afflicts many elderly people stems not only from natural processes of physical deterioration but also from atrophy due to inactivity. We often remark on the continuing emotional strength of elderly individuals who go on with life in an active way. The nature of the activities will vary with individual interests and capabilities, but the general positive effect of activity is undeniable.

These two beneficial functions of recreation—restorative and preventive—can be incorporated into any activity. Your parent may readopt hobbies that she enjoyed in the past, or may be stimulated to undertake something new. A combination of both—reinforcement of old skills and stimulation of new interests—is probably best. You may notice that some nursing home activities are designated for men only or for women only. These sex-segregated involvements can also be a morale booster, since maintenance of one's sexual identity is associated with continuation of past roles, and can help to sustain feelings of dignity.[13]

Group Sessions

Another goal of activities in the nursing home should be to assist your parent in the initial *adjustment* to the nursing home environment. Adjustment in these circumstances can be a tremendously demanding task, because the environment is radically new, and because adjustments typically become more difficult as people get older. These two factors, working in conjunction, can trigger an emotional slump that is hard to counteract. Some nursing homes offer group support sessions in which residents are encouraged to exchange ideas, feelings, and memories. These sessions may be particularly important to your parent when she is newly admitted because she may feel overwhelmed by her new environment and disconnected with the past.[14] Of course, in order for group sessions to be effective, your parent has to willingly participate in them and not just "be physically there." The component of willingness is an internal one. You and the nursing home staff can, and should, encourage your parent to join others and to become a part of the nursing home social network. But you cannot make it happen. Whether at 8 or at 80, we are all ultimately responsible for ourselves. It is just as true, however, that your parent will be a more willing member if group experiences successfully touch on emotional needs.

It will be hard for you to evaluate from the outside what the effects of these group sessions in nursing homes are, since you are removed from the experience of being old, infirm, and disoriented. But, as was discussed in Chapter 6, "Emotional/Psychological Concerns," an important task of old age is to resolve issues of the past, through the process of life review. Sessions aimed at clarifying and justifying past roles provide an opportunity for reconciliation with the past and subsequent adjustment in the present.

One final note about group sessions—some nursing homes conduct what is termed "reality orientation," which may be classified as an activity by the nursing home administration. This program involves a gathering of residents for orientation to the facts of nursing home life. Questions like "What time is dinner?" are asked in order to reinforce continuing awareness of day-to-day realities and cooperation with them. Residents who give incorrect answers are corrected, those who give no answers are reminded, and those who give correct answers are praised. Such programs may aid the administration in the smooth running of the home (since cooperative patients are manageable ones), but they have been the subject of controversy.[15] Critics maintain that residents who appear confused may be doing so purposefully out of resentment at having to participate in this kind of drill. In addition, it should be noted that there are other realities besides those of the nursing home. An elderly individual preoc-

cupied with coming to terms with the past may give answers that
are throwbacks to another time in her life. Reality orientation
may not be "bad," but it is not necessarily a constructive pro-
grammed activity. The debate over whether it is effective or
demeaning brings up another point. You cannot assess the quality of activities in a nursing home merely by perusing a list. It is
a good idea to stick around and see what actually goes on. With
the exception of group therapy sessions, to which admittance is
and should be exclusive, viewing of activities in process is a
worthwhile step to take.

When a Decision Is Made

Even with all reason pointing to the nursing home alternative,
arriving at a commitment may be difficult. As is often the case,
doubts about the home itself may linger, and remnants of guilt at
the prospect of being the coordinator of this move will be painful. A sense of loss and mourning on your part will be justified
and natural.

When your parent moves, you should remember that humans
are symbolic creatures. By this it is meant that from a very
young age, we are able to represent to ourselves large concepts
and feelings by small concrete items. For instance, small children away from their mother find comfort in carrying an item
that she gave them, a treasure that brings her to mind. Similarly,
people of all ages carry pictures in their wallets as portable symbols of the closeness they feel to and with others. Whether for a
move to a smaller apartment where you can't fit all your athletic
trophies, and so choose the most important ones to "stand for"
the rest, or a move to a nursing home, the same process is
required. The memories and comforts elicited by the symbols
are real.

Helping your parent to decide what to bring to the nursing home
can be a very important, though painful, task. You can expect that
you and your parent will each experience loss, change, guilt, and
anger. A religious statue may represent a lifetime of commitment
and values that still offer comfort and are lovingly passed on. A
special lamp may symbolize years of family dinners, evening talks,
or bedtime readings. Despite the changed proportions of your par-

ent's room, the presence in the nursing home environment of items that are personal and meaningful to her may go a long way toward emotional reassurance.

Helping after Admission

Research suggests that there is a positive relationship between family involvement with nursing home patients and the quality of care they receive. In other words, it seems that when more attention is drawn to a patient by involved relatives—visiting, phoning, talking with staff—more care and concern are likely to be elicited from the nursing home staff. Many adult children feel uncomfortable and unsure about how often and when to visit. Keep in mind that your presence—whether by phone, mail, or in person, will be a tremendous support for your parent. It is also through your involvement with the nursing home staff that you can actively contribute to your parent's care plan.

Some tasks are not routinely undertaken by the nursing home. It is important to determine what tasks the home can be relied upon to perform, and which are left for the resident and her family. You should clearly state which tasks and responsibilities you intend to take on; otherwise the nursing home staff may resent your efforts as an intrusion. If there is uncertainty about whose responsibility a particular task might be, there is also the chance that it will be left undone. The following is a list of "gray" areas—areas that are frequently not clearly understood as being either the staff's or the relatives' responsibility.[16]

1. Personalizing care: providing special or extra food; making sure the resident's room is attractive; giving birthday parties for resident.

2. Monitoring and ensuring the provision of care: reporting any abuse or neglect to the authorities; ensuring that drugs/medication not covered by Medicare or Medicaid are ordered; making a telephone accessible to resident; filing claims for resident benefits; transporting resident to doctor; providing adequate supplies (facial tissues, etc.).

3. Maintaining clothes: laundering resident's personal clothing; marking resident's personal clothing; keeping resident's clothing inventory up-to-date.

4. Grooming: clipping fingernails and toenails; arranging for hair grooming.

5. Providing reading materials: making current newspapers available; keeping books and magazines available.

Remember the importance of clear communication as well as cooperation and support between the family and the nursing home staff.

If Your Parent Is Unhappy in the Nursing Home

You may approach visits to your parent with optimism and good intentions, expecting to find her engaged in the activities and programs which impressed you on your initial tour, only to feel beaten down and bewildered by your parent's complaints and expressed wish to go home. This can be a very difficult time even for the most well-prepared child.

Complaints about the home may be justified, and you may need to investigate and act upon them in some way. Certainly even the best of nursing homes isn't infallible or incapable of hiring an incompetent or uncaring person. In order to be an effective advocate for your parent, you will need to be familiar with the avenues for voicing grievances. Probably the most useful way to express the complaint would be through a discussion with the nursing home personnel. Before or immediately following admission, it is a good idea to familiarize yourself with the structure and hierarchy of the nursing home personnel, so that you are aware of who is responsible for what. If your complaint is of a relatively minor nature, you should start with the staff member who is directly involved. For instance, if your parent is upset about being the first patient on the floor to be given morning medicine and would prefer to sleep longer, you could express this to the head nurse on your parent's floor. If your concern, however, is of a major or persistent nature, you may need to approach administrative personnel. In extreme cases you could present the matter in question to an outside party. An appropriate place to start would be your local office of the aging or health department. They will either register and respond to your complaint or they will redirect it.

Your parent's unhappiness with and complaints about the home may be due to factors other than the characteristics of the home. Many elderly people continue to lose independence, vigor, and strength while adult children feel helpless and unable to quell their parent's fears and sorrow. Parents may complain about the home as a way of stirring up lingering guilt, or as a way of bringing the family close—as if to say, "I've tried, but no one can replace you." In a similar fashion, family members can angrily voice complaints to the nursing home as a way of dealing with their own feelings of guilt and helplessness, as well as to communicate to their parent, "I'm still on your side."

It is quite possible that your parent will have a difficult time adjusting to the nursing home. You may initially feel broken or shaken by your parent's unhappiness. Nonetheless, it is important for you to listen, comfort, and understand. You may need to remind yourself and your parent of the reasons why the decision was made and what benefits you hope can be derived from the experience. It may also be a good idea for you to join in discussions with support groups for family members of nursing home residents.

As time goes on, it is possible for your visits and contacts, and those of other family members and friends, to provide you and your parent with support in the present and a link to the past. Your parent will probably want to see pictures of the family, of the dog, of the new car. Your parent will want to see your child's report card, and hear the family news—both good and bad. Your parent will benefit most from feeling like a vital part of the family. If you can help your parent to continue to feel this connection to you and the family, the nursing home can be a place of residence rather than a place of isolation.

Chapter 12_____
Dying, Death, and Funerals

This chapter is intended to provide information and guidance. No one can really know what your experiences with your dying parent, with a funeral director, or with bereavement will be like. Personal circumstances, beliefs (especially religious beliefs), and philosophies will all contribute to the experiences that you and your family have.

When does dying begin, and when is the most appropriate time for thinking about the end of life? These questions have concerned philosophers for centuries, and may be touching on your life now, with the aging of your parent. It is hoped that the points of view presented here will encourage you to explore these questions for yourself and your family and to become more comfortable with your own answers.

If your parent is elderly, it is likely that she has already considered the end of life, and that—to some degree or in some corner of your mind—you have begun to think about what it will be like to lose your parent. The beginning of this realization may have come when a physician revealed that your parent has a terminal illness. It may have occurred with slow acknowledgment and dread as you observed her increasing debility. Or it may have confronted you directly, as a topic that your parent wanted to talk about. In any case, for children of aging parents, facing and preparing for death is as much a part of care as all of the other matters that have been discussed in this book.

Thinking about Your Parent's Death

Death is a subject that most people are afraid of, or that, at least, they would like to avoid. Sometimes adult children believe that the safest course is to act as if nothing has changed. If the topic of death sneaks into a conversation somehow, they quickly change the subject or say that such ideas are silly. But making death a taboo subject may prevent your parent from coming to terms with it. Dying people have a great need to talk, and to experience honest intimacy with loved ones so that the generations can mourn together, and even plan for the future.[1] In fact, a person who knows that loved ones understand and will readjust is likely to have a less emotionally painful death. One woman reported that her father could only die comfortably when his grandchildren were able to say a proper "good-bye" and let him know that he could go and they would be OK.

Some children think that if the situation's true hopelessness is expressed, a parent's will to live will plummet. Children may also avoid facing up to a parent's impending death out of fear that their feelings of hopelessness will negatively affect the quality of care they provide for their parent. Not so. Facing your parent's death means, in part, accepting the limits of your efforts without actually doing less.

Your Feelings

While helping your parent—and yourself—through this time, you will probably experience many changes and some turbulence. You may, for example, feel accepting of your parent's impending death one day and totally outraged by it the next. In a similar way, your feelings at a given time may correspond closely to those of your parent, creating an atmosphere of harmony, whereas at another time, the two of you may suddenly clash, as your feelings go in one direction and your parent's in another. Like living, dying occurs in a context filled with other people. The dying person, friends, and family all struggle through fears and grief together.

In order for you to support your parent, it is important to spend some time working with and understanding your own feelings. This is a time when it is imperative to talk with friends and family and not to keep your confusion and sorrow to yourself. It is often the case that families of the dying person feel an initial sense of anguish that gradually becomes specified. You might begin to focus on particular occasions or moments that you will miss. Sunday morning visits, seeing your parent hold your children, or simply the opportunities to continue "making memories" might stand out most in your mind. Whatever your thoughts are of, these are the elements in your relationship that contribute to the pain of loss.

Children of aging parents often experience loss and mourning in a gradual rather than a sudden fashion.[2] You may, for example, pinpoint your parent's sense of humor as a characteristic that you will miss, and then find that it is not actually death but increasing infirmity that has caused this important quality to ebb. Gradual adjustment is often easiest to handle, since an extended period of anticipation allows survivors to mentally prepare themselves for what is to come. As you continue to further define what the death of your parent will mean to you, what specific characteristics or situations you will miss, be aware of your feelings. The overwhelming sensation is probably one of loss and emptiness. But it is not uncommon for survivors to experience a range of bitter feelings, as well. Fear, anger, resentment, or a mixture of these may coexist with the anguish.[3]

The loss of a parent represents a definite transition for you. It takes away from your status as "child of" and places you in a different category within your family. As you come to accept your new status, you are more likely to anticipate your future role as an "oldster." Facing your parent's death also brings you closer to a realization of your own mortality.

Another possible source of negative feelings is the fact that relationships are never ideal. As the death of your parent approaches, you may experience regret or even anger about what was wrong in the relationship. Your parent may not have always been as warm and supportive or as understanding as you wished. Part of the process of accepting your parent's death is becoming comfortable with these disappointments. If you have moments when you experience these negative feelings, try to be aware of them, instead of cringing from them out of fear or guilt.

You may determine that you can still take action to change aspects of your relationship or at least resolve differences and soothe feelings through discussion with your parent. Remember, though, that neither of you can go back in time to amend the wrongs. Criticizing your parent now for perceived past neglects will cause only harm. In fact, criticism in general is not likely to be productive. The goal here is to come to an understanding and acceptance of each other. You might tell your parent that you know it hasn't always been easy for the two of you to agree, say, on a particular issue, but that the moments of discord don't mean that you do not feel caring or love. Whether or not that discord will then be the subject of further conversation will depend upon the issue and your personalities. Once your message is out, allow your parent room to come to terms with it in her own way.

Guilt also frequently comes into play in dealing with a dying parent. Not uncommonly, adult children feel that it would be best for their parent to die quickly.[4] This sentiment may be appropriately expressed as "I hate to see her suffer." But beyond this selfless concern is often a weariness stemming from the heavy burdens of care and worry. This conflict—the pushing and pulling of your own and your parent's needs—can be handled in a number of ways. The most effective way is for you as a caregiver to moderate and balance the two, keeping in mind that although your parent needs you, you need not go beyond your limits. In fact, you will be more honestly giving if you consider your own needs, as well. Sometimes, children of aging and dying parents give so much—probably out of a feeling that there will be time for themselves later—that resentment develops. Children then feel guilty about their feelings of resentment. They attempt to alleviate this guilt by doing more for the parent. Doing more leads to more guilt, and so on. The only way to break this vicious cycle is to do less. Your negative emotions will then be less likely to erode the quality of the relationship at this critical time.

Finding Out How Your Parent Wants to Die

What, then, should be your goals as you approach this period, of undetermined length, during which your parent is to die? You may have formulated the goal of amending or coming to terms with unsatisfactory aspects of your relationship. These thoughts and wishes should be communicated to your parent directly.

Another very important goal is to be a supportive listener for your parent. Dying parents often have intense needs to communicate, and it is helpful for them to have a close family member to share feelings with. It is also very important to find out about how your parent wants to die.

One woman watched while her father, dying of lung cancer, repeatedly struggled to remove the respirator that was covering his mouth. "He is in so much pain," she lamented. "He can't speak. If only he were able to tell me what he wanted, I would help him in any way I could." Fortunately, there was a social worker there who told the woman, "Perhaps he is telling you what he wants and what to do and you aren't listening." The woman then realized that her father's constant attempts to remove the respirator were expressions of discomfort and pain and of his wish to die more peacefully.

As physical illness or deterioration takes hold of your parent and the end of life gets closer, decisions concerning life-support or life-sustaining measures often need to be communicated to medical personnel. When the prognosis is very bad, most doctors will ask whether aggressive care (that which seeks cure) or supportive care (a euphemism for keeping the patient comfortable) is wanted. Very often, the dying person is not able to speak for herself at that point.

If you have not discussed this topic with your parent before the time that a decision needs to be made, you will be left in the difficult position of determining what is most appropriate. You might try to recall your parent's feelings about how other dying patients were treated or base a decision on the values your parent has espoused. But such determinations are never easy. Sometimes it happens in those cases that adult children provide the maximum in life-support and life-sustaining measures simply to avoid feeling guilty. Many parents, however, if given the chance, would prefer to have a peaceful and natural death, rather than a laborious and dehumanizing one. If no discussions have taken place, children need to be tuned in to the signals that their dying parent gives.

It should also be kept in mind that some parents want every attempt made to keep them alive. If this is so, this is what you should do. One woman complained that although she knew that she herself did not want to be kept alive at all costs, her mother did not want to talk about when to stop heroic measures to save her life. After some reflection, the daughter realized that her mother really wanted everything done that could be done. It is sometimes hard for us to accept the fact that what seems right to us may not be what our parent wants. It is very important to listen carefully to your parent's messages regarding how she wants to die.

Most often the parent does know what she wants and does give you signals. But in some cases the parent is physically unable to communicate. This is why it is so important to discuss these matters beforehand. Some parents really don't know what they want and ask that you make the decision. This is the most difficult situation of all. You should talk with friends, family, and physicians about possible options.

A parent who feels especially strongly about wanting a natural death, without reliance upon life-support machinery, and who is able to express these feelings beforehand might make out a *living will*.[5] This document delineates an individual's wishes, and can be used to communicate those wishes at the appropriate time. A copy of a standard version of the living will can be found in Appendix D, but it is a flexible document and can be changed to suit the individual. If your parent utilizes a living will, the document should be signed by her and by two nonrelatives or nonbeneficiaries.

Although it has not yet been tested in the courts of all states, the living will is widely recognized as a statement of an individual's desires. If your parent makes out such a document, be sure that her doctor has been informed and is willing to cooperate.

Hospice

There was a time when most people died at home. Today nearly 65 percent of Americans die in hospitals, and the percentage is rising. This is due to a number of factors. The hospital is the place to go when a person is sick. Physicians not only provide medical care, they are thought to possess knowledge, wisdom, and power. There are also financial incentives for choosing the hospital as a place to die. Medicare will cover the cost of dying in a hospital.[6]

Often deaths occur with no family and friends present, with the dying person strapped down, attached to tubes and respirators. Many of us would prefer to die with dignity, with the opportunity to choose whether we want medication or more aggressive treatments, and to hold the hand of a loved one.

If, in your discussions, you find that your parent does not want her life extended by life-support systems or heroic measures and that she does not want to die in a hospital environment, you might consider the hospice concept of care. *Hospice* is a system of care for dying patients and their families. The focus in hospice is not on seeking cure but on caring for patients and supporting both patients and families with respect to a variety of needs. In keeping with the hospice philosophy, patients are allowed to die with dignity, unencumbered by life-support machinery or heroic resuscitation measures. A peaceful death is not the only goal of hospice. Another is to help patients to live the remainder of their lives as fully and as free of pain as possible. Carefully tailored pain-management plans are the hallmark of good hospice care.[7]

These goals are met through agencies that coordinate services to dying patients, providing medical and mental health personnel as well as volunteers and clergy, if desired. Most care is given in the patient's home, although some agencies are based within nursing homes or hospitals. In the typical case, patients are cared for by family members, with regular visits from a doctor, a social worker, nurses, home health aides, and other hospice staff—whatever is required by the family. The aims are to strengthen the family and foster cohesiveness as death approaches, and to extend support, through bereavement counseling, to the family after the patient's death.[8]

What to Look for in Hospice Care

If your parent qualifies for hospice care (generally, the patient must have a terminal illness, but some agencies specialize in a particular illness), you will need to find out what is available in your area. Some areas have just one hospice service available, but if you are fortunate, you will have a choice among several. In comparing hospice agencies, you might consider the following questions:

1. Is help available on a 24-hour emergency basis? Your sense of security will be increased if it is.

2. What type of backup inpatient facilities cooperate with the hospice program? There should be a nearby hospital that will admit hospice patients and agree to cooperate with hospice philosophies.

3. How adequate is the pain-management program of the agency? The better programs do not routinely increase dosages of medication as pain increases, but consider other factors—such as how alertness will be affected— as well.

4. What kinds of orientation and training programs are provided for staff members? The understanding and sense of conviction of hospice personnel will dictate the success of the program.

5. What types of counseling services will be provided? Ideally, coverage will include full counseling services for all family members, both before and after the patient's death.

6. Will your parent be allowed to continue to use the services of her private physician, in conjunction with the hospice physician? This is an important factor, because many elderly people feel that they have established a special relationship with their doctor and do not want to give that up.

Hospice Costs

Hospice costs are considerably lower than the costs of hospital or nursing home care because neither room and board nor life-support machinery is needed. The exception to this is when hospice agencies provide shelter or are based within hospitals. Even in these cases, though, the cost is considerably less than that of traditional hospital care.

The federal government has recognized hospice care as a viable and cheaper alternative to regular hospital care. Currently, those eligible for Medicare are provided hospice coverage when the following conditions are met.[9]

1. A private doctor and the hospice medical director must certify that the patient has a life expectancy of 6 months or less.

2. The patient must sign a statement choosing hospice care instead of regular hospital care (this decision can be reversed at any time).

3. The hospice agency selected must be certified by Medicare.

This last factor, Medicare certification, can be a problem, because only a small percentage of hospice agencies take part in Medicare programs. The reason for this lack of interest is that the Medicare rate is based on a flat maximum fee which, for a full 6 months of service, is relatively low. In addition, if the patient lives for more than 6 months, the hospice agency must continue to provide services without reimbursement.

Many insurance companies now recognize the need for hospice coverage and meet hospice costs either fully or in part. It is best to check with your parent's insurance agent for advice.

Finally, if payment is to be made on an individual, private basis, fees are based on a sliding scale and are generally reasonable. Further information about hospice programs and listings of Medicare-certified and non-Medicare-certified agencies can be obtained from a number of sources. Addresses of these sources are given in Appendix C.

Overcoming Your Own Denial

Elderly people often have much less of a problem in overcoming denial of death than their children. You may notice that by the time the seriousness of your parent's condition becomes apparent to you, your parent has progressed beyond denial and anger. Through the loss of loved ones or friends, elderly parents typically have had more experience than their middle-aged children in facing death. This and the increasing likelihood of pain and infirmity have already weakened their mechanisms for denying mortality. Thoughts of death, then, may not be as unbearable to your parent as they are to you. In fact, research indicates that the older we get, the less we are afraid of death.[10] Courage on the part of your parent can ease the way for your own shedding of denial. Two points should be remembered here. First, shedding of denial in the face of strong evidence that your parent's condition is serious and fatal does not mean abandoning your parent or minimizing your involvement. It may simply mean, from your standpoint, that you recognize the implications of the illness and are willing to face those new demands. Second, it is expected that you, like your parent, will hold out hope without denial throughout the course of the illness. Hope is always justified.

The Dying Process

A widely held view of dying, first presented by Elisabeth Kübler-Ross, defines the process of accepting one's impending death as a gradual one. According to this view, the dying person moves through a series of stages—beginning with denial and encompassing phases of anger, bargaining, and depression—before arriving at eventual acceptance.[11]

Denial tends to occur most vehemently as an initial reaction, and acceptance tends to be displayed to a greater degree as time goes on. Beyond that, though, dying is a delicate process that does not obey strict expectations. Still, the notion of a range of emotions and reactions, regardless of the sequence in which they occur, is likely to provide a helpful framework for understanding your parent.

According to Kübler-Ross, the individual tends to experience different emotions at different times; however, there is one emotion—hope—that is said to transcend the boundaries of all stages. Hope, never dying, can be thought of as an emotion that, to some degree and in one form or another, is always clung to.

Denial

In the first, or denial, stage, the individual strongly believes that death is unthinkable, and so is able to cushion the shock that news of impending death must bring. The patient might reason that the diagnosis must be wrong or that treatment will be curative. The strength of this denial may vary, but the emotion will probably reemerge from time to time, even after the patient seems willing to accept the diagnosis. In a way, denial represents hope, even though denial fights against belief in illness, while hope is retained in spite of such belief.

During the stage of intense denial, it is important to allow your parent these defenses. This does not mean agreeing with your parent if you know that her beliefs are unfounded. Although you may be struggling with denial of your own, sharing in her denial will not do your parent any good, and in fact, will only impede her efforts to come to terms with her approaching death. Allowing your parent her defenses means being willing to listen without constantly pointing out the irrational or contradictory nature of her statements. By being a nonjudgmental listener, you will not risk becoming the "enemy," and your parent will be more likely to turn to you when her denial begins to break down.

Anger

In the second stage, anger is the predominant emotion. The dying patient, having accepted the news at face value, reacts with utter horror, anger, and resentment—feelings that are often directed at family members, as well as at doctors, nurses, and God. This venting of feelings can take on subtle forms, such as noncooperativeness, or aggressive forms, such as outright hostility.

It shouldn't be difficult to understand these feelings. Who wouldn't be resentful of a visitor or a doctor who cheerily comes by, trying to make one feel that dying isn't so bad? Who wouldn't feel betrayed by a God who is seen as purposefully taking away what He has the ability to give? The patient is likely to feel at this point that it is simply not fair for life to end. Protest—sometimes loud, verbal protest—is a patient's way of showing that she is still alive and wants to express feelings.

Family members at this point need to be empathic, and to realize that anger is indeed justified. Again, a key is to be a nonjudgmental listener. You can't change what is, but you can show that you understand your parent's feelings, without being defensive.

Bargaining

As these intense emotions give way and the patient is able to concede to the inevitability of death, a third stage appears, in which the patient "bargains," often with God, for more time. The patient may say, for example, "If only I could see my grandson graduate, I could die happy." Such extensions of time may be possible, either because of the patient's strong will to fulfill a final desire or because of medical treatment. But it also happens that one bargain may follow another and that sooner or later, the progression of the illness does not allow for bargains to be fulfilled.

At this point, it is helpful to share your own feelings of disappointment with your parent. If it seems unlikely, for instance, that your parent will live to see a grandson graduate, it may be helpful to acknowledge that you understand the meaning of this, and that the value she places on education is one which won't be forgotten.

What needs to be examined further is the possibility that pleas for an extension of time result from unresolved guilt. A dying person sometimes pleads for more time so that the wrongs of his or her life can be corrected before death. If this seems to be the case for your parent, the kindest thing you can do is to help your parent identify and express those feelings, especially to the party who is directly involved. Such coming to terms can greatly ease a heavy heart. (See Chapter 6, "Emotional/Psychological Concerns," especially the material on life review.)

Depression

When the patient has given up denial and the active emotionality of anger, and has left bargaining behind, depression—the fourth stage—often sets in. This depression can be of two kinds. The first, and probably the easiest to handle from the family's point of view, stems from a sense of helplessness that develops when the patient feels that loose ends have not been tied. Your parent may be depressed because she does not know which adult child will look after her surviving spouse, or even who will take care of her pet after her death. Uncertainties such as these can weigh heavily on the dying person's mind, and you can certainly help your parent to "put things in place." Her thoughts are also likely to center on the funeral arrangements. While your parent may not want to attend to all funeral details, it is very possible that she will want to convey her general wishes. Talking over her wishes and assuring your parent that you will follow them can help to set her mind at ease.

The second type of depression is not as easy to deal with. In working with dying patients, Kübler-Ross noted that a sort of mourning often takes place before peaceful acceptance is achieved. To the dying individual, loss is everywhere—music that will no longer be heard, beauty that will no longer be seen, tasks that will no longer be accomplished, loved ones who will no longer be near to comfort and bring happiness. The world may seem beautiful, but fast slipping out of reach.

This type of overwhelming depression, as your parent prepares to die, will have powerful effects on family members as well. It is likely that you will feel helpless during this phase. The helplessness is real. You can't give back to your parent what is about to be lost.

Dealing with this grief most effectively is a matter of simply being there. There may not be words to "make it better," but feelings can be conveyed through your gestures. Touching or holding hands as your parent grieves for all the joys, hopes, and loves of life that will be lost can bring comfort to you both.

Acceptance

The final stage—acceptance—is one of quiet resolution, characterized by a near lack of emotions. The patient who has achieved acceptance and is prepared to die has come a long way. Yet families of these patients are sometimes in great pain. Because the patient who has reached this point tends to detach herself from others—to look ahead rather than behind—families may have the feeling that their loved one is already partially lost.

For you, this phase will probably mark the transition between acceptance of the reality of your parent's dying and your mourning of the actual loss. For your parent, it might be useful to keep in mind that although her great need for communication has probably diminished, the desire for supportive contact remains. Just being there and showing your own form of quiet resolution can go a long way toward assuring your parent that you will be all right.

To work in opposition to that peace which your parent has attained, to beg your parent to hold on or to fight harder, is to put a great burden on the dying patient. When acceptance has come, it should be cherished, not fought against.

When Your Parent Dies

Even if your parent is old and her death long anticipated, the end can come suddenly. Depending upon where your parent lives and your own proximity, you may or may not be with her in those last moments. For those who are able to be with their parent as death takes place, the experience has been reported as one of great closeness. One middle-aged woman commented that being afforded the opportunity to comfort and be close to her father at the end seemed to her like a reward for having endured through the dying process. Not all children are given this opportunity. Your parent may not reside close by, or may die before you arrive, or suddenly, while you are preoccupied with something else. Yet, if you have prepared yourself emotionally, and feel confident that your parent has reached acceptance, your pain at her actual death can be greatly eased.

Carrying Out Your Parent's Wishes

Some adult children find after a parent dies that the parent has already arranged and paid for his or her own funeral. Many parents who purchase such pre-need funeral plans do so with the intention of sparing their survivors agony, uncertainty, and financial obligation. They may also feel that by selecting the elements of their own funeral, they are making their presence deeply felt and having their final say, and that the service will therefore be more meaningful to the survivors.

Such arrangements can work in a number of ways. Sometimes, details of the funeral and services are chosen and then financed or prepaid. Charges are based on costs at the time the arrangements are made, with the expectation that the interest-which accrues on the money paid (through trust fund invest-ment) will make up for inflationary increases that have occurred between the time of the arrangements and the time of death. Your parent may have purchased such a plan or may have dis-cussed options with an undertaker, made choices, and left behind instructions to be followed. In either case, you and your family should be able to carry out your parent's wishes regarding funeral arrangements.

Your parent may have had a desire to make a body or organ donation. If so, she probably made arrangements in advance by signing a donor card in the presence of two witnesses. This card is a legal document and specifies your parent's wishes. (For addresses of sources to contact for more information, see Appendix D.) Your parent should have notified her physician, lawyer, and close rela-tives about the decision. Even if your parent has donated organs, it is still possible for survivors to hold a funeral, with either cremation or burial, and, in some cases, to have a viewing.

For a great variety of reasons, many parents do not make arrangements and do not even discuss these issues with their children. You may therefore find yourself in a position of respon-sibility with respect to your parent's funeral arrangements. What follows is the information you are likely to need in order to make what are often very painful decisions. One source of assistance might be a memorial society. You can probably find one by looking in the yellow pages of your phone book under the head-ing "Funeral Services" or "Memorial Societies."

Cremation

Cremations—although still outnumbered by burials and entomb-ments—are gaining in popularity. For the most part, these are "no-frills" funerals. Unless viewing takes place prior to the cre-mation, embalming usually need not be done. Further, the price of the coffin chosen for cremation is generally lower than that of one chosen for burial. Eliminating the costs of both embalming and a traditional coffin greatly reduces the overall funeral costs and simplifies the process. Ashes can be placed in an urn and given to survivors, buried in a special section of the cemetery, stored in a special compartment (similar to a mausoleum), or scattered in a desired location.[12]

Making Funeral Arrangements

Funeral costs can range from less than $1000 to $10,000, depending largely on the price of the coffin. Most coffins cost roughly between $1000 and $2000. Cemetery costs can range from several hundred to several thousand dollars.[13] Critics of the funeral industry contend that funeral directors often coax survivors into arranging a costly funeral. This criticism may sometimes be justified. One woman reported that when her mother died she thought about what type of arrangements would best suit her mother's wishes as well as her own budget. She was determined not to spend more than she could afford on the funeral. Yet, when she and her brother described the kind of arrangements they had in mind, the funeral director said it sounded like they wanted a "welfare funeral." This prompted them to buy a more expensive funeral than they could afford.

It should be remembered, though, that survivors often come into the funeral home in a distraught state, expecting direct guidance from the undertaker. One woman reported that when her mother died she was relieved that the funeral director made all the arrangements and decisions. She said she felt like a "zombie" and was glad to be a player in, rather than the director of, the proceedings. You may not know in advance what your frame of mind will be or what subtle pressures might be used by the undertaker. You can allow yourself to take comfort in accepting advice and guidance from a funeral director, but you should not be manipulated into spending more money than you want, or into having more elaborate services than you think are necessary or in good taste. The best approach is to choose a funeral director you can trust. It may be possible to make a reasonably informed choice based on the reputation of the director or on how long the home has been serving the community. In some cases, you may be able to obtain information about the reputations of the funeral homes in the area through your community or occupational affiliations, such as clergy or even labor unions.

If you choose burial, once a home has been selected, the process of making the arrangements begins. Many people assume that survivors will opt for an open casket. It is with that assumption that an exploration of options begins.

Open versus Closed Caskets

In favor of an open casket, it is said that mourners benefit from seeing the body of their loved one, that viewing encourages acceptance of the reality of death and provides survivors an opportunity to say good-bye. Critics of the funeral industry contend that undertakers endorse this view because they earn additional profits when an open casket is chosen. Critics further believe that viewing the body in whatever state or age it last existed arrests the process of remembering the fullness of an individual's life. They argue that freely sparked recollections and the feelings stirred by these memories are needed for eventual acceptance to take place. They also argue that open coffins represent denial rather than acceptance of the death state, since the mortician's job is to make the deceased look as "lifelike" as possible. Whatever position you are inclined to take, you should know that open-casket viewing can substantially add to overall funeral costs, owing to preparation work and use of the home's facilities.

If you choose an open casket, cosmetic restoration will be done in order to create an acceptable appearance for viewing. In order to carry this out, the undertaker will need to embalm the body, or replace the blood with preserving fluids. The undertaker will also need to ask you about burial clothes, hairstyle, and other details of grooming. Clothing can be purchased from the funeral home, which saves the anguish of going shopping for just that purpose, although such clothing will be more expensive than you would ordinarily expect. Or you can select clothing from the wardrobe of your deceased parent.

If you choose a closed coffin, the decision about whether or not to embalm may be left up to you. You should be aware that the funeral director will probably advise you to have this service performed, or even assume that you want it done. You can protect your right to choose by inquiring about legal requirements in your state and insisting that it not be done if that is your option and your wish. Also, remember to see that charges for services not carried out are dropped from your final bill.

Choosing a Coffin

A second decision, and probably the major one in terms of expense, will be in purchasing a coffin. Coffins are made in three basic materials—softwoods (such as pine, chestnut, or cedar) covered with cloth, finely finished hardwoods, and metals of various kinds. Interior materials vary also, with linings ranging from broadcloth to silk, and foundations made of different-quality mattresses or even spring-and-mattress sets.

Because of the diversity of possible exterior and interior combinations, pricing is highly variable. You can expect the coffins that are made out of softwoods to be the least expensive, while those made from hardwoods will be substantially higher. Metal units will vary in price according to the type of metal used.

Because coffins are the major hard commodity that undertakers sell, you may expect to encounter a certain amount of sales finesse. Not infrequently, undertakers imply that the quality or cost of the coffin can be equated with the quality and depth of the relationship that existed between the purchaser and the deceased. This approach often succeeds in inducing the consumer to look at more expensive coffins. A second approach often taken is to appeal to a survivor's desire to "protect" the loved one's body. Undertakers and casket manufacturers stress the secure, airtight features of more expensive caskets. "Airtight" warranties may even be given for up to 50 years on some models, leading the purchaser to believe that the body will endure for a long period of time in them. This has not been proved.

If you are seeking an inexpensive to moderately priced coffin, you may have to show firmness and even insist on being shown models in your price range. Remember that the undertaker is not a dictator of morality, or a judge of the quality of your relationship with your parent. Resist being made to feel that there is an equation between your love and the value of the coffin or the long-term preservation of the body.

Coffin Enclosures

Caskets disintegrate in time, and the ground above tends to slowly cave in. Because of this, many cemeteries require that a coffin enclosure be used—either a vault or a grave liner. These are made from wood or cement and surround the coffin within the earth. As you might expect, cement enclosures are more durable than those made from wood. Undertakers can also sell you a vault, which is a one-piece enclosure. It is likely that you will be able to purchase a grave liner, or a sectional enclosure, directly from the cemetery. This second choice tends to be less expensive when available. Before purchasing either, it is a good idea to check with your parent's cemetery to see if an enclosure is required. Some cemeteries do not stipulate that an enclosure must be used, giving you the option of avoiding that expense.

Cemeteries

Many cemeteries are now expanding their offerings to include, in addition to traditional interments, community mausoleums and facilities for cremation. These options are growing in popularity as burial space is becoming scarcer.[14]

Traditional burial plots are still most favored. These can be loosely divided into two types: those that allow tombstones (restrictions are often placed on the material and size of the stone) and those that allow only flat plaques as memorials. This latter type may be found in what is sometimes referred to as a "memorial park," and generally this name is appropriate. Because the landscaping and the inconspicuous flat plaques tend to blend, these areas resemble parks more than they do our usual picture of cemetery grounds.

When calculating the cost of your parent's interment, to the price of the burial plot or entombing crypt must be added the charges for a coffin enclosure (if that is to be purchased from the cemetery), opening and closing of the grave or crypt, and purchase and setting of a memorial stone or plaque. There may be an extra, one-time charge for perpetual care of the grave site or crypt.

Comparison shopping among cemeteries is relatively easy, because cemetery personnel are generally willing to disclose price information over the phone. Assessing services and costs, then, will be a matter of contacting and comparing individual cemeteries. In addition to cost factors, you might also consider location, proximity of the plot to those of other relatives or friends, religious affiliation of the cemetery, and the attractiveness of the particular plot.

Funeral Services

Funeral services are designed to honor the deceased and to convey to those present the significance of his or her life. They also encourage the family to renew bonds among themselves. The coming together of family members can be a display of cohesion and mutual support. Services have a way of assuring those in grief that they are not alone.

In some religious faiths, funeral rites are well-established. They involve ceremonies that are based on an affirmation of faith and hope on the part of survivors. While such services often follow a format, it is generally the case that family members are permitted to choose scriptures, music, and messages, so that the memorial suits their personal tastes and needs and those of the deceased relation. In other faiths, funeral rites are based on a less-structured plan and depend to a greater degree on the wishes of family members. A specific clergy member may be chosen, for instance, because of his or her unique perspective or special relationship to the deceased.

For families who do not desire a religious service, a memorial service can still be conducted. Funeral directors can help to make arrangements so that individuals who were particularly close to your parent can speak, sharing thoughts and memories. Or you or the funeral director can conduct a more open style of service in which those gathered have the opportunity to share ideas and memories.

Remember that the choices belong to you and your family. The type of service you decide to hold in memory of your parent should be one which pleases and comforts you.

Experiencing Grief

We tend to think that the word "grief" is self-explanatory, that grieving begins and ends with extreme sadness and anguish. But, although sorrow is a major component of the grieving process, a range of emotions often make themselves felt during mourning. In addition to the sorrowful and related feelings of heartache, anguish, and emptiness, survivors often experience a mixture of self-related concerns. Many adult children feel relief that the burdens are finally over, or self-pity for all the worries, demands, and life upheavals that they have endured throughout their parent's illness. Anger may be felt at the realization that time with the parent passed so quickly, or so slowly. A child may feel anger at the perceived unjustness of the loss, or displeasure that the final days didn't go just the way the child had hoped.

It is important not to disallow feelings that don't "seem right." Some adult children believe, for instance, that it is disrespectful to feel relieved when a parent dies. They may fight back these emotions when they surface, refusing to acknowledge the relief component of their grief. Survivors who filter out such reactions are not likely to fully come to terms with their loss. Grief is a complex and very personal process, one that must be lived through honestly before resolution is possible.

There is no rule concerning how long the grieving process lasts. It is generally expected that the most intense period of emotional turmoil will not last for more than 6 months. Symptoms of grief, however, tend to reappear periodically during the first year or so of bereavement. Somatic disturbances such as weakness, chills, tremors, sleeplessness, loss of appetite, and even hallucinations (seeing the deceased everywhere) are a part of the grieving process, and, along with the feelings discussed, can be expected to cause discomfort during this time.

You should not berate yourself for failing to "get over" your loss in a short period of time. Despite the fact that you probably anticipated the death of your parent, the loss may feel very heavy. After all, your parent may well have been your principal source of comfort, moral support, and advice. The relationship between the two of you was built over many years and represents an intimacy that can't be replaced. It is sometimes even more difficult to mourn the loss of a parent you did not have a good relationship with. Sometimes a troubled relationship leaves a bereaved child feeing angry, guilty for feeling angry, and, ultimately, exhausted or depressed.

You should be cautious about your own physical well-being. It is a well-recognized fact that the death of a loved one carries with it a stress that can precipitate serious illness.[15] Religious customs such as the Catholic wake or the Jewish "sitting shiva" allow friends and family to mourn together and remind us that feelings of grief have their rightful place in life. The memories, fantasies, and dreams that you and your family have of your parents should not only be mulled over privately but also shared. It has been shown that it is helpful to have a confidant—someone with whom you can share a wide range of feelings. If you mourn alone, you may find yourself talking exclusively to the memory of your deceased parent. If the stress of grief is great for you over an extended period of time, it would be wise to seek counseling to facilitate the grieving process.

Chapter 13 _____

Conclusions and New Directions

> The lord hath decreed that ye worship none save him, and that ye show kindness to parents.... Lower unto them the wing of submission through mercy and say, "My lord, have mercy on them as they took care of me when I was little."
>
> *The Koran*

Fewer people are reaching the end of their life without experiencing some form of dependency, and yet the stress and strain on adult children caring for elderly parents has only very recently begun to receive attention. One study reported in 1986 concluded that "new research on the family responsibilities of workers shows that an unexpectedly high percentage of full-time office employees spend significant amounts of time caring for elderly relatives and friends." In a sample of employees at the Travelers Insurance Company in Hartford, Connecticut, it was found that 28 percent of those studied spent an average of 10.2 hours a week caring for elderly relatives or friends. Some full-time employees spent as many as 80 hours a week helping an elderly parent, and the vast majority said that caregiving had a negative impact on social and emotional well-being, as well as on fulfillment of other family responsibilities. In this study, as in others, most of the caregiving adults were between the ages of 41 and 56 (many still caring for their own children), and most were women (only 29 percent of men were primary caregivers to an elderly person). Of those receiving care, the average age was 77, close to 70 percent were women (most were mothers), and the majority lived independently in their own homes or apartments.[1]

All of the available evidence indicates that adult children do as much for their parents as was ever done by preceding generations, and yet middle-aged children feel guilty about how little help they give to their parents. One study showed that 60 percent of caregiving daughters felt guilty about not doing enough for their parents, and 75 percent agreed that children don't take care of their elderly parents as well as they did in the old days. Elaine Brody, a leading gerontologist, believes that the guilt adult children feel is based on myth. She suggests that "the good old days" are really the memories that adult children have of the time in which their parents cared for them. The level of care that an adult child offers a parent does not live up to the child's memory of the nurturance and support that was received from the parent. The roles of parent and child can never be totally reversed. You can never care for your parent the way she cared for you, and thus you may feel that you can never do or give enough. If you believe that other adult children today similarly do not do enough for their parents, your own guilt is likely to be somewhat diminished. "I don't do enough for my parent, and everybody else does what I do or even less." This attribution to others may be a kind of defensive operation.[2] If you accept your feeling that the debt of gratitude owed to your nurturing parent is beyond repayment, you may more easily appreciate the help you are *able* to give.

Adult children have not abandoned their elderly parents, but public and social policies have not fully recognized the strains on middle-aged children who are caring for their parents. Policymakers must first acknowlededge that the problems of old age do not strictly belong to elderly people, but that the entire family unit is involved. As political and social policy is made concerning the elderly population, it cannot be ignored that, for example, more and more middle-aged women are entering the work force. Much has already been written about how difficult it is for women to juggle career and child-care responsibilities. Soon there will be articles on how the "sandwich generation" can balance career, child-care, and parent-care responsibilities. As medical technologies continue to extend the lives of elderly parents, we had better make corresponding improvements in social and public policy or else come up with a new generation of pills to cope with massive burnout among the middle-aged population.

The Changing Status of Elderly People

Although elderly people have not been abandoned by their adult children, it is true that they enjoy less status than they did decades ago. One reason for this diminished status is that elderly people are more numerous.

Decades ago, when someone lived to a ripe old age it was a rare occurrence. People thought the elderly person was doing something right, and often attributed his or her longevity to wisdom. Now that there are so many elderly people, we know that it may not take any special ability to reach old age.

Although elderly people may have more money than ever before, a high percentage (25 percent) still live at or near the poverty level. But it is not only lack of money and an increase in numbers that has contributed to a loss of status among the elderly in our society. There is general agreement among social gerontologists that the status of the elderly in other industrial societies is also low. It seems that as a society becomes more technologically advanced, more complex, and more modern, the status of its elderly people correspondingly declines. In less complex, agricultural societies, the elderly are afforded more status, in part because they control the property rights, which they can pass on to their descendants. It would also seem that in societies where there is rapid change, the elderly are less sought after for information and advice. This is because so much information becomes quickly out-of-date or irrelevant. In agricultural societies an elderly person might be consulted about the weather or when to plant. In contemporary American society, on the other hand, one would probably not go to an elderly person to inquire about career opportunities, real estate, or home computers. The prevailing myth that science and technology, which is constantly changing, will inevitably lead us to happier, more fulfilled lives has contributed to elderly people's loss of status. Perhaps when it becomes apparent that technology alone does not have the power to save our souls, the elderly will be afforded more respect.

The status of the elderly isn't simply inversely related to the complexity of a culture. In some of the least complex societies—

hunting-and-gathering societies in particular—the elderly were in fact abandoned. "Abandonment occurs when older persons become so frail that their continued presence hinders the mobility of their band or tribe, which must move in pursuit of subsistence." Yet this abandonment does not appear to be related in any way to the notion of status. "Sometimes the frail elderly are considered quite useless and left by the side of the trail quite casually; sometimes with great pomp and ceremony. Often the elderly choose their own time of departure, preferring the anticipated benefits of the hereafter to the suffering of continued physical existence."[3] In some cultures the practice of abandonment was valued as a positive transition. In other words, the fact that in this culture we do not abandon our old is certainly not a sign that we grant them any more status than those who did.

Since ours is not a subsistence or nomadic culture, it may be that children who discuss the anthropological literature on abandonment are being indirectly aggressive, and that parents who do so may be indirectly looking for sympathy or attempting to engender guilt. If your parent brings up the fact that elderly Eskimos were left on the ice floes and that this may not be a bad idea, it is more likely that she is saddened by her chronic illnesses and the problems of growing old. Some impaired and disabled people have a very hard time adjusting to their new, less independent role. Although it is good for elderly people to resist dependency, some absolutely refuse to believe that anyone would love them if they needed care. A shift in roles may be difficult for adult children, but it is often more difficult for elderly parents. Some believe that only when they are nurturing and helping can they possibly be loved. It is important to reassure your parents that you do not only love them when they take care of you, and that their presence is important to you as an adult child. It is important to communicate this feeling precisely, because it is a hard one for many aging parents to fully accept.

Fading Support Systems

In the "good old days" the support systems for older people consisted of adult children, extended family, and friends and neighbors. Although the commitment of adult children has remained high, there are fewer of them. The extended family has become less extended, and the nature of the American community and neighborhood has changed.

One 85-year-old man I spoke with remembered that when he first came to this country, he was enormously impressed by the fact that Americans had porches in front of their homes and that many had front lawns as well as backyards. In Europe, he recalled, privacy was valued most and everyone's porches faced the back, whereas in the United States there was much more of a neighborly spirit. When an elderly American needed help in the early 1900s, he said, there were always neighbors on their front porches who were involved in the life of the community and who were able to help. There may not have been as many ideal communities at the turn of the century as this man remembers, but there may be even fewer today.

New Support Systems

Many adult children who at the present time do not need to provide much care for their parents are nonetheless worried that they may one day have to. Adult children beset with their own anxieties and responsibilities often think, "I'm barely managing to keep myself and my family halfway afloat. If there comes a time when I have to care for my parent, I will definitely go under." Examining how elderly people have been treated in other times and cultures will not take us far in our understanding of what is needed here and now. Adult children have very good reasons to be anxious about their parents getting old. The demographic facts, the sheer number of old, frail, impaired people alive today presents us with an unknown and unexplored situation. Clues and cues from the past can be of only limited help. Solutions involving a combination of informal supports (family, friends, and neighbors) and formal supports (governmental and professional agencies) are needed. A new working relationship between these two types of support systems must be established.

Studies have shown that there is a relationship between the kind of help that is provided by adult children and their economic status. Adult children at the lower income levels are more likely to provide services directly to a parent who needs help, whereas adult children at the higher income levels are more likely to hire people to help a parent. Adult children are perhaps the best coordinators of service providers. You are probably in the best position to determine what services can be obtained from friends, other family members, and the government agencies. In addition to being a coordinator of services, you may be especially good at providing emotional support. This means that you have to find a way to allow your parent to confide in you.

At present it appears that future research on informal support systems needs to focus on how to enable elderly parents and their children to confide in each other, and also how to enable siblings to cooperate and work together better. There are many more problems with formal support systems.

The Importance of Informal Support Systems

Adult children honor their parents. How much help do elderly parents receive from government? Research indicates that families provide 80 to 90 percent of medically related and personal care, in addition to help with household tasks, shopping, and transportation. Research in the 1960s and '70s showed that when an elderly parent was institutionalized it was because there was no family, or because the family's caregiving capacities were stretched to the limit by the parent's chronic physical or mental impairment. "After prolonged and strenuous efforts to care for their parents, adult children reached the limits of endurance."[4] The family also provides the social and emotional support, the affection and the warmth that goes beyond what can be tabulated numerically.

More and more research is pointing to the fact that confiding in others improves not only mental but physical health. Psychotherapists have always known that there is value in getting things off your chest, but only recently has there been a substantial amount of scientific evidence to back up this assertion. If your parent is carrying around fears, guilt, or unspoken remorse, she is better off confiding in someone. It may not be easy or painless for her to express these feelings, and it may be just as difficult for you to listen, but if your parent has no one else to confide in, you would be doing her a great service by allowing her to confide in you. One researcher contacted the spouses of people who had died in car accidents or suicides. He found that those who had kept their grief to themselves were much more likely to have developed physical problems. Although it is a topic of ongoing debate, insurance companies have found that people in psychotherapy are much less likely to go to physicians.[5]

New Directions for Informal Support Systems

Not all adult children are equally gifted at being able to listen effectively to their parents' troubles. For some families there is no problem; for other families, the introduction of effective listening could be the most important change. One question that researchers have virtually ignored is how to assist adult children in becoming more effective listeners. Parallel assistance should also be given to elderly parents who need to learn to listen better to their children. *The available evidence indicates that when parents and children are better able to confide in each other, health costs in this country will go down.*

Another important area on which interest and research should be focused is the relationship between the siblings of elderly parents. There is some research that indicates that as siblings mature they mellow a bit and are better able to cooperate with each other when a parent needs help.[6] However, this is not always the case. The pressures of parent care often stir up unresolved sibling conflicts that were dormant for decades. It is not so unusual for a 55-year-old to yell, "I do everything for mommy and she still likes you better! It's just not fair!" More effort needs to be devoted to finding ways for siblings to resolve rivalries and cooperate more effectively when a parent needs help. So far, virtually no research has addressed this most important question.

It should be pointed out, however, that problems that siblings have with their elderly parents cannot and need not always be resolved by a family therapist. There is nothing unusual or "abnormal" about many of the families who are pressed to the breaking point by their responsibilities. They often don't need therapists, but they need and have a right to expect help from the government. When you care for an aging parent, even in the very best of circumstances, you still have to confront the fact that she will soon be leaving you and that you are mortal as well. You also recognize that you may someday need help or be dependent on your own children. These are not experiences that can be negotiated easily. Even the strongest, healthiest, and most emotionally mature adult children sometimes are unable to meet the needs of a dependent impaired parent. The healthiest and most normal families may need help from government and professional agencies.

New Directions for Formal Support Systems

Although children in our society honor their parents, it sometimes seems that government does not. Today, the government makes pious speeches about the family, but adult children do not need to be cheered on and encouraged to help their parents. They already do as much as can be expected. Politicians sometimes talk about creating incentives for children to assist their parents. Such talk is insulting, because it implies that adult children do not adequately fulfill their filial responsibilities when, in fact, they do.

Government policies designed to address the needs of elderly citizens sometimes operate as though there are no adult children, as though there are no families. The adult child who is caring for a parent, performing chores and duties, and offering emotional and possibly financial support so that her parent does not use Medicaid, is not likely to get any recognition or support from the government. In fact, adult children who put time into helping their parents when they might otherwise be working are likely not only to make less money, but to get less social security income when they retire. Thus, adult children who assist their parents by taking time from work are currently being penalized by the system.

Social security has been extremely effective in many respects. In 1937, one out of every two elderly people in the United States received some form of economic support from family members. By 1979 that figure had dropped to 1.5 percent. However, the future of social security is cloudy. The anxiety of adult children is not alleviated by their widely held suspicion that social security will no longer be functioning by the time they get to retirement age. In one survey of over 1000 adults, only 30 percent of those not yet of retirement age believed that there will be enough money in social security to pay them benefits when they retire.

The newest Medicare regulations are already creating more serious problems not only for the elderly but for adult children. There is every indication that older hospital patients will continue to be discharged "quicker and sicker" than ever before. The additional stress and strain this puts on adult children has not yet been well publicized.

More backup services are needed for responsible caregiving children, and for working women in particular. The stress and strain that is experienced by working children who care for parents is in many cases too great a burden. Counseling for the adult child, self-help groups, respite, and adult day care are very much needed and hardly available in many parts of the country. In fact, where they do exist, such services—though already quite minimal—are being cut back, sometimes with the justification that they are not consistent with "old-time family values." Research has shown, however, that services which offer some relief, such as respite, strengthen the family's ability to care for an elderly parent. Not only family, but government, too, has a responsibility for impaired or frail elderly people. When government officials call for more sacrifice from family members, they are not helping elderly people or their children. They are instead disguising their own irresponsibility!

Just Enough Help

As has been pointed out, one of the most difficult dilemmas you will face as an adult child is knowing how much help to provide for your parent. Although it is best to help your parent do for herself, there are times when she may need to lean on you heavily. It is important not to avoid this because you feel it will create too much dependency. The loss of a loved one or a serious illness or injury could force your parent to be dependent on you for a period of time. At some point after your parent regains some strength, though, it is best to encourage her to be more independent. If this is physically impossible, she should be encouraged to do as much as she can for herself for as long as she can. It is important to periodically review your parent's care needs and the care you provide. Sometimes a service provided is no longer needed and sometimes more care is necessary. Remember that what was effective a year ago may not be today.

It is a mistake to go beyond your own limits in caring for a parent. Some adult children refuse to consider nursing home placement, even when continuing to care for an impaired parent may mean destroying the rest of the family. An unfavored child may do this if she or he is still trying to gain the approval of the parent, whereas favored children may go to unreasonable extremes because they feel they can never do enough to repay a loving parent.

Another reason why it is important not to do too much for your parent is that parents do not want to be overly dependent on their children. In a nationwide poll of 1476 adults, 6 out of 10 young adults (those between the ages of 18 and 34) said they believed that it is better for older people who cannot take care of themselves to live with their children than to be placed in a nursing home. In the over-65 age group, only 3 in 10 agreed. In other words, most of the over-65 group think it is preferable to be in a nursing home than to live with their children.[7]

Helping Your Parent to Stay Self-Sufficient

The current situation suggests that families and government will both have to pay closer attention to the prevention of problems than to their remediation. No matter what age your parent is, it is useful to provide emotional support, to provide inspiration, to encourage your parent to be ambitious and to look forward. Not enough attention has been given to the issue of postponing and even preventing elderly parents from having to depend on their families or on governmental supports. Whatever you can do to help your parent to remain independent and able to care for herself is important.

Some adult children discourage their parents from beginning new relationships, learning new skills, developing new interests. It is a big mistake to try to obstruct your parent's attempts at growing and being autonomous. It is not so unusual for someone who is 75 years old to first learn how to drive, and it certainly makes more sense to encourage your parent to brush up on driving skills than to chauffeur her around. If your parent can maintain a sense of self-sufficiency by being with friends or making new ones, or developing a relationship with a member of the opposite sex, you should be supportive and encouraging.

Today's young adults believe that their parents were too permissive about such things as dating and sexuality. Let us hope these adult children do not attempt to stunt the growth of their parents. The widespread ageism in our society should be recognized and fought against by adult children, who should encourage their parents to try new things and to take risks.

Although there are reasons to be concerned about where our society is headed, in regard to the increasing numbers of elderly parents and the stress that this puts on their families there are reasons to be optimistic. There is a great incentive to help elderly parents and to work out solutions to the problems. Elderly people themselves make up a large constituency, and they tend to vote more than other age groups. Even politicians and social planners have parents. Although, as I stated, the past can only be of limited assistance as we seek solutions to the problems facing families with aging parents, there are basic guidelines and rules that were formulated centuries ago. We must remind our legislators, our policymakers and social planners, of these rules, which, if followed, can allow us to live a more satisfying life. One such rule states simply, "Honor thy mother and thy father: that thy days may be long upon the land which the Lord thy God giveth thee."

Appendix A_____
State Agencies on Aging

ALABAMA

Emmett W. Eaton
Executive Director
Commission on Aging
State Capitol
Montgomery, AL 36130
(205) 261-5743

ALASKA

Mr. Jon B. Wolfe
Executive Director
Older Alaskans Commission
Pouch C. Mail Stop 0209
Juneau, AK 99811
(907) 465-3250

ARIZONA

Mr. Michael Slattery
Director
Aging and Adult Administration
P.O. Box 6123
1400 W. Washington Street
Phoenix, AZ 85005
(602) 255-4446

ARKANSAS

Herb Sanderson
Director
Arkansas State Office on Aging
Donaghey Building, Suite 1428
7th and Main Streets
Little Rock, AR 72201
(501) 371-2441

CALIFORNIA

Ms. Alice Gonzales
Director
Department of Aging
1020 19th Street
Sacramento, CA 95814
(916) 322-5290

COLORADO

Mr. William J. Hanna
Director
Aging and Adult Services Division
Department of Social Services
Room 503
1575 Sherman Street
Denver, CO 80220
(303) 866-2586

CONNECTICUT

Mary Ellen Klincke
Director
Department on Aging
175 Main Street
Hartford, CT 06106
(203) 566-7725

DELAWARE

Ms. Eleanor L. Gain
Director
Division of Aging
Department of Health and Social
    Services
1901 N. Dupont Highway
New Castle, DE 19720
(302) 421-6791

DISTRICT OF COLUMBIA

Ms. E. Veronica Pace
Director
Office on Aging
Office of the Mayor
1424 K Street, N.W.
Washington, DC 20005
(202) 724-5622

FLORIDA

Ms. Margaret Lynn Duggar
Director
Program Office of Aging and Adult
    Services
Department of Health and
    Rehabilitation Services
1323 Winewood Boulevard
Tallahassee, FL 32301
(904) 488-8922

GEORGIA

Mr. Fred McGinnis
Office of Aging
878 Peachtree Street, N.E.
Room 632
Atlanta, GA 30309
(404) 894-5333

HAWAII

Mr. Renji Goto
Director
Executive Office on Aging
Office of the Governor
1149 Bethel Street, Room 307
Honolulu, HI 96813
(808) 548-2593

IDAHO

Ms. Maria Salazar
Acting Director
Idaho Office on Aging
Room 114-Statehouse
Boise, ID 83720
(208) 334-3833

ILLINOIS

Ms. Janet S. Otwell
Director
Department on Aging
421 E. Capitol Avenue
Springfield, IL 62706
(217) 785-3356

INDIANA

Ms. Jean Merritt
Executive Director
Indiana Department on Aging &
    Community Services
115 N. Pennsylvania Street
Suite 1350
Indianapolis, IN 46204
(317) 232-7006

IOWA

Ms. Karen L. Tynes
Executive Director
Commission on Aging
Jewett Building
914 Grand Avenue, Suite 236
Des Moines, IA 50319
(515) 281-5187

KANSAS

Ms. Sylvia Hougland
Secretary
Department on Aging
610 W. 10th Street
Topeka, KS 66612
(913) 296-4986

KENTUCKY

Ms. Marge Brock
Division for Aging Services
Department of Human Resources
DHR Building, 6th Floor
275 E. Main Street
Frankfort, KY 40601
(502) 564-6930

LOUISIANA

Ms. Sandra Adams
Director
Office of Elderly Affairs
4528 Bennington Avenue
P.O. Box 80374
Baton Rouge, LA 70898-0374
(504) 925-1700

MAINE

Ms. Patricia Riley
Director
Bureau of Maine's Elderly
Department of Human Services
State House, Station No. 11
Augusta, ME 04333
(207) 289-2561

MARYLAND

Ms. Rosalie Abrams
Director
Office on Aging
State Office Building
301 W. Preston Street
Baltimore, MD 21201
(301) 383-5064

MASSACHUSETTS

Richard Rowland
Secretary
Department of Elderly Affairs
38 Chauncy Street
Boston, MA 02111
(617) 727-7751

MICHIGAN

Ms. Olivia Maynard
Director
Office of Services to the Aging
P.O. Box 30026
Lansing, MI 48909
(517) 373-8230

MINNESOTA

Mr. Gerald A. Bloedow
Executive Director
Metro Square Building, Room 204
7th and Roberts Streets
St. Paul, MN 55101
(612) 296-2544

MISSISSIPPI

Dr. David K. Brown
Executive Director
Mississippi Council on Aging
Executive Building, Suite 301
Jackson, MS 39201
(601) 354-6590

MISSOURI

Mr. Rick Westphal
Director
Division on Aging
Department of Social Services
Broadway State, P.O. Box 570
Jefferson City, MO 65101
(314) 651-3082

MONTANA

Ms. Norma Harris
Administrator
Community Services Division
P.O. Box 4210
Helena, MT 59604
(406) 444-3865

NEBRASKA

Ms. Helen Boosalis
Executive Director
Department on Aging
P.O. Box 95044
301 Centennial Mall South
Lincoln, NE 68509
(402) 471-2306

NEVADA

Myla C. Florence
Administrator
Division for Aging Services
Department of Human Resources
505 E. King Street
Kinkhead Building M, Room 101
Carson City, NV 89710
(702) 885-4210

NEW HAMPSHIRE

Ms. Anna M. Pluhar
Director
Council on Aging
14 Depot Street
Concord, NH 03301
(603) 271-2751

NEW JERSEY

Ms. Ann Zahora
Director
Division on Aging
Department of Community Affairs
363 W. State Street
CN 807
Trenton, NJ 08625-0807
(609) 292-4833

NEW MEXICO

George Ellis
Executive Director
State Agency on Aging
La Villa Rivera Building
224 E. Palace Avenue, 4th Floor
Santa Fe, NM 87501
(505) 827-7640

NEW YORK

Mr. Eugene Callendar
Director
Office for the Aging
New York State Executive
    Department
Empire State Plaza
Agency Building No. 2
Albany, NY 12223
(518) 474-5731

NORTH CAROLINA

Mr. Ernest B. Messer
Director
Division of Aging
708 Hillsboro Street, Suite 200
Raleigh, NC 27603
(919) 733-3983

NORTH DAKOTA

Mr. Larry Brewster
Director
Aging Services
Department of Human Services
State Capitol Building
Bismark, ND 58505
(701) 224-2577

OHIO

Joyce F. Chapple
Executive Director
Ohio Department of Aging
50 W. Broad Street, 9th Floor
Columbus, OH 43215
(624) 466-5500

OKLAHOMA

Mr. Roy R. Keen
Supervisor
Special Unit on Aging
Department of Human Services
P.O. Box 25352
Oklahoma City, OK 73125
(405) 521-2281

OREGON

Mr. Richard C. Ladd
Administrator
Oregon Senior Services Division
313 Public Service Building
Salem, OR 97310
(503) 378-4728

PENNSYLVANIA

Ms. Alma R. Jacobs
Secretary of Aging
Department of Aging
Finance Building
231 State Street, Room 307
Harrisburg, PA 17120
(717) 783-1550

RHODE ISLAND

Mrs. Adelaide Luber
Director
Department of Elderly Affairs
79 Washington Street
Providence, RI 02903
(401) 277-2858

SOUTH CAROLINA

Mr. Harry Bryant
Executive Director
Commission on Aging
915 Main Street
Columbia, SC 29201
(803) 758-2576

SOUTH DAKOTA

Mr. Michael Vogel
Administrator
Office of Adult Services and Aging
Department of Social Services
Richard F. Kneip Building
700 N. Illois Street
Pierre, SD 57501-2291
(605) 773-3656

TENNESSEE

Ms. Emily M. Wiseman
Executive Director
Commission on Aging
703 Tennessee Building
535 Church Street
Nashville, TN 37219
(615) 741-2065

TEXAS

Mr. O. P. (Bob) Bobbit
Executive Director
Texas Department on Aging
210 Barton Springs Road
5th Floor
Austin, TX 78704
(512) 475-2717

UTAH

Dr. Robert Ward
Division of Aging and Adult
  Services
Department of Social Services
150 W. North Temple
Salt Lake City, UT
84110-2500
(802) 533-6422

VERMONT

Mary Ellen Spencer
Director
Office on Aging
103 Main Street
Waterbury, VT 05676
(802) 241-2400

VIRGINIA

Ms. Wilda Ferguson
Director
Office on Aging
101 N. 14th Street, 18th Floor
James Monroe Building
Richmond, VA 23219
(804) 225-2271

VIRGIN ISLANDS

Mrs. Gloria M. King
Director
Commission on Aging
6F Havensight Mall
Charlotte Amalie
Saint Thomas, VI 00801
(809) 774-5884

WASHINGTON

Mr. Charles Reed
Director
Bureau of Aging and Adult Services
Department of Social and Health
  Services
OB-43G
Olympia, WA 98504
(206) 753-2502

WEST VIRGINIA

Mr. Phil Turner
Director
Commission on Aging
State Capitol
Charleston, WV 25305
(304) 348-3317

WISCONSIN

Ms. Donna McDowell
Director
Bureau on Aging
1 W. Wilson Street, Room 685
Madison, WI 53702
(608) 272-8606

WYOMING

Mr. Scott Sessions
Director
State of Wyoming
Wyoming Commission on Aging
Hathaway Building, #139
Cheyenne, WY 82002
(307) 777-7986

AMERICAN SAMOA

Mr. Tali Maae
Director
Territorial Aging Program
Government of American Samoa
Office of the Governor
Pago Pago, American Samoa 96799
Samoa 3-1254 or 3-4116

GUAM

Mr. Franklin Cruz
Director
Office of Aging, Social Services
Department of Public Health
Government of Guam
Agana, Guam 96910
749-9901, Ext. 423

PUERTO RICO

Ms. Alicia Ramirez Suarez
Executive Director
Gericulture Commission
Department of Social Services
P.O. Box 11398
Santurce, PR 00910
(809) 722-2429

TRUST TERRITORY OF THE
PACIFIC ISLANDS

Mrs. Erlinda T. Dumatol
Director
Office on Aging
Trust Territory of the Pacific Islands
Saipan, CM 96950
9335-9328

Appendix B

Information on Nursing Homes

ALABAMA

Fred Draper
Executive Vice President
Alabama Nursing Home Association
4140 Carmichael Road
Montgomery, AL 36106
(205) 271-6214

ALASKA

Dennis L. DeWitt
President
Health Association of Alaska
319 Seward Street
Juneau, AK 99801
(907) 586-1790

ARIZONA

William Walker
Executive Director
Arizona Nursing Home Association
124 W. Thomas Road, Suite 101
Phoenix, AZ 85013
(602) 277-0813

ARKANSAS

Jack Riggs
Executive Director
Arkansas Long Term Care
   Association
1324 W. Capitol Avenue
Little Rock, AR 72201
(501) 374-4422

CALIFORNIA

Ronald M. Kurtz
Executive Vice President
California Association of Health
   Facilities
1401 21st Street, Suite 202
Sacramento, CA 95814
(916) 444-7600

COLORADO

Arlene Linton
Executive Director
Colorado Health Care Association
1390 Logan Street, Suite 316
Denver, CO 80203
(303) 861-8228

CONNECTICUT

Louis Halpryn
Executive Vice President
Connecticut Association of Health
  Care Facilities
131 New London Turnpike, Suite 18
Glastonbury, CT 06033
(203) 659-0391

DELAWARE

Rev. Richard Stazesky
Executive Director
Delaware Health Care Facilities
  Association
3801 Kennett Pike
Building 200
Wilmington, DE 19807
(302) 571-0822

FLORIDA

Bill Phelan
Executive Director
Florida Health Care Association
215 S. Bronough Street
Tallahassee, FL 32301
(904) 224-3907

GEORGIA

J. Wendell Brigance
Executive Vice President
Georgia Health Care Association
3735 Memorial Drive
Decatur, GA 30032
(404) 284-8700

HAWAII

Lynda Johnson
Vice President
Hospital Association of Hawaii
320 Ward Avenue, Suite 202
Honolulu, HI 96814
(808) 521-8961

IDAHO

Dale C. Shirk
Executive Vice President
Idaho Health Care Association
820 W. Washington
Suite 206
Boise, ID 83701
(208) 343-9735

ILLINOIS

Rick L. Middleton
President
Illinois Health Care Association
1029 S. 4th Street
Springfield, IL 62703
(217) 528-6455

INDIANA

Richard L. Butler
Executive Director
Indiana Health Care Association
One North Capitol, Suite 1115
Indianapolis, IN 46204
(317) 636-6406

IOWA

Larry L. Breeding
Executive Vice President
Iowa Health Care Association
950 12th Street
Des Moines, IA 50309
(515) 282-0666

KANSAS

Richard (Dick) Hummel
Executive Director
Kansas Health Care Association
221 Southwest 33rd
Topeka, KS 66611
(913) 267-6003

KENTUCKY

James S. Judy
Executive Vice President
Kentucky Association of Health
  Care Facilities
903 Collins Lane
Frankfort, KY 40602 (40601)
(502) 875-1500

LOUISIANA

Steven E. Adams
Executive Director
Louisiana Health Care Association
7921 Picardy Avenue
Baton Rouge, LA 70809
(504) 769-3705

MAINE

Ronald Thurston
Executive Director
Maine Health Care Association
303 State Street
Augusta, ME 04330
(207) 623-1146

MARYLAND

Fred D. Chew
Executive Director
Health Facilities Association of
  Maryland
10400 Connecticut Avenue
Suite 300
Kensington, MD 20895
(301) 933-5550

MASSACHUSETTS

Ned Morse
Executive Director
Massachusetts Federation of
  Nursing Homes
886 Washington Street
Dedham, MA 02026
(617) 326-8967

MICHIGAN

Charles Harmon
Executive Vice President
Health Care Association of
  Michigan
501 S. Capitol Avenue, Suite 335
Lansing, MI 48933
(517) 371-1700

MINNESOTA

Rick Carter
Executive Vice President
Minnesota Association of Health
  Care Facilities
2850 Metro Drive, Suite 429
Minneapolis, MN 55420
(612) 854-2844

MISSISSIPPI

Martha Carole White
Executive Director
Mississippi Health Care Association
4444 N. State Street
Jackson, MS 39206
(601) 362-2527

MISSOURI

Earl Carlson, Jr.
Executive Director
Missouri Health Care Association
263 Metro Drive
Jefferson City, MO 65101
(314) 635-9283

MONTANA

Rose Skoog
Executive Director
Montana Health Care Association
36 S. Last Chance Gulch, Suite A
Helena, MT 59601
(406) 443-2876

NEBRASKA

Sandra Hockley
Executive Director
Nebraska Health Care Association
3100 "O" Street, Suite 7
Lincoln, NE 68510
(402) 435-3551

NEVADA

Dave Nicholas
Executive Director
Nevada Health Care
  Association
1150 E. Williams
Suite 203
Carson City, NV 98702
(702) 885-1006

NEW HAMPSHIRE

Jean Claude Sakellarios
Executive Director
New Hampshire Health Care
  Association
130 Silver Street
Manchester, NH 03103
(603) 669-1663

NEW JERSEY

James Cunningham
President
New Jersey Association of Health
  Care Facilities
2131 Route 33
Lexington Square Commons
Trenton, NJ 08690
(609) 890-8700

NEW MEXICO

Jan Wiltgen
Executive Director
New Mexico Health Care
  Association
1024 Eubank N.E.
Suite B
Albuquerque, NM 87112
(505) 296-0021

NEW YORK

James Mullaley
Executive Director
New York State Health Facilities
  Association
290 Elwood Davis Road
Syracuse, NY 13221-4938
(315) 457-9100

NORTH CAROLINA

J. Craig Souza
Executive Vice President
North Carolina Health Care
  Association
5109 Bur Oak Circle
Raleigh, NC 27612
(919) 782-3827

NORTH DAKOTA

Allan B. Engen
Executive Director
North Dakota Health Care
  Association
513 East Bismarck Avenue
Bismarck, ND 58501
(701) 222-0660 or 222-4867

OHIO

Stephen G. Cochran
Executive Vice President
Ohio Health Care Association
50 Northwoods Boulevard
Worthington, OH 43085
(614) 436-4154

OKLAHOMA

Jon Hitt
Oklahoma Health Care Association
7707 South Memorial Drive
Tulsa, OK 74133
(918) 250-8571

OREGON

Dr. Hartzell J. Cobbs
Executive Director
Oregon Health Care Association
12200 N. Jantzen Avenue
Suite 380
Portland, OR 97217
(503) 285-9600

PENNSYLVANIA

Robert Benedict
Executive Vice President
Pennsylvania Health Care
  Association
1200 Camp Hill By-Pass
Camp Hill, PA 17011
(717) 763-7053, Extension 253

RHODE ISLAND

Alfred Santos
Executive Director
Rhode Island Health Care
  Association
144 Bignall Street
Warwick, RI 02888
(401) 785-9530

SOUTH CAROLINA

J. Randall Lee
Executive Director
South Carolina Health Care
  Association
1122 Lady Street, Suite 1118
Columbia, SC 29201
(803) 256-2681

SOUTH DAKOTA

Dennis Callies
Executive Director
South Dakota Health Care
  Association
301 S. Garfield, Suite 6
Sioux Falls, SD 57104-3198
(605) 339-2071

TENNESSEE

Richard T. Sadler
Executive Director
Tennessee Health Care Association
2809 Foster Avenue
Nashville, TN 37210
(615) 834-6520

TEXAS

Bob Conkright
Acting President
Texas Health Care Association
6225 U.S. 290 East
Austin, TX 78761 (78723)
(512) 458-1257

UTAH

Dennis McFall
President
Utah Health Care Association
1255 East 3900 South
Salt Lake City, UT 84124
(801) 268-9622

VERMONT

Edwin J. Foss
Executive Director
Vermont Health Care Association
58 E. State Street
Montpelier, VT 05602
(802) 229-5700

VIRGINIA

Peter Clendenin
Executive Director
Virginia Health Care Association
2112 W. Laburnum Avenue
Suite 206
Richmond, VA 23227
(804) 353-9101

WASHINGTON

Leonard G. Eddinger, Jr.
Executive Director
Washington State Health Facilities
  Association
410 E. 11th, Suite 201
Olympia, WA 98507
(206) 352-3304

WEST VIRGINIA

Charles W. Caldwell
Executive Director
West Virginia Health Care
  Association
1115 Quarrier Street
Charleston, WV 25301
(304) 346-4575 or 346-4576

WISCONSIN

George F. MacKenzie
Executive Director
Wisconsin Association of Nursing
  Homes
14 S. Carroll Street, Suite 200
Madison, WI 53703-3376
(608) 257-0125

WYOMING

Dan J. Lex
Executive Director
Wyoming Health Care Association
809 Silver Sage Avenue
Cheyenne, WY 82003
(307) 635-2175

*Appendix C*_____
Hospice Information

The National Hospice Organization
1901 N. Fort Myer Drive, Suite 902
Arlington, VA 22209
(703) 243-5900

The Joint Commission on the Accreditation of Hospitals
875 N. Michigan Avenue
Chicago, IL 60611
(312) 642-6061

The American Cancer Society
90 Park Avenue
New York, NY 10016
Offers a free booklet, *The Hospice Concept*

The National Consumers League
815 15th Street, Suite 516
Washington, DC 20005

The Institute of Consumer Policy Research
  (a branch of Consumers Union)
256 Washington Street
Mount Vernon, NY 10553

Appendix D ————————
Uniform Donor Cards

American Medical Association*
535 N. Dearborn Street
Chicago, IL 60610
Attention: Order Department

Deafness Research Foundation*
366 Madison Avenue
New York, NY 10017

Eye Bank Association of America*
3195 Maplewood Avenue
Winston-Salem, NC 27103

Medic Alert*
P.O. Box 1009
Turlock, CA 95380

National Kidney Foundation*
116 E. 27th Street
New York, NY 10016

National Pituitary Agency*
210 West Fayette Street, Suite 503
Baltimore, MD 21201

National Temporal Bone Banks Center of the Deafness
  Research Foundation*
550 N. Broadway, Room 103
The Johns Hopkins University School of Medicine
Baltimore, MD 21205

Tissue Bank at Naval Medical Research Institute
Bethesda, MD 20814-5055

———————
*Will accept requests for uniform donor cards.

My Living Will
To My Family, My Physician, My Lawyer
and All Others Whom It May Concern

Death is as much a reality as birth, growth, maturity and old age—it is the one certainty of life. If the time comes when I can no longer take part in decisions for my own future, let this statement stand as an expression of my wishes and directions, while I am still of sound mind.

If at such a time the situation should arise in which there is no reasonable expectation of my recovery from extreme physical or mental disability, I direct that I be allowed to die and not be kept alive by medications, artificial means or "heroic measures". I do, however, ask that medication be mercifully administered to me to alleviate suffering even though this may shorten my remaining life.

This statement is made after careful consideration and is in accordance with my strong convictions and beliefs. I want the wishes and directions here expressed carried out to the extent permitted by law. Insofar as they are not legally enforceable, I hope that those to whom this Will is addressed will regard themselves as morally bound by these provisions.

(Optional specific provisions to be made in this space — see other side)

DURABLE POWER OF ATTORNEY (optional)

I hereby designate _____ to serve as my attorney-in-fact for the purpose of making medical treatment decisions. This power of attorney shall remain effective in the event that I become incompetent or otherwise unable to make such decisions for myself.

Optional Notarization:

"Sworn and subscribed to

before me this _____ day

of _____, 19_____."

_____
Notary Public
(seal)

Signed_____

Date _____

Witness _____

_____
Address

Witness _____

_____
Address

Copies of this request have been given to _____

_____   _____

(Optional)   My Living Will is registered with Concern for Dying (No. _____)

Distributed by Concern for Dying, 250 West 57th Street, New York, NY 10107 (212) 246-6962

Notes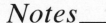

Chapter 1

1   D. Callahan, What do children owe elderly parents? *The Hastings Center Report,* April 1985, pp. 32–37.

2   D. Yankelovich, *New Rules: Searching for Self-Fulfillment in a World Turned Upside Down.* New York: Random House, 1981.

3   M. Sussman & J. Romeis, Willingness to assist one's elderly parents: Responses from United States and Japanese families. *Human Organization,* 1982, *41*(3), pp. 56–259.

4   E. Shanas, The family relations of old people. *The National Forum,* Fall 1982, *62,* p. 10.

Chapter 2

1   S. Minuchin, *Families and Family Therapy.* Cambridge: Harvard University Press, 1974.

2   E. A. Carter & M. McGoldrick, *The Family Life Cycle: A Framework for Family Therapy.* New York: Gardiner Press, 1980.

3   J. Haley, *Problem Solving Therapy: New Strategies for Effective Family Therapy.* New York: Harper Colophon, 1978.

Chapter 3

1   N. Darnton, Women and stress on job and at home. *The New York Times,* August 8, 1985, p. C1.

2   Study finds elderly women more susceptible to poverty. *The New York Times.* September 24, 1984, p. A17.

3   M. Cantor, *Caring for frail elderly: Impact on family, friends, and neighbors.* Paper presented at the 33rd annual scientific meeting of the Gerontological Society of America. San Diego, November 1980.

4   Ibid.

5   J. Kreps, Intergenerational transfers and the bureaucracy. In E. Shanas & M. Sussman (Eds.), *Family Bureaucracy and the Elderly*. Durham, N.C.: Duke University Press, 1977.

6   P. Laslett, *Family Life and Illicit Love in Earlier Generations*. Cambridge, England: Cambridge University Press, 1977.

7   The White House Conference on Aging. *Chartbook on Aging In America*, Washington, D.C.: U.S. Government Printing Office, 1981, p. 50.

8   Ibid, p. 56.

Chapter 4

1   C. G. Jung, *Memories, Dreams, Reflections*. New York: Vintage Books, 1961.

2   C. Rogers, *On Becoming a Person: A Therapist's View of Psychotherapy*. Boston: Houghton Mifflin, 1970.

3   M. E. P. Seligman, *Helplessness: On Depression, Development, and Death*. San Francisco: W. H. Freeman, 1975.

4   A. Miller, *The Drama of the Gifted Child*. New York: Basic Books, 1981.

5   J. Halpern & I. Halpern, *Projections: Our World of Imaginary Relationships*. New York: Seaview/Putnam, 1983.

6   Quoted by I. Kristol in a review of *The Good News Is the Bad News Is Wrong* by B. Wattenberg. *The New Republic*, October 29, 1984, p.37.

Chapter 5

1   B. L. Neugarten, Quoted in E. Hall, Acting one's age: New rules for old. *Psychology Today*, April 1980, pp. 66–80.

2   C. G. Jung, The practice of psychotherapy. In *The Collected Works of C. G. Jung*. (Vol. 16). Princeton, N.J.: Princeton University Press, 1954.

3   E. Erikson, *Childhood and Society*. New York: Norton, 1950.

4   G. Sheehy, *Passages: Predictable Crises of Adult Life*. New York: Dutton, 1976.

5   D. Levinson, *The Seasons of a Man's Life*. New York: Knopf, 1978.

6   C. Gilligan, *In a Different Voice: Psychological Theory and Women's Development*. Cambridge: Harvard University Press, 1982, p. 8.

7   M. Cantor, Strain among caregivers: A study of experience in the United States. *The Gerontologist*, 1983, *23*, 6, 597–604.

8   E. Stoller, Parental caregiving by adult children. *Journal of Marriage and the Family*, November 1983, *45*, (4), 851–858.

9   A. M. Lang & E. M. Brody, Characteristics of middle-aged daughters and help to their elderly mothers. *Journal of Marriage and the Family,* February 1983, *45* (1), 192–202.

10   Stoller. Loc. cit.

11   T. H. Holmes & R. H. Rahe, The social readjustment rating scale. *Journal of Psychosomatic Research,* 1967, *11,* 213–218.

12   R. S. Lazarus & J. B. Cohen, Environmental stress. In I. Altman & J. F. Wohlwill (Eds.), *Human Behavior and Environment: Current Theory and Research,* pp. 89–127. New York: Plenum, 1977.

13   A. D. Kanner, J. C. Coyne, C. Schaefer, & R. S. Lazarus, Comparison of two different modes of stress measurment: Daily hassles and uplifts vs. major life events. *Journal of Behavioral Medicine,* 1971, *4,*(9), 1–39.

14   H. Selye, *The Stress of Life.* New York: McGraw-Hill, 1956.

15   A. Bandura, Self-efficacy mechanism in human agency. *American Psychologist,* 1982, *37,*(2), 122–147.

16   C. J. Holahan & R. H. Moos, Social support and psychological distress: A longitudinal analysis. *Journal of Abnormal Psychology,* 1981, *90,*(4), 403–413.

17   C. J. Holahan & R. H. Moos, Social support and adjustment: Predictive benefits of social climate indices. *American Journal of Community Psychology,* 1982, *10,*(4), 403–413.

18   L. F. Berkman & S. L. Syme, Social networks, host resistance, and mortality: A nine year follow-up study of Alameda county residents. *American Journal of Epidemiology,* 1979, *109,* 186–224.

19   H. Benson, *The Relaxation Response.* New York: Morrow, 1975.

FOR FURTHER READING

Brody, E. M., Johnsen, P. T., Fulcomer, M. C., & Lang, A. M. Women's changing roles and help to the elderly: Attitudes of three generations of women. *Journal of Gerontology,* 1983, *38,* pp. 597–607.

Cicirelli, V. G. A comparison of helping behavior to elderly parents of adult children with intact and disrupted marriages. *The Gerontologist,* 1983, *23,*(6), pp. 619–625.

Lang, A. M. & Brody, E. Patterns of family support to middle-aged, older and very old women. Paper presented at the 33rd annual scientific meeting of the Gerontological Society of America, San Diego, November 1980.

Chapter 6

1   J. Weinberg, Quoted in *The National Institute of Senior Centers* (memo.) Washington, D.C.: National Council on the Aging, June/July 1975, p. 3.

2   Z. Rubin & E. B. McNeil, *The Psychology of Being Human* (4th ed.). New York: Harper & Row, 1985.

3   The Dialogues of Plato, Quoted in Morris, W., Understanding the aging process: Psychological aspects and their implications for economic need. In A. Hoffman (Ed.), *The Daily Needs and Interests of Older People*. Springfield, Ill.: Charles C. Thomas, 1970, p. 135.

4   E. Cumming & W. E. Henry, *Growing Old: The Process of Disengagement*. New York: Basic Books, 1961, pp. 14–15.

5   S. Freud, *Civilization and Its Discontents*. New York: Norton, 1962, p. 27.

6   United Nations, *The Aging: Trends and Policies*. New York: United Nations Department of Economic and Social Affairs, 1975, p. 11.

7   B. L. Neugarten, Personality and the aging process. *The Gerontologist*, 1972, *12*, 9–15.

8   K. W. Schaie, The Seattle longitudinal study: A twenty-one year exploration of psychometric intelligence in adulthood. In K. W. Schaie (Ed.), *Longitudinal Studies of Adult Development*. New York: Guilford Press, 1982.

9   P. R. Bruce, A. C. Coyne, & J. Botwinick, Adult age differences in metamemory. *Journal of Gerontology*, 1982, *3*, pp. 354–357.

10   B. F. Skinner, *A Matter of Consequences: Part 3 of an Autobiography*. New York: Random House, 1983.

11   J. Meer, Loneliness. *Psychology Today*, July 1985, pp. 28–33.

12   B. Houser & S. L. Berkman, Aging parent/Mature child relationships. *Journal of Marriage and the Family*, 1984, *46*, pp. 295–299.

13   A. J. Walker & L. Thompson, Intimacy and intergenerational aid and contact among mothers and daughters. *Journal of Marriage and the Family*, 1983, *45*,(4), pp. 841–849.

14   Ibid.

15   R. N. Butler, The life review: An interpretation of reminiscence in the aged. *Psychiatry*, 1963, *26*(1), 65–76.

16   E. Erikson, *Childhood and Society*. New York: Norton, 1950.

17   K. King, Reminiscing, dying, and counseling: A contextual approach. In I. Burnside (Ed.), *Working with the Elderly: Group Processes and Techniques* (2d ed.). Monterey, Calif.: Wadsworth Health Science, 1984.

18   A. W. McMahon & P. J. Rhudick, Reminiscing: Adaptational significance in the aged. *Archives of General Psychiatry*, 1964, *10*(3), 292–298.

Chapter 7

1   L. Cartwright, Sources and effects of stress in health careers. In G. C. Stone, F. Cohen, & N. E. Adler (Eds.), *Health Psychology*. San Francisco: Jossey-Bass, 1979.

2   M. R. DiMatteo & D. D. DiNicola, Social science and the art of med-
     icine: From Hippocrates to holism. In H. S. Friedman & M. R. DiMatteo
     (Eds.), *Interpersonal Issues in Health Care*. New York: Academic Press,
     1982.

3   C. Dunkel-Schetter & C. B. Wortman, The interpersonal dynamics of
     cancer: Problems in social relationships and their impact on the cancer
     patient. In H. S. Friedman & M. R. DiMatteo (Eds.), *Interpersonal
     Issues in Health Care*. New York: Academic Press, 1982.

4   S. E. Taylor, Hospital patient behavior: Reactance, helplessness, or
     control? In H. S. Friedman & M. R. DiMatteo (Eds.), *Interpersonal
     Issues in Mental Health Care*. New York: Academic Press, 1982.

5   R. M. Kaplan, Coping with stressful medical examinations. In H. S.
     Friedman & M. R. DiMatteo (Eds.), *Interpersonal Issues in Health
     Care*. New York: Academic Press, 1982.

6   E. J. Langer, I. L. Janis, & J. A. Wolfer, Reduction of psychological
     stress in surgical patients. *Journal of Experimental Social Psychology*,
     1975, *11*, 155–165.

7   R. N. Butler & M. I. Lewis, *Aging and Mental Health: Positive Psy-
     chological and Biomedical Approaches* (3rd ed.). St. Louis: Mosby,
     1982.

8   C. K. Holahan, C. J. Holahan, & S. S. Belk, Adjustment in aging: The
     roles of life stress, hassles and self-efficacy. *Health Psychology*, 1984,
     3(4), 315–328.

9   B. L. Cohen & F. Lee, *Health Physics*, 1982, *36*(6).

10   Holahan, Holahan, and Belk. Op. cit., p. 325.

11   Public Health Service, Change in cigarette smoking and current smok-
     ing practices among adults: United States, 1978. *Advance Data*, 1979,
     52, pp. 1–16.

12   S. Schacter, Recidivism and self-cure of smoking and obesity. *American
     Psychologist*, 1982, *37*,(4), 436–444.

13   E. Lichtenstein, The smoking problem: A behavioral perspective. *Jour-
     nal of Community and Consulting Psychology*, 1982, *50*,(6), 804–819.

14   R. S. Paffenbarger, R. T. Hyde, A. L. Wing, C. H. Steinmetz, A natural
     history of athleticism and cardiovascular health. *JAMA: Journal of the
     American Medical Association*, 1984, *252*,(4), 491–495.

15   C. H. Folkins & W. E. Sime, Physical fitness training and mental health.
     American Psychologist, 1981, *36*,(4), 373–389.

16   I. L. McCann & D. S. Holmes, Influence of aerobic exercise on depres-
     sion. *Journal of Personality and Social Psychology*, 1984, *46*,(5),
     1142–1147.

17   S. Kra, *Aging Myths: Reversible Causes of Mind and Memory Loss*.
     New York: McGraw-Hill, 1986.

18   E. Eckholm, Malnutrition in elderly: Widespread health threat. *The New York Times,* August 23, 1984, p. C1.

Chapter 8

1   Heckler links fears on health fees to aging. *The New York Times,* August 23, 1984, p. A23.

2   U.S. Senate Special Committee on Aging. *Developments in Aging: 1983.* Washington, D.C.: U.S. Government Printing Office, 1984.

3   S. V. Saxon & M. J. Etken, *Physical Change and Aging: A Guide for the Helping Professions.* New York: Tiresias Press, 1978.

4   E. C. Gioiella, Healthy aging through knowledge and self care. *Prevention in Human Services,* 1983, *3*(1), 39–51.

5   Saxon & Etken. Op. cit.

6   F. Shumer, *Abnormal Psychology.* Lexington, Mass.: D. C. Heath, 1983.

7   D. L. Price, P. J. Whitehouse, R. G. Stuble, J. T. Coyle, A. W. Clark, M. R. Delong, L. C. Cork, & J. C. Hedreen, Alzheimer's disease and Down's syndrome. *Annals of the New York Academy of Sciences,* 1982, *396,* 145–169.

8   F. M. Sinex & R. H. Myers, Alzheimer's disease, Down's syndrome and aging: The genetic approach. *Annals of the New York Academy of Sciences,* 1982, *396,* 3–13.

9   A slow death of the mind. *Newsweek,* December 3, 1984, *104*(24), pp. 56–62.

10   R. L. Walford, Immunological studies of Down's syndrome and Alzheimer's disease. *Annals of the New York Academy of Sciences,* 1982, *396,* 95–103.

11   J. E. Birren, (Ed.), *Handbook of Aging and the Individual: Psychological and Biological Aspects.* Chicago: University of Chicago Press, 1959.

12   O. J. Kaplan, *Mental Disorders in Later Life.* Stanford, Calif.: Stanford University Press, 1945.

13   Sinex and Myers. Loc. cit.

14   A slow death of the mind. Loc. cit.

15   S. H. Zarit, N. K. Orr & J. M. Zarit, *The Hidden Victims of Alzheimer's Disease: Families under Stress,* New York: New York University Press, 1985.

16   E. Roberts, Potential therapies in aging and senile dementias. *Annals of the New York Academy of Sciences,* 1982, *396,* 165–178.

17   Ibid.

18   A slow death of the mind. Loc. cit.

FOR FURTHER READING

Braumstein, J. T. *Medical Applications of the Behavioral Sciences.* Chicago: Yearbook Publishers, 1981.

Brusse, E. W. *Behavior and Adaptation in Later Life* (2nd ed.). Boston: Little, Brown, 1977.

Cameron, P., & Biber, H. Sexual thought throughout the life-span. *The Gerontologist,* 1973, *13,* 144–147.

Goldman, R. Decline in organ function with aging. In J. Rossman (Ed.), *Clinical Geriatrics* (2nd ed.). Philadelphia: Lippincott, 1979.

Henker, F. O. All aging is psychosomatic. *Psychosomatics,* March 1983, *24*(3), 231–233.

Masters, W., & Johnson, V. *Human Sexual Response.* Boston: Little, Brown, 1966.

Mergler, N. L., & Goldstein, M. D. Why are there old people? *Human Development,* 1983, *26,* pp. 72–90.

Chapter 9

1   J. Brody, Personal health. *The New York Times,* January 22, 1986, p. C4.

2   *Family Caregiving and the Elderly.* New York: New York State Office for the Aging, 1983.

3   *Housing Options for Older Americans.* Washington, D.C.: American Association of Retired Persons, 1984.

4   I. Molotsky, Advice on helping the elderly. *The New York Times,* February 23, 1985, p. 17.

5   J. Z. Nassif, *The Home Health Care Solution.* New York: Harper & Row, 1985.

6   J. Elder, For the elderly, private care increasing. *The New York Times,* November 31, 1985, pp. C1; C10.

7   For aging parents alone in New York. *The New York Times,* December 26, 1985, p. C12.

8   F. Hathaway, Elder concern can ensure peace of mind. *The Palm Beach Post,* March 3, 1985.

9   Elder. Op. cit.

FOR FURTHER READING

Hare, P. H., & Ostler, J. N. *Creating an Accessory Apartment.* New York: McGraw-Hill, 1986.

Chapter 10

1 A. M. Lang & E. M. Brody, Characteristics of middle-aged daughters and help to their elderly mothers. *Journal of Marriage and The Family,* 1983, *45,* 193–202.

2 G. C. Eggert, R. Morris, & S. Pendleton, Caring for the patient with long-term disability. *Geriatrics,* 1977, *22,* 102–114.

3 A. Horowitz, *Families Who Care: A Study of Natural Support Systems of the Elderly.* Paper presented at the 31st annual scientific meeting of the Gerontological Society of America, Dallas, November 1978.

4 D. L. Frankfather, M. J. Smith, & O. Capers, *Family Maintenance of the Disabled Elderly.* Paper prepared for presentation at meeting of the American Orthopsychiatric Association. Washington, D.C., April 4, 1979.

5 E. S. Wiggins, Live-in help. A realistic option for dual career families. *Aging,* Fall 1983, pp. 9–11.

6 Ibid., p. 11.

Chapter 11

1 C. Johnson & F. Johnson, A micro-analysis of "senility": The response of the family and health professionals. *Culture, Medicine, and Psychiatry,* 1983, *7,* 77–96.

2 P. T. Sassi & H. J. Sanadaraj, Old people living in home for the aged: A study on certain variables of adjustment. *Psychological Studies,* 1982, *27,* 77–80.

3 L. Alan, The importance of including the family in the comprehensive psychiatric assessment of the nursing home bound person. *Journal of Gerontological Social Work,* 1984, *7,* 31–80.

4 *Thinking about a Nursing Home?* Washington, D.C.: The American Health Care Association, 1984.

5 Ibid.

6 R. Brent, E. Brent, & R. Mauksch, Common behavior patterns of residents in public areas of nursing homes. *The Gerontologist,* 1984, *24,* 186–192.

7 N. Feil, Group work with disoriented nursing home residents. *Social Work with Groups,* 1982, *5,* 57–65.

8 J. Erber & C. A. Dye, A profile of the newly admitted nursing home resident. *International Journal of Aging and Human Development,* 1982, *15,* 307–313.

9 E. Langer & J. Rodin, The effects of choice and enhanced personality responsibility for the aged—A field experiment in an institutionalized setting. *Journal of Personality and Social Psychology,* 1976, *34,* 191–198.

10   M. Ryden, Morale and perceived control in institutionalized elderly. *Nursing Research,* 1984, *33,* 130–136.

11   R. Schultz, The effects of control and predictability on the physical and psychological well being of the institutionalized aged. *Journal of Personality and Social Psychology,* 1976, *33,* 563–573.

12   R. MacNeil & M. Teague, Bingo and beyond: A rationale for recreation services within nursing homes. *Activities, Adaptation, and Aging,* 1983, *3,* 39–46.

13   H. Citron & L. Kartman, Preserving sexual identity in the institutionalized aged through activities. *Activities, Adaptation, and Aging,* 1982, *3,* 55–63.

14   N. Feil. Op. cit.

15   D. Buckholdt & J. Gubrium, Therapeutic pretense in reality orientation. *International Journal of Aging and Human Development,* 1983, *16,* 167–181.

16   A. Rubin & G. Shuttlesworth, Engaging families as support resources in nursing home care: Ambiguity in the subdivision of tasks. *The Gerontologist,* 1983, *23,* 632–636.

Chapter 12

1   E. Kübler-Ross, *On Death and Dying.* New York: Macmillan, 1969.

2   R. Kalish, Death and dying in a social context. In R. Binstock & E. Shanas (Eds.), *Handbook of Aging and the Social Sciences.* New York: Van Nostrand, 1976.

3   Kübler-Ross. Op. cit.

4   Kalish. Op. cit.

5   R. Kastenbaum, *Death, Society and Human Experience.* St. Louis: Mosby, 1977.

6   E. Kleiman, Hospital care of the dying: Each day painful choices. *The New York Times,* January 14, 1985, pp. A1;B4.

7   Hospice: Not to cure but to help. *Consumer Reports,* 1986, *51,* 24–26.

8   S. Stoddard, *The Hospice Movement: A Better Way of Caring for the Dying.* New York: Vintage Books, 1978.

9   Hospice: Not to cure but to help. Op. cit.

10   H. Wass, Death and the elderly. In H. Wass (Ed.), *Dying: Facing the Facts.* Washington, D.C.: Hemisphere, 1979.

11   Kübler-Ross. Op. cit.

12   The editors of *Consumer Reports. Funerals: Consumers' Last Rights.* New York: Pantheon Books, 1977.

13   L. DeSpelder, *The Last Dance: Encountering Death and Dying*. Palo Alto, Calif.: Mayfield, 1983.

14   The editors of *Consumer Reports*. Op. cit.

15   DeSpelder. Op. cit.

Chapter 13

1   G. Collins, Many in work force care for elderly kin. *The New York Times,* January 6, 1986, p. B5.

2   E. Brody, Parent care as a normative stress. *The Gerontologist,* 1985, *25,* 19–29.

3   G. R. Lee, Status of the elderly: Economic and familial antecedents. *Journal of Marriage and the Family,* May 1984, p. 269.

4   Brody. Op. cit., p. 20.

5   D. Goleman, Emotional support has its destructive side. *The New York Times,* August 27, 1985, p. C1.

6   V. G. Cicirelli, *Helping Elderly Parents: The Role of Adult Children.* Boston, Mass.: Auburn House, 1981.

7   Old and young differ over issues of aging. *The New York Times,* January 17, 1985, p. C9.

Index